"Consumer culture poses one of the most comprehensive and subtle challenges to Christian faith and discipleship. While many books have offered general accounts of this tension, *The Sacraments and Consumer Culture* focuses on each sacrament: the challenges that each face in a consumer culture and the resources they provide for the Church to live its mission more fully. Along the way, Brunk considers both the history and contemporary practice of the sacraments. This helpful book speaks to both academic and pastoral audiences."

—Vincent Miller, author of *Consuming Religion:*
Christian Faith and Practice in a Consumer Culture

"This book reads as a compelling plea for deep connections. In an era where advertisements and commercialization are no longer dominating the world of trade only, but also the areas of politics, education, and health, and where the commodification of the life-world slowly but surely reaches a certain level of absurdity, Brunk proposes to take a step back and thoroughly rethink the relation between Christian faith and culture. He lucidly observes that there have been perilous evolutions in society which have alienated us from the cosmos, from God, the Church and, most saliently, and tragically, from each other. The response to what he describes as consumerism and its concomitant individualism is, however, not massive rejection but subtle discernment. Brunk brilliantly shows how the built-in sacramental principle of Christianity offers an enormous but virtually unexplored potential to uphold a truthful vision where emptiness rules, to undermine rhetoric without love or against life, and to promote solidarity in misery. Put differently, the gist of Brunk's book is as sagacious as it is thought-provoking in today's world: sacraments establish much deeper connections than any consumerist ideology is capable of."

—Joris Geldhof
Faculty of Theology and Religious Studies
Katholieke Universiteit Leuven, Belgium

"Christian sacraments only exist in the practice of real parishioners, living the faith in social environments affecting and even dominating their response to the Gospel. Timothy Brunk invites us to reflect with him on two decades of theological criticism of the pervasive consumerism of our time to assess the problems it poses to our participation in the graces each sacrament affords. Brunk's expert enlistment of historical and contemporary theological sources on the sacraments provides readers greater knowledge and insight for more effective pastoral-liturgical practice."

—Bruce T. Morrill, SJ
Vanderbilt University

D0840523

The Sacraments and Consumer Culture

Timothy Brunk

LITURGICAL PRESS ACADEMIC

Collegeville, Minnesota

www.litpress.org

Scripture quotations are from the *New Revised Standard Version Bible*, copyright © 1989 National Council of the Churches of Christ in the United States of America. Used by permission. All rights reserved worldwide.

Excerpts from the English translation of *Rite of Penance* © 1974, International Commission on English in the Liturgy Corporation (ICEL); excerpts from the English translation of *Pastoral Care of the Sick: Rites of Anointing and Viaticum* © 1982, ICEL; excerpts from the English translation of *Order of Christian Funerals* © 1985, 1989, ICEL; excerpts from the English translation of *Rite of Christian Initiation of Adults* © 1985, ICEL; excerpts from the English translation of *Rites of Ordination of a Bishop, of Priests, and of Deacons* © 2000, 2002, ICEL; excerpts from the English translation of *The Roman Missal* © 2010, ICEL; excerpts from the English translation of *The Order of Celebrating Matrimony* © 2013, ICEL; excerpts from the English translation of *The Order of Confirmation* © 2013, ICEL. All rights reserved.

Excerpts from Pope John Paul II's *Familiaris Consortio* © Libreria Editrice Vaticana. Used with permission.

Excerpts from the English translation of the *Catechism of the Catholic Church* for use in the United States of America copyright © 1994, United States Catholic Conference, Inc.—Libreria Editrice Vaticana. English translation of the *Catechism of the Catholic Church: Modifications from the Editio Typica* copyright © 1997, United States Catholic Conference, Inc.—Libreria Editrice Vaticana. Used with Permission.

Excerpts from documents of the Second Vatican Council are from *Vatican Council II: Constitutions, Decrees, Declarations; The Basic Sixteen Documents*, edited by Austin Flannery, OP, © 1996. Used with permission of Liturgical Press, Collegeville, Minnesota.

Excerpts from *St. John Chrysostom: Baptismal Instruction* translated and annotated by Paul W. Harkins, Copyright © 1963 by Rev. Johannes Quasten and Rev. Walter J. Burghardt, S.J., Paulist Press, Inc., New York/Mahwah, NJ. Reprinted by permission of Paulist Press, Inc. www.paulistpress.com.

1   2   3   4   5   6   7   8   9

Library of Congress Cataloging-in-Publication Data

Names: Brunk, Timothy M., 1965– author.
Title: The sacraments and consumer culture / Timothy Brunk.
Description: Collegeville, Minnesota : Liturgical Press Academic, 2020. | Includes index.
  | Summary: "An examination of how consumer culture has had a corrosive effect on the seven sacraments of the Catholic Church, also assessing how sacramental worship can provide resources for responsible Christian discipleship in today's consumer culture"— Provided by publisher.
Identifiers: LCCN 2019040772 (print) | LCCN 2019040773 (ebook) | ISBN 9780814685082 (paperback) | ISBN 9780814685327 (epub) | ISBN 9780814685327 (mobi) | ISBN 9780814685327 (pdf)
Subjects: LCSH: Sacraments—Catholic Church. | Consumption (Economics) | Catholic Church—Doctrines.
Classification: LCC BX2203 .B784 2020 (print) | LCC BX2203 (ebook) | DDC 234/.16—dc23
LC record available at https://lccn.loc.gov/2019040772
LC ebook record available at https://lccn.loc.gov/2019040773

To

Laura and David Ash
Betsey Beckman
St. Patrick's Parish, Seattle, WA
John Laurance, SJ

They helped me think about liturgy.

Vincent Miller
Participants in the 2014 Lilly Seminar on Consumer Culture

They helped me think about consumerism.

CONTENTS

ACKNOWLEDGMENTS

I would like to thank the Symbol, Ritual, and Sacrament section of the College Theology Society for the opportunity to present parts of this book as works in progress. I am similarly grateful to members of the Delaware Valley contingent of the North American Academy of Liturgy.

Thanks are also due to Stephany Annor for reading through the manuscript and to Charlie Soule for preparing the index.

Chapter 1 originally appeared as "Baptism and Consumerism," *Studia Liturgica* 43, no. 1 (2013): 1–31.

Chapter 2 originally appeared as "The Sacrament of Confirmation in a Consumer Culture," *Worship* 88, no. 4 (2014): 333–52.

Chapter 3, "Eucharist and Consumerism," is the fruit of participation in the 2014 Lilly Seminar "What Does It Mean to Be a Human in Consumer Culture?"

Chapter 4 originally appeared as "Consumer Culture and Sacramental Reconciliation," *Worship* 92, no. 4 (July 2018): 337–60.

All citations from the Rite of Christian Initiation of Adults (RCIA), Rite of Baptism for Children, General Introduction to Christian Initiation, Rite of Confirmation (1971), Rite of Penance, Rite of Marriage (1969), Order of Christian Funerals, and Rites of Ordination (1968) are from *The Rites of the Catholic Church as Revised by the Second Vatican Council*, 2 vols. (Collegeville, MN: Liturgical Press, 1990).

INTRODUCTION

Pointing out the many flaws and weaknesses he found in the teachings of Plato, the Stoics, the Epicureans, and other Greek philosophers, the third-century Christian apologist Tertullian asked, "What indeed has Athens to do with Jerusalem? What concord is there between the [Greek] Academy and the Church? What between heretics and Christians?"[1] Readers of the present work may wonder, "What indeed has consumerism to do with the sacraments?" In the following pages, I will argue that consumer culture has a great deal to do with the understanding and practice of the sacraments of the Catholic Church in the North Atlantic context in which I live. The heart of the argument is two-fold. First, consumer culture lives and breathes a form of individualism that is hostile to a shared world of meaning. Second—and related to the first point—consumer culture involves relating to a world of objects shorn of larger contexts. Each of these claims deserves expansion before proceeding.

Concerning a shared world of meaning, Bernard Lonergan writes:

> For what is community? It is not just a number of men within a geographical frontier. It is an achievement of common meaning, and there are kinds and degrees of achievement. Common meaning is potential when there is a common field of experience, and to withdraw from that common field is to get out of touch. Common meaning is formal when there is common understanding,

---

1. Tertullian, *Prescription against Heretics* 7, in Alexander Roberts and James Donaldson, eds., *Ante-Nicene Fathers The Writings of the Fathers Down to A.D. 325,* vol. 3: *Latin Christianity: Its Founder, Tertullian I. Apologetic; II. Anti-Marcion; III. Ethical* (Peabody, MA: Hendrickson, 2004), 246.

and one withdraws from that common understanding by mis-understanding, by incomprehension, by mutual incomprehension. Common meaning is actual inasmuch as there are common judgments, areas in which all affirm and deny in the same manner; and one withdraws from that common agreement when one disagrees, when one considers true what others hold false and false what they think true. Common meaning is realized by will, especially by permanent dedication, in the love that makes families, in the loyalty that makes states, in the faith that makes religions. Community coheres or divides, begins or ends, just where the common field of experience, common understanding, common judgment, common commitments begin and end.[2]

Rather than forming or engaging a common meaning realized by will, love, loyalty, and faith, consumer culture fosters what James K. A. Smith identifies as a "strange configuration of sociality,"[3] which encourages people to assess themselves against standards of youth, beauty, and taste relentlessly promoted in advertising. More to the point, this configuration of sociality also forms people to assess *others* by these standards.

If we could somehow analyze ourselves as a friend of a friend approaches "our circle" for the first time, we might catch ourselves looking him up and down, noting clothes that seem to be from Old Navy instead of Abercrombie & Fitch (and from last season at that!); he's got a big clunky cell phone that's about two years old; his tastes in music seem a bit dull and dated; and he's from a part of town we wouldn't walk through at night. Or while we're sitting at the Starbucks in the food court, we might find that our eyes are constantly darting to watch the other girls and women passing by. In just the blink of an eye, we find that we've sized them up from top to bottom.[4]

2. Bernard Lonergan, "*Existenz* and *Aggiornamento*," in Lonergan, *Collected Works of Bernard Lonergan*, vol. 4: *Collection*, ed. Frederick Crowe and Robert Doran (Toronto: University of Toronto, 1993), 226.

3. James K. A. Smith, *Desiring the Kingdom: Worship, Worldview, and Cultural Formation* (Grand Rapids, MI: Baker Academic, 2009), 96, 98. I return to this "strange configuration" again on pp. 67, 76, 83, and 200.

4. Smith, *Desiring the Kingdom*, 98.

What is "in common" here is a sense of individual competition, alienation from each other, and even alienation from ourselves as beings created in the divine image and called to communion with the triune God.

Sacramental celebrations, on the other hand, are precisely manifestations of communion, as Augustine points out: "People could not be gathered together under the name of any religion, whether true or false, if they were not bound together by some sharing of visible signs or sacraments. The power of these sacraments is great beyond description."[5] Indeed, the "power" of sacraments in the Christian tradition is rooted in the life, death, and resurrection of Jesus Christ: the paschal mystery.[6] The communal element of the paschal mystery is stressed in the *Catechism*: "By his word, through signs that manifest the reign of God, and by sending out his disciples, Jesus calls all people to come together around him. But above all in the great Paschal mystery—his death on the cross and his Resurrection—he would accomplish the coming of his kingdom. 'And I, when I am lifted up from the earth, will draw all men to myself.' [John 12:32] Into this union with Christ all [people] are called."[7]

I have stated that consumer culture involves relating to a world of objects shorn of larger contexts. For example, if I had the means I could in principle purchase the Mona Lisa from the Louvre and then use it as a welcome mat for my house. As the purchaser / owner of this piece of art, I could do with it whatever I wish. I determine its use and application. I would be free to ignore its place in the history of art—I could make it into a dartboard—or I could choose to display it publicly for others to appreciate. This example is perhaps a bit overdrawn so let's choose something closer to

5. Augustine, *Answer to Faustus, a Manichean*, 19, 11, in *The Works of Saint Augustine: A Translation for the 21st Century*, vol. I/20: *Answer to Faustus, a Manichean*, ed. Boniface Ramsey, trans. Ronald Teske (New Rochelle, NY: New City, 2007), 244–45.

6. *Sacrosanctum Concilium* 61 teaches: "For well-disposed members of the faithful the liturgy of the sacraments and sacramental sanctifies almost every event of their lives with the divine grace which flows from the paschal mystery of the passion, death and resurrection of Christ. From this source all sacraments and sacramental draw their power."

7. *Catechism of the Catholic Church* 542.

home, say, items for sale at a supermarket. In ages past, shoppers knew the farmers who tended the livestock now for sale as cuts of meat. They knew those who planted and harvested the fruits and vegetables. How many of us can say the same of the food we buy at our local supermarkets? Vincent Miller writes about eating "beans from nowhere,"[8] appearing on store shelves as if by magic. The context that produced these beans is closed to the shopper.

This book argues that, being formed by the many-times repeated purchasing of items whose context of origin is closed to them, people in North Atlantic cultural contexts can and do transfer this mindset to religious objects and practices. Miller points out that consumers can purchase Tibetan prayer flags and display them on their front porches with no connection to or understanding of the lives of prayer of Buddhist monks facing Chinese cultural oppression.[9] Perhaps one is in fact a practicing Buddhist—or perhaps the color of the flags nicely sets off the blue trim on one's porch. What can happen to prayer flags can happen to sacraments. Is baptism fundamentally about being plunged into the death and new life of Jesus Christ or is it about sentimentality and fancy $600 baptismal gowns?[10] Is confirmation about God's gift of the Spirit or about being rewarded for mastering elements of one's catechism?[11] Is weekly Mass a time for parishioners to outdo one another in their "Sunday best" or is it a time of corporate prayer in which individualism is shunned?[12] Is the Rite of Marriage fundamentally concerned with a display of one's sense of style (reflected in one's choice of garment, for example) or is it a matter of taking up with one's spouse the mission of the church in and to the world?[13]

---

8. Vincent Miller, *Consuming Religion: Christian Faith and Practice in a Consumer Culture* (New York: Continuum, 2005), 38. I expand on this point in section II of the first chapter, p. 3.

9. Vincent Miller, *Consuming Religion: Christian Faith and Practice in a Consumer Culture* (New York: Continuum, 2005), 4. I reference these prayer flags again in section IV of chapter 3, p. 76.

10. See section IV of the first chapter, p. 10.

11. See section IV of the second chapter, p. 48.

12. See section II of the third chapter, p. 64. See also Tissa Balasuriya, *The Eucharist and Human Liberation* (Maryknoll, NY: Orbis Books, 1977), 149.

13. See section IV of chapter 6, p. 148.

Pope Leo the Great, who helped to steer the Catholic Church through the Christological controversies of the fifth century, taught in one of his sermons that

> after all had been fulfilled that belonged to the preaching of the Gospel . . . our Lord Jesus Christ was raised to heaven. He made an end to his bodily presence in the sight of his disciples on the fortieth day after the Resurrection . . . . What was to be seen of our Redeemer has passed over into the Sacraments.[14]

What was to be seen of our Redeemer, according to a passage from the *Catechism* cited above, is that Jesus calls all people to come together around him. Vincent Miller contends that with respect to consumerism sacramentality may "provide the cultural basis, both in belief and practice, for an oppositional sensibility."[15] By examining the words and gestures of the seven sacraments of the Catholic Church, I argue in this book that what is to be experienced in these sacraments does indeed provide a basis for resisting consumerism.

14. St. Leo the Great, *Sermon 74*, 2 as quoted in *Fathers of the Church: A New Translation*, vol. 93: *Saint Leo the Great: Sermons*, ed. Thomas Halton (Washington, DC: Catholic University of America Press, 1996), 326. I refer again to this sermon in section IV of chapter 5, p. 126.

15. Vincent Miller, *Consuming Religion: Christian Faith and Practice in a Consumer Culture* (New York: Continuum, 2005), 189.

Chapter One

BAPTISM
AND CONSUMER CULTURE

I. Introduction

Tom Beaudoin, Patrick McCormick, Vincent Miller, and William Cavanaugh (among others), have argued persuasively that an important facet of consumer culture is its production and marketing of commodities that appear before us on store shelves as if by magic, shorn of all apparent connection to the conditions under which the items were made, harvested, packaged, shipped, and so on, in order to arrive at the market.[1] Ignorance of the contexts under which consumer goods are produced is a basic feature of late-modern society, at times perhaps verging on deliberate indifference to those contexts. When one becomes accustomed to the abstraction of products from the people and

1. See Tom Beaudoin, *Consuming Faith: Integrating Who We Are with What We Buy* (New York: Sheed & Ward, 2003), 68–69; Patrick McCormick, *A Banqueter's Guide to the All-Night Soup Kitchen of the Kingdom of God* (Collegeville, MN: Liturgical Press, 2004), 17; Vincent Miller, *Consuming Religion: Christian Faith and Practice in a Consumer Culture* (New York: Continuum, 2005), 37; William Cavanaugh, *Being Consumed: Economics and Christian Desire* (Grand Rapids, MI: Eerdmans, 2008), 36–37; Miller, "The Body Globalized: Problems for a Sacramental Imagination in an Age of Global Commodity Chains," in *Religion, Economics, and Culture in Conflict and Conversation*, ed. Laurie Cassidy and Maureen O'Connell, The Annual Publication of the College Theology Society 56, (Maryknoll: Orbis Books, 2011), 116. In various ways, the theme of commodities from "nowhere" runs throughout each of the works cited above.

1

places that produced them, one becomes accustomed to living in a world of brute things with very little by way of social meaning or significance. Miller in particular has sounded warnings about what this acclimation to abstraction might mean for religious symbols, beliefs and practices, but he also sees in the principle of sacramentality "an interesting example of a religious resource for countering consumer culture, because it challenges consumer culture not by critiquing consumption but by challenging the abstracting dynamisms of commodification itself."[2]

In this book, I want to examine this challenge to commodification and in this chapter, I will treat baptism. In what ways might we understand baptism as a religious practice subject to abstraction from the religious context in which it is properly located? In what ways does this sacrament offer a means to counter and challenge the "abstracting dynamisms of commodification"? I will first present a summary of the arguments made by Miller and others about commodification. I will argue that attending to the paschal mystery as the root element at work in baptism (and indeed all the sacraments) is one approach to resisting commodification. I contend that in a consumer culture the practice of infant baptism can complicate attempts to resist commodification. On the other hand, attending to the rich context of the ancient preparation for baptism known as the catechumenate (significantly revived with the 1972 promulgation of the Rite of Christian Initiation of Adults), allows one to appreciate baptism as associated with quite specific practices as well as having very clear social significance (and not merely significance for the individual being baptized). The ancient and still current practices of exorcisms and the baptismal renunciation of Satan will be other elements to bring into the discussion of resisting consumerism. Finally, I will argue that the church's baptismal practice can be a springboard for social concern about the pollution and privatization of water.

---

2. Miller, *Consuming Religion*, 189. See also Andy Crouch, "Life after Postmodernity," in *The Church in Emerging Culture: 5 Perspectives*, ed. Leonard Sweet (Grand Rapids, MI: Zondervan, 2003), 84.

II. The Veil of the Commodity

In the late fourth century, Ambrose of Milan sounded an early warning about the dangers of ignorance of and indifference to the conditions under which goods are produced as he discoursed about Lazarus and Dives:

> More endurable was that rich man from whose table the beggar Lazarus was collecting what fell, desiring to be filled; but his table also was made from the blood of many poor and his cups dripped with the blood of many whom he had driven to the halter. How many are killed, so that what delights you may be secured! Deadly is your hunger; deadly, your luxury. One fell from a roof top when he was building spacious store-homes for your grain. Another fell from the highest branches of a lofty tree while he was searching for the kinds of grapes to bring down, from which wines worthy of your table might be pressed. Another was drowned in the sea because he feared that a fish or an oyster might be wanting to your table. Another was frozen stiff by the cold of winter while he was intent on tracking hares and catching birds in cribs.[3]

Tom Beaudoin allows us to fast-forward to the early twenty-first century:

> To stay competitive, global corporations are attempting to distance themselves from earthbound issues like workers, wages, unions, and factories. More and more, they turn their focus to the construction of an ethereal brand-image. Their logos must be globally recognizable, symbolizing an attitude, a feeling, a value, or a lifestyle, while avoiding conjuring up any images of the earthly origins of the products that bear their logo. The logo must suggest a certain ethos but not remind the consumer that someone somewhere actually makes the products that bear the logo. The logo should float freely above and beyond the way it was actually produced.[4]

---

3. Ambrose, *De Naboth* 5.19–20, in Martin R. P. McGuire, "S. Ambrosii De Nabuthae: A Commentary, with an Introduction and Translation" (PhD diss., Catholic University of America, 1927), 57.

4. Beaudoin, *Consuming Faith*, 68–69. See also Miller, "The Body Globalized," 115; Cavanaugh, *Being Consumed*, 36–37. Beaudoin may be overgeneralizing

The suppression of the human and social context that gives birth to the commodity is now a high art. Thus, what matters is not the working conditions of those who stitched together my sneakers with their stylish swoop designs but whether I embrace the philosophy that I should "just do it." Miller observes that "the formation of our imaginations on this side of the veil of the commodity makes us appear autonomous, unrelated to anything. We are not implicated in the world, but rather are individual, sovereign subjects who choose from a range of objects at our disposal."[5] Advertisements purporting to lift the veil give us happy elves making cookies[6] or employees in a cereal factory waxing enthusiastic about the "joy we put in every spoonful."[7] Viewers of ads may be "unrelated to anything" or to a world of production that does not really exist! In any event, whether the process of production in question is socially meritorious or socially scandalous remains out of sight. The web of social implications and human relationships is hidden or falsified.

Beaudoin uses the phrase "economic docetism" to describe the abstraction of commodities from their contexts of origination in the skill, sweat, and labor of human beings. For Beaudoin, this term refers to "Christian participation in the economy that denies the facticity, holiness, and potential revelatory character of our bodiliness or the bodiliness of others."[8] What happens when the docetism of commodification is applied to religious beliefs and practices? Miller argues that religious "traditions are pillaged for their symbolic content, which is then repackaged and recontextualized in a way that jettisons their communal, ethical, and political

---

here, for there are companies such as Patagonia that do seek to be socially responsible. However, there is a clear sense in which the exceptions prove the rule.

5. Miller, "The Body Globalized," 116.

6. Videos of television ads for Keebler cookies in which happy (and magical) elves make cookies are available online. See, for example, "Keebler Town House Crackers: 80's," I Love TV Commercials, June 16, 2010, 0:30, http://www.you tube.com/watch?v=m0KRNCb83ZU.

7. See "Honey Bunches of Oats - Our Latest Commercial!," WeLoveHBOO-cereal, April 15, 2009, 0:30, http://www.youtube.com/watch?v=em9thvkiS7I.

8. Beaudoin, *Consuming Faith*, 75.

consequences."[9] Drawing upon the work of Katherine Bergeron, Miller writes of the commercial success of the 1993 *Chant* album: "The use of chant is particularly informative, as this music forms part of the ritual prayer of the monastic community. There it is tied to a host of practices and institutions that link it as a cultural object to the life of the community. She argues that such nostalgic uses of religious music remove it from its liturgical context and transform it into 'virtual' rituals that make no demands on the listener."[10] Of course, the Spanish Benedictine monks of Santo Domingo de Silos featured on the album pray and chant together in a regular daily cycle featuring not only the Liturgy of the Hours but shared participation in sacramental life, notably the Mass. The monks are also committed to lives of poverty, chastity, and obedience to their religious superiors. None of these strings come attached for those who merely listen to the album in their cars or at work. Certainly, some who listen to *Chant* may find themselves drawn to prayerful contemplation, even specifically Christian prayer. The album might renew or reinvigorate one's Christian faith, perhaps inspiring a vocation to monastic life. Or it might be just one of many options on the shelf, an album with soothing and non-demanding sounds that connote nothing religious at all. In the latter case, the songs in praise of God have been well and truly commodified.

Can the sacrament of baptism be commodified? Two elements of commodification are relevant here. One concerns the sense in which baptism is (or is not) understood by the parties involved as a commercial transaction. The other concerns the extent to which baptism is (or is not) separated from the religious context that gives it meaning. Of course, the church has always condemned in principle the notion that grace could be bought and sold, going back to Peter's rebuke of Simon the magician in Acts 8. Just as

---

9. Miller, *Consuming Religion*, 84. Here Miller is writing with specific reference to Joseph Campbell.

10. Ibid., 76. Miller is using Katherine Bergeron, "The Virtual Sacred," *New Republic* 212 (February 7, 1995): 29–34. What is said here about this album also applies to the Cistercian Monks of Stift Heiligenkreuz, *Chant: Music for Paradise*, Universal Music 1766016, 2008, which reached #1 on the Billboard classical charts.

clearly, certain members of the church were in effect crossing the line with the sale of medieval indulgences. Even in the present day, the practice of stipend masses is subject to critique.[11] Our focus, however, is baptism. Of the twenty-two parishes I contacted in a survey about monetary gifts and infant baptism, eleven make a point of *not* mentioning finances at all to those inquiring about baptism. Two parishes always mention a specific amount for a customary gift. One parish provides information about specific amounts only if the parents ask. These last three parishes also make it clear that financial gifts are not required. The remaining parishes did not respond to the survey.[12] Insofar as this sampling of American parishes is representative, then it seems safe to say that American parishes successfully avoid giving the impression that baptism is somehow for sale, although one may ask about the degree to which identifying a customary amount nevertheless connotes the expectation of a financial gift.[13]

In what ways might baptism be dissociated from the religious context that gives it meaning in the way that the *Chant* album is torn from its religious moorings? Apart from the exceptional circumstance of a person who is at the point of death foreseen in the Rite of Christian Initiation of Adults (RCIA) 373, the rite of baptism always involves a renunciation of Satan and a profession of faith, whether these are uttered by the one to be baptized (in the case of

11. See Edward J. Kilmartin, *The Eucharist in the West: History and Theology*, ed. Robert Daly (Collegeville, MN: Liturgical Press, 1998), 205–37.

12. My admittedly non-scientific research involved contacting twenty-two parishes around the United States: Arkansas (one); California (one); Colorado (one); Delaware (one); Florida (one); Georgia (one); Indiana (one); Kansas (one); Michigan (one); Nebraska (one); New York (one); Ohio (one); Oklahoma (one); Pennsylvania (two); South Dakota (one); Texas (one); Washington state (two); West Virginia (two); Wisconsin (one).

13. In this connection it is interesting to note that the third-century writer Tertullian had to contend with people who disdained Christian baptism because it was a relatively simple rite that was offered at no cost. The thinking of his opponents was that the price of a rite was connected to the significance of the rite. See Tertullian, *On Baptism* 2., quoted in Mark Searle, "Faith and Sacraments in the Conversion Process," in *Conversion and the Catechumenate*, ed. Robert Duggan (New York: Paulist, 1984), 64.

mature persons) or by the parents and godparents of the one to be baptized (in the case of infants).[14] Baptism is thus almost always celebrated in an explicitly named context of shared religious faith, marked above all by belief in the saving triune God. On the other hand, when baptism is celebrated apart from Sunday Mass (e.g., on Saturday mornings or Sunday afternoons), then the full depth of its connection to the rest of the sacramental life of the church is obscured. The practice of infant baptism, for its part, runs the risk of directing attention to sentimentality and away from what is quite literally a life-and-death event. It is a life-and-death event rooted in the life and death of Jesus of Nazareth.

III. Paschal Mystery as Context of Production of Baptism

If commodities conceal the contexts of their production (fair wages? sanitary working conditions?), one way to resist commodification is to attend as best one can to those hidden contexts.[15] It follows, then, that one path to pursue to resist the potential commodification of baptism is to attend to what might be called its context of production: the paschal mystery. What God effects through the paschal mystery of the life, death, and resurrection of Jesus is the reconciliation of God and human, lost first of all in the sin of Adam and Eve. It is interesting to note Alexander Schmemann's observations on that first sin: "The fall of man is the rejection by him of [his proper] calling, his refusal to be priest. The original sin consists in man's choice of a non-priestly relationship with God and the world. And perhaps no word better expresses the essence of this new, fallen, non-priestly way of life than the one which in our own time has had an amazingly successful career, has truly become the symbol of our culture. It is the word *consumer*. After having glorified himself as *homo faber*, then as *homo sapiens*, man

---

14. RCIA 373 reads thus: "In the case of a person who is at the point of death, that is, whose death is imminent, and time is short, the minister, omitting everything else, pours natural water (even if not blessed) on the head of the sick person, while saying the usual sacramental form."

15. A point made in Beaudoin, *Consuming Faith*, 102–104, and Miller, *Consuming Religion*, 184–86.

seems to have found his ultimate vocation as 'consumer.' "[16] We will return to the notion of redemption as including overcoming a consumerist worldview but for the moment, let us simply note that belief in the paschal mystery goes hand in hand with denial of docetism. Jesus, the human being, really suffered and died on the cross. He had a social context of friends, religious teachings, opponents and supporters. If the old adage is true that it was from the side of Christ as he slept the sleep of death on the cross that there came forth the wondrous sacrament of the whole church, then perhaps there is something about the principle of sacramentality that can work to resist economic docetism.[17]

To begin this assessment of baptism and the paschal mystery, a good place to start is the well-known passage in Rom 6 according to which those who are baptized are baptized into the death of Christ so that like him they may walk in newness of life. Although Christian writers of the first few centuries did not exploit this theme, after the third century or so it became more and more prominent.[18] The same fourth-century Ambrose who warned about indifference to the fate of workers bringing food to one's table also had counsel to offer about abstracting baptism from the paschal mystery. "For what," he asks, "is water without the cross of Christ except a common element without any sacramental effect?"[19] Reading Scripture allegorically, he draws similar lessons

---

16. Alexander Schmemann, *Of Water and the Spirit* (Yonkers, NY: St. Vladimir's Seminary, 1974), 96.

17. The adage is quoted approvingly by St. Thomas Aquinas in *Summa Theologiae* III, q. 62, a. 5, sed contra. See also *Sacrosanctum Concilium* 5. Tom Beaudoin makes the bodiliness of Jesus part of his argument about how to address consumerism; my analysis differs insofar as I am considering the specifically sacramental practice of baptism. See Beaudoin, *Consuming Faith*, 74–76.

18. See Mark Searle, "Response: The RCIA and Infant Baptism," *Worship* 56, no. 4 (1982): 327–32 at 329. Thomas Finn theorizes that the "absence of Pauline influence in the baptismal theology of the more orthodox writers of the second century may be a reaction to the gnostic sects who were fond of citing Paul as the authority for their speculations." Citation from Thomas Finn, "Baptismal Death and Resurrection: A Study in Fourth Century Eastern Baptismal Theology," *Worship* 43, no. 3 (1969): 175–89 at 175n2.

19. St. Ambrose, *The Mysteries* 1.4.20, in *Fathers of the Church: A New Translation*, vol. 44: *Saint Ambrose: Theological and Dogmatic Works*, ed. Roy Deferrari (Washington, DC: Catholic University of America Press, 1963), 12.

about baptism from the unpalatable water at Marah, purified by a piece of wood: "So the water is bitter, but when it has received the cross of Christ, when the heavenly sacrament, it begins to be sweet and pleasant, and worthily sweet, in which fault is withdrawn."[20] The bishop of Milan makes the same point when he draws on a curious incident involving Elisha and an axe-head that had fallen to the bottom of the Jordan River. "Then Eliseus threw a piece of wood [into the river], and the head of the axe was raised. So do you see that in the cross of Christ the infirmity of all men is raised?"[21]

Remembrance of the cross of Christ is a feature of Christian initiation, notably in the rite of consignation. The sign of the cross is made on or over those who are accepted into the order of catechumens: "The cross is traced on the forehead of the candidates (or, at the discretion of the diocesan bishop, in front of the forehead for candidates in whose culture the act of touching may not seem proper . . .); at the discretion of the celebrant the signing of one, several, or all of the senses may follow."[22] Michael Witczak observes: "The minister touches each inquirer, at least on their forehead, but also, optionally, on each of their senses. When one enters Christ, Christ's Body, the church, one does so completely and bodily. No aspect of one's person is left out."[23] In the case of infants, consignation (by the minister, parents, and godparents) takes place on the day of baptism.[24] The child, writes Witczak, "is marked with the most dramatic image of Christ's love: his total self-giving on the cross when he revealed his love for the Father and the world."[25]

Remembrance of the cross of Christ in baptism is not a matter of gesture only. There is the baptismal profession of faith, which

20. St. Ambrose, *The Sacraments* 2.4.13, in *Saint Ambrose: Theological and Dogmatic Works*, 283. See Exod 15:23-25.

21. St. Ambrose, *The Sacraments* 2.4.11, in *Saint Ambrose: Theological and Dogmatic Works*, 282. See 2 Kgs 6:1-6.

22. RCIA 54.

23. Michael Witczak, *The Sacrament of Baptism* (Collegeville, MN: Liturgical Press, 2011), 19.

24. 1969 Rite of Baptism for Children (RBC) 41; 79. The 2020 Order of Baptism of Children (OBC) retains this language in 41 and 79. See *The Order of Baptism of Children for Use in the Dioceses of the United States of America* (Washington, DC: United States Conference of Catholic Bishops, 2020), which will be the source for all references to the OBC.

25. Witczak, *The Sacrament of Baptism*, 59.

includes the question: "Do you believe in Jesus Christ . . . our Lord, who was born of the Virgin Mary, was crucified, died, and was buried, rose from the dead and is now seated at the right hand of the Father?"[26] In this connection, what St. Augustine had to say about the word of faith is reminiscent of St. Ambrose's words about the cross: "Take away the word, and what is the water except water? The word is added to the elemental substance, and it becomes a sacrament, also itself, as it were, a visible word . . . . 'This is the word of faith which we preach,' says the Apostle. 'For if you confess with your mouth that Jesus is Lord and believe in your heart that God has raised him up from the dead, you will be saved.' "[27] In baptism, the paschal mystery is present in both word and gesture. Indeed, the RCIA itself proclaims that "the whole initiation must bear a profoundly paschal character."[28] The question, then, is to what degree this context of production for baptism is clearly perceived and grasped by late-modern believers.

IV. Infant Baptism

The vast majority of late-modern Roman Catholics are initiated into the church in infancy and as infants they do not do much perceiving and grasping of the paschal mystery on display in their baptisms. My aim in pointing this out is not to challenge the legitimacy or validity of infant baptism, a practice of immemorial

26. RCIA 225; see also RBC 58 and 85 and OBC 58 and 95 where the parents and godparents make the same profession of faith.

27. Augustine, *Tractates on John* 80.3.1–3.2 in *Fathers of the Church: A New Translation*, vol. 90: *Saint Augustine Tractates on the Gospel of John*, 55–111, trans. John W. Rettig (Washington, DC: Catholic University of America Press, 1994), 117, 118. In *The Mysteries* 3.14, Ambrose makes a similar point, drawing, as earlier, on the incident at Marah: "Marah was a bitter fountain. Moses cast the wood in it, and it became sweet. For water without the preaching of the cross of the Lord is to no advantage for future salvation; but when it has been consecrated by the mystery of the saving cross, then it is ordered for the use of the spiritual laver." *Saint Ambrose: Theological and Dogmatic Works*, 10.

28. RCIA 8. This leads Aidan Kavanagh to wonder whether the Easter Vigil, the culmination of the RCIA, might really be the only suitable time for baptisms. See Kavanagh, *The Shape of Baptism: The Rite of Christian Initiation* (Collegeville, MN: Liturgical Press, 1978), 135.

custom in the church. Rather, I want to highlight at least two ways in which the practice of infant baptism can contribute to a sense of commodification of baptism. One way involves the passivity of the infant as recipient of the sacrament; the other involves the role of sentimentality as obscuring the paschal mystery.

As noted earlier, the commodification of objects involves abstracting them from the web of human relations whence they come. Another aspect of consumer culture is how it attempts to foster the belief that once one has purchased the consumer item in question, enjoying the promised good (whether this is a savory taste or a new "you") is a matter of effortlessness—not just "rice" but "Minute Rice." Ads for sports cars feature spine-tingling rides along scenic roads; only the fine print clarifies that the road had been closed to other traffic that might complicate one's excursion. The consumer invests no effort; the product simply delivers the satisfaction for which it was obtained.

I argue that a similar dynamic is potentially at work in infant baptism. The "goods" of remission of original sin, incorporation into the church as body of Christ and so forth, are delivered to the infant who makes no effort towards these goods. The infant is not even aware of the fact that he or she is making no effort—but others at the baptismal ceremony can be left with the impression that sacraments can be a matter of what God does to (imposes on?) passive recipients. To be clear, I am not attempting to argue that baptismal grace is given by God (only) as a reward for human effort. I am not seeking to get the nose of the Pelagian camel under the flap of the sacramental tent. I *am* suggesting that in a consumer culture that is quite different from the culture in which infant baptism first emerged, Christians may need to articulate how infant baptism is not after all just another form of passive enjoyment of a consumer good.

A second risk with respect to infant baptism is sentimentality. John Burgess contends: "It is easy to make baptism little more than a sentimental ritual of welcoming a newborn baby into a congregation. The pastor sprinkles a few drops of water on the baby's head and parades her up and down the aisle. Those in the pews smile approvingly, as the organist finds the register with tinkling bells and plays, 'Jesus Loves Me.' But baptism is not simply a gentle anointing that makes everything about the baby innocent and clean."[29] Indeed, as William Strange observes, Christian parents in the early church likely hesitated to bring their children forward for baptism: "Augustine's mother agonised over this decision when her son was ill in childhood, and came down against it (*Confessions* 1:17). Her reason is instructive: she did not want to lay the heavy demands of discipleship on her child. . . . Parents from the second to fourth centuries did not regard baptism as a blessing for their children, but as a burden placed upon them. Probably, the more pious the parents, the more reluctant they were to baptise their children."[30] Part of the "demands of discipleship" in the church of this earlier epoch was the notion that the forgiveness of postbaptismal sin was at best a difficult affair.[31] There was as yet no practice of repeatable confession. Having had one's sins erased once in baptism, one would have a single additional opportunity in the form of canonical penance, which was quite stringent. One was committed to the high wire of discipleship with a small safety net. There was a vivid sense that baptism involved matters of life-and-death seriousness. One present-day homilist observes: "In the domestic beauty of our lovely ritual of Baptism, with proud parents and grandparents and godparents beaming joyfully at the innocent charm of a white-gowned child, it can be hard to recognize the radical nature of the act of Baptism. But if your nostrils were spiritually energized, they would be filled with the smell of death."[32]

The passive reception of baptism on the part of the infant can reinforce notions of consumerist passivity. The sentimentality associated with infant baptism, though not directly an aspect

---

29. John P. Burgess, *After Baptism: Shaping the Christian Life* (Louisville, KY: Westminster John Knox, 2005), 3.

30. William Strange, "Entering the Sheepfold: A New Look at Infant Baptism," in *Joining and Leaving Religion: Research Perspectives*, ed. Leslie J. Francis and Yaacov Katz (Leominster, UK: Gracewing, 2000), 48–49.

31. In his *On Baptism* 18, Tertullian provides a classic example of this kind of thinking.

32. Lowell Grisham, "The Baptism of Jesus by John," sermon preached at St. Paul's Episcopal Church, Fayetteville, Arkansas, January 7, 2001, as quoted in Debra Dean Murphy, "Identity Politics: Christian Baptism and the Pledge of Allegiance," *Liturgy* 20, no. 1 (2005): 5–10 at 8.

of consumerism, can serve a consumerist function insofar as it removes baptism from the paschal mystery that gives it its meaning. Consumer culture is also all too happy to capitalize on this sentimentality, however. It took me a very short time online to find a baptismal gown costing $625.[33] Again, I want to emphasize that I am not denying the validity or legitimacy of infant baptism. I simply want to point out that in a consumer culture the potential complications of this practice go beyond sixteenth-century debates about whether only adults should be baptized.

V. The Catechumenate I: Public Persons

In the early centuries of the church, of course, most baptisms involved adults. This section of this chapter directs attention to how the ancient catechumenate allows one to appreciate baptism as far from being an event abstracted from a context of meaning. The catechumenate, first of all, was a public affair and not private. It involved attention to the practice of almsgiving, and it was a matter of energizing the faith not only of those seeking baptism but of the rest of the Christian community as well—and even non-Christians.

The New Testament provides a number of examples in which only minimal preparation preceded adult baptism (e.g., the three thousand or so who were baptized in Acts 2, the eunuch in Acts 8, the household of Cornelius in Acts 10), but the Didache, parts of which have been dated to the first century, provides basic catechetical instruction in the Ways of Life and Death as a prelude to baptism.[34] By the third century, the catechumenate was well-established in at least some regions as a prerequisite for initiation into the church. In the ancient catechumenate as well as the restored RCIA, baptism is associated with quite specific practices as well as having very clear social significance beyond the importance the rite has for the individual(s) being baptized.

33. See "Silk Christening Gowns," *One Small Child*, https://www.onesmallchild .com/product-category/christening-gowns/luxurious-fabrics/silk-christening -gowns .
34. See *Didache* 1–6.

If consumer culture emphasizes the private enjoyment of goods (think of family members watching television programs in their own individual bedrooms), the catechumenate emphasizes the public quality of Christian faith. William Harmless offers this summary of the impact of the restoration of the Rite of Christian Initiation of Adults:

> RCIA reverses a centuries-old habit: privatizing Christian initiation. No longer is the formation of converts a few hasty months of private instruction in doctrine. No longer is their conversion a private matter—worked out in hushed anonymity between convert and parish priest. No longer is their baptism to be a quiet little affair, a small gathering of family and friends held any Saturday afternoon. Rather their initiation is to assume once more the honor, the centrality, and the symbolic richness it enjoyed in the patristic era.
>
> Because of the new rite, converting individuals assume center stage in the assembly's worship. Before the whole assembly, their motives and commitments are examined. Before it, they are lavished with blessings, healed with exorcisms, strengthened with anointings. Week after week, they are solemnly dismissed in a vivid, even threatening, gesture meant to catechize the faithful and catechumen alike on the high dignity of their baptism. . . . Candidates are to be public persons, and the witness of their conversion, a matter of public record.[35]

Candidates are "public persons"—in the present day, for example, their names are publicly entered into the Book of the Elect during the Rite of Election[36]—and their conversion is public.

VI. The Catechumenate II: Almsgiving

In a late-modern culture characterized by consumerism and the hectic pursuit of more and more things, it is worth noting that

---

35. William Harmless, *Augustine and the Catechumenate* (Collegeville, MN: Liturgical Press, 1995), 9–10. See also Kavanagh, *The Shape of Baptism*, 128.

36. RCIA 130–33. Notably, 130 specifically indicates that the elect are to be called by name out loud.

an important part of the public conversion process was the practice of almsgiving, a practice quite opposed to consumerism. The Didache, for example, directs would-be Christians to give alms: "Give to everyone that asks thee, and do not refuse, for the Father's will is that we give to all from the gifts we have received. Blessed is he that gives according to the mandate; for he is innocent. Woe to him who receives; for if any man receives alms under pressure of need he is innocent; but he who receives it without need shall be tried as to why he took and for what, and being in prison he shall be examined as to his deeds, and 'he shall not come out thence until he pay the last farthing.'"[37] Centuries later, the theme of almsgiving as a practice associated with baptism would be emphasized by St. Basil of Cappadocia, St. Augustine, St. John Chrysostom and St. Maximus of Turin. Addressing himself to Basil's treatise on baptism, Aidan Kavanagh directs attention to

> Basil's repeated use of the story of the rich young man to illustrate for the catechumen what is necessary to be a disciple of Christ. One must first obey the commandments. Then one must sell all and follow him, since ". . . whoever of you does not renounce all that he has cannot be my disciple" (Luke 14:33). This attitude becomes the *leitmotiv* of the entire treatise, and it is directed not only to monastic ascetics but to all who are made *christoi* by baptism. "Not only should we not endeavor to increase our possessions and to acquire greater gains, as do men of the world, but we should not even lay claim to the property which has already been acquired and is our own. Let us be zealous in giving to the needy."[38]

37. *Didache* 1.5 in *The Apostolic Fathers*, vol. 1: *I Clement, II Clement, Ignatius, Polycarp, Didache, Barnabas*, trans. Kirsopp Lake (Cambridge, MA: Harvard University Press, 1959, reprint), 311. The passage in quotes here is from Matt 5:36. See also the commentary on almsgiving in Aaron Milavec, *The Didache: Text, Translation, Analysis, and Commentary* (Collegeville, MN: Liturgical Press, 2003), 50–51.

38. Aidan Kavanagh, *On Liturgical Theology* (New York: Pueblo, 1984), 155. Kavanagh is quoting from Basil, *Concerning Baptism* 1.2, in *Fathers of the Church: A New Translation*, vol. 9: *Saint Basil: Ascetical Works*, trans. Monica Wagner (Washington, DC: Catholic University of America Press, 1962), 364. Kavanagh adds here that "according to the precedent stated in Acts 4:32-37, this was not absolute poverty but the possession of all things in common, from which distribution was made according to need."

Basil refers to the passage in which Luke 14:33 is found (i.e., Luke 14:25-33) at least six times in *Concerning Baptism*, including three direct citations of verse 33. One of those citations is presented as part of what Basil calls the teaching that catechumens must receive before baptism thus "making ourselves fit to receive the instruction."[39]

Writing on the catechumenate in the time of Augustine, William Harmless notes that of the many Lenten ascetical disciplines associated with those seeking entrance into the church—fasting, attention to one's sins, and so forth—it was almsgiving that "received the most catechetical attention."[40] Augustine was fond of referring to giving alms and offering forgiveness as the "two wings" upon which prayer may rise to God. Two such references are found in Augustine's Lenten homilies, during which the *competentes*—those petitioning for baptism—were present.[41]

Speaking to those seeking baptism, John Chrysostom also referred to almsgiving. God "has commanded you, too, to do this as far as you can in the things which have been entrusted to you—to increase the sanctity which you have received, to render more shining your justice after the bath, and to make your grace more lustrous."[42] Warning especially women preparing for the sacrament, he urged "pay no attention to garments made from the silkworm's thread, nor to necklaces of gold,"[43] and in language reminiscent of Ambrose's warning about the fate of fishers and hunters who try to gather food for the wealthy, Chrysostom noted that in order "that you may wear a single ruby, countless poor are

---

39. Basil, *Concerning Baptism*, I.2 as in *Saint Basil: Ascetical Works*, 383–84.

40. Harmless, *Augustine and the Catechumenate*, 64. The practice of fasting, of course, also has ramifications in a consumer culture but here I will focus on almsgiving. The chapter on confirmation will direct attention to fasting.

41. Augustine uses the image of the two wings of prayer in Sermons 58.10; 205.3; 206.2–3; *Exposition on Psalm 42* 8. Sermons 205 and 206 were delivered at the beginning of Lent.

42. John Chrysostom, *Twelfth Instruction on Baptism* 8, in Paul Harkins, ed., *St. John Chrysostom: Baptismal Instructions* (Westminster, MD: Newman, 1963), 176.

43. John Chrysostom, *First Instruction on Baptism* 34, in Harkins, *St. John Chrysostom*, 36.

starved and crushed."[44] He urged his listeners to "strip off your adornment and put it into Christ's hands through the hands of His poor."[45]

In the fifth century, St. Maximus of Turin drew an especially close connection between baptism and almsgiving: "Almsgiving is another kind of washing of souls, so that if perchance anyone has sinned through human frailty after baptism, there is still the possibility of being cleansed by almsgiving, as the Lord says: Give alms, and behold, everything is clean for you. But (with due regard to the faith) I would say that almsgiving is more indulgent than baptism. For baptism is given once and bestows pardon once, whereas as many times as alms are bestowed pardon is granted. These are two fonts of mercy, which give life and forgive sins."[46] Boniface Ramsey is careful to point out that Maximus may well have been engaging in a rhetorical flourish when he spoke this way about baptism and almsgiving,[47] but for present purposes it suffices to observe that, in the words of St. Jerome, "almsgiving does the very thing that baptism does."[48] It should also be noted that Maximus is addressing cases of postbaptismal sin and not the situation of catechumens as such. Nevertheless, Maximus associated the practice of baptism with the practice of giving alms to the poor. Each of these practices is a manifestation of a desire to turn from sin. Perhaps there is something to be said for understanding these practices in light of each other in a culture marked by consumerism.[49]

---

44. John Chrysostom, *Twelfth Instruction on Baptism* 41, in Harkins, *St. John Chrysostom*, 185. In Chrysostom's admonitions to women, one finds an echo of 1 Tim 2:9, which he explicitly cites on p. 187 of the Harkins text.

45. John Chrysostom, *Twelfth Instruction on Baptism* 46, in Harkins, *St. John Chrysostom*, 187.

46. St. Maximus of Turin, *Sermon 22A*, quoted in Boniface Ramsey, "Almsgiving in the Latin Church: The Late Fourth and Early Fifth Centuries," *Theological Studies* 43, no. 2 (1982): 226–259 at 242. Maximus is citing Luke 11:41.

47. Ramsey, "Almsgiving in the Latin Church," 243.

48. Jerome, *Tractate on Psalm 134 [133]*, lines 197–200, quoted in Ramsey, "Almsgiving in the Latin Church," 243.

49. Parishes that introduce catechumens to the stewardship of time, talent, and treasure are an important present-day analogue to the ancient emphasis on almsgiving.

VII. The Catechumenate III: Shining for Others

We have already had occasion to note that in the catechumenate (both ancient and present-day), the process of becoming Christian is public and how this public quality can offer a measure of resistance to a culture that is marked by consumerist individualism. Here, I want to turn to how the catechumenate culminating in Christian initiation is a matter of significance not only for those to receive baptism and the other sacraments of initiation. The catechumens also have importance for the community into which they are received and beyond. "Catechumens," writes Aidan Kavanagh, "occupy an overt place in Church structure and discharge a real ministry to the Church by witnessing in their own lives to the never-ending need of conversion in Christ that is requisite for the whole Church, universal as well as local."[50] In turn, the church has the responsibility of welcoming catechumens and providing for their formation.[51] The RCIA repeatedly draws attention to the supportive role that the baptized faithful are to play in the formation of newcomers. For example, there is this prayer to be offered in these or similar words as part of the rite of acceptance into the order of catechumens:

> Assisting minister: That they may have our sincere and unfailing support every step of the way, let us pray to the Lord.
>
> R. Lord, hear our prayer.
>
> Assisting minister: That they may find in our community compelling signs of unity and generous love, let us pray to the Lord.
>
> R. Lord, hear our prayer.[52]

50. Kavanagh, *The Shape of Baptism*, 130. Reflecting on Lent as the season during which candidates take their final steps toward baptism, André Resner remarks that "Lent insistently reminds us that baptism, by the mystery of God's stubborn grace, is never done with us." André Resner, "Casting Our Mammon on the Baptismal Waters: Preaching Economic Justice during Lent," *Journal for Preachers* 27, no. 2 (2004): 42–50 at 45.

51. This is a point made by Michael Witczak, who adds: "In this very act, the community will find its own faith articulated anew and challenged to grow." Witczak, *The Sacrament of Baptism*, 18.

52. RCIA 65. Other examples may be found in paragraphs 4, 9, 67B (dismissal at the conclusion of the rite of acceptance into the order of catechumens), 114

Among those dealing with the catechumenate in the early church, Augustine and John Chrysostom were particularly eloquent concerning the ways in which those about to be baptized or just recently baptized were to have an effect on the church. Both figures drew upon the theme of light as found in Matt 5; Augustine also draws on Genesis 1. Here is the relevant portion of Augustine's Sermon 226:

> In the original foundation of the world we read that *darkness was upon the deep, and the Spirit of God was skimming over the water. And God said, let light be made; and light was made. And God divided between the light and the darkness; and he called the light day, and the darkness he called night* (Gn 1:2-5). There you have the day which the Lord has made. But that's not the one, is it, in which we should exult and be joyful? There's another day which the Lord has made, which we ought rather to acknowledge as the one in which to exult and be joyful; since the faithful who believe in Christ have been told, *You are the light of the world* (Mt 5:14). If light, then of course also day, because he called the light day.
>
> Yesterday here too the Spirit of God was skimming over the water, and darkness was upon the deep, when these *infants* were still carrying their sins. So when their sins were forgiven them through the Spirit of God, that's when God said, *Let light be made; and light was made.* There they are, *the day which the Lord has made; let us exult and be joyful in it.*[53]

Thus, for Augustine baptism is connected to the theme of new creation and a cause for celebration and exultation on the part of those who now behold the newly baptized shining with the light of the day God has made. The bishop of Hippo does not view the baptism of the infants as an exclusively self-regarding event.

(intercession at the rite of sending for election), 134 (intercession at the rite of election), 136B (dismissal at the conclusion of the rite of election), 155B (dismissal after the first scrutiny), and so on. See also RBC 4 and OBC 4.

53. Augustine, Sermon 226, in John Rotelle, ed., *The Works of Saint Augustine: A Translation for the 21st Century: Sermons III/6 (184–229Z) on the Liturgical Seasons,* trans. Edmund Hill (New Rochelle, NY: New City, 1993), 252.

This theme is even more pronounced in the preaching of the Golden Tongue. Reflecting on his own baptism, Chrysostom addresses those soon to be baptized with a concern for himself:

> Now tears and bitter groans assail me. For I thought of the day on which I too was judged worthy to speak those words. When I consider the burden of my sins I have accumulated from that day to this, my mind is confounded; my reason is cut to the quick when I see what shame I have poured on myself by my subsequent negligence. Wherefore, I beg all of you to show some generosity to me, especially since you are about to meet the King. He will receive you with great eagerness; He will put upon you the royal robe; He will give you gifts, as many as you could wish and of whatever kind you wish, but only if we ask for spiritual things. Ask for a grace on my behalf, that He may not demand from me an accounting of my sins, but granting me pardon, He may hereafter judge me worthy of His favor.[54]

Chrysostom's humility here allows him to make an important point, namely, that baptism involves doing, praying, and being for others. Unlike the *Chant* album discussed earlier, it is clear that baptism is associated with other concrete practices.

Chrysostom also urges those about to be baptized to take seriously the gleaming robes they will don after the rite:

> Now the robe you wear and the gleaming garments attract the eyes of all; if you should will to do so, by keeping your royal robes shining even more brightly than it now does, you will always be able to draw all who behold you to show the same zeal and praise for the Master.
>
> It was on this account that Christ said: *Let your light shine before men, in order that they may see your good works and give glory to your Father who is in heaven.* Did you see how He urges us to let the light within us shine forth not by garments but by deeds? After He said: *Let your light shine,* He added: *in order that they may see your good works.* This light does not stop with the bodily senses but illumines the soul and understanding of those who see it;

---

54. John Chrysostom, *Second Instruction on Baptism* 19, in Harkins, *St. John Chrysostom,* 50–51. The reference to "those words" is to the profession of faith.

after it dispels the darkness of evil, it draws those who find it to shine with their own light and to imitate the life of virtue.

Let your light shine before men, He says. And He was right in saying *before men*. Let your light be so bright, He says, that it not only illumines yourselves but shines before men who need it to guide them. Just as light for the bodily eyes puts darkness to flight and keeps on the right path those who travel a material road, so the light for the mind which comes from the excellence of your conduct lights the way for those whose mental vision is so muddled by the darkness of error that they cannot see the path of virtue. This light clears away the mist from the spiritual eyes of these travelers, puts them on the right road, and makes them walk thenceforth on the path of virtue.

That they may see your good works and give glory to your Father who is in heaven. Let your virtue, He says, and your well-disciplined conduct, and the uprightness of your deeds move those who behold you to praise the common Master of us all. I exhort you: let each one of you be eager to live his life with such exactness that prayers of worship may ascend to the Master from all who behold you.[55]

Preaching on another occasion, Chrysostom imagines the Lord Jesus speaking to his followers about the light that has been given to them: " 'For I,' saith He, 'it is true, have kindled the light, but its continuing to burn, let that come of your diligence: not for your own sakes alone, but also for their sake, who are to profit by these rays and to be guided unto the truth.' "[56]

In the context of the ancient catechumenate, then, baptism was not simply a matter of an individual seeking salvation the way

---

55. John Chrysostom, *Fourth Instruction on Baptism* 18–21, in Harkins, *St. John Chrysostom*, 73–74. See also the *Sixth Instruction on Baptism* 11, in Harkins, *St. John Chrysostom*, 97. The preaching of Basil of Cappadocia on almsgiving earlier in this chapter takes place in the context of his urging his hearers to let their light shine before others. See *Concerning Baptism* 1.2, in *Saint Basil: Ascetical Works*, 364. See also the citation from John Chrysostom in n. 42 of this chapter in which he, too, connects almsgiving to the theme of shining before other men and women.

56. John Chrysostom, *Homilies on Matthew* 15.11, in Philip Schaff, ed., *Nicene and Post-Nicene Fathers of the Christian Church*, vol. 10: *St. Chrysostom: Homilies on the Gospel of Saint Matthew* (Grand Rapids, MI: Eerdmans, 1986, reprint), 98.

that an individual consumer today looks for a product that suits his or her own tastes and then enjoys it privately. Augustine, for example, referred to those seeking baptism as *competentes*, because they are petitioning for baptism *together* (*com-peto* = to ask together).[57] Beyond that, those to be baptized were made aware of the expectations associated with preparation for baptism and life after baptism. Among these expectations is that they will by their conduct demonstrate that their life with God in Christ is a matter of witnessing before others in their righteous and just conduct, and this for the sake of the others.

VIII. Exorcisms and The Renunciation of Satan

We can also examine exorcisms and the baptismal renunciation of Satan as aspects of baptism that resist consumerism. The renunciation of Satan is by extension a renunciation of all forms of false worship. Exorcisms are rites designed to assist people in the struggle to be followers of Christ and to resist false desires.

William Harmless points out that on at least one occasion when St. Augustine was preaching on the need for Christians to distinguish themselves from pagans, his hearers burst out with the chant "Down with Roman gods! Down with Roman gods!"[58] Issues of present-day decorum aside, it is unlikely that one would hear similar cries in a church today. There is no question that in antiquity, Christians and would-be Christians were quite clear—at least in theory—about the pagan practices they were rejecting: worship of idols, adoration of the Emperor, and of course the "shows."[59] Writing around the year 200, Tertullian devoted an entire treatise to the evils of the shows and spectacles put on by Roman municipalities, which often featured savage brutality and/ or enactment of pagan myths. For Tertullian, such activities were plainly incompatible with baptism:

---

57. See the reference to Augustine's Sermon 216.1, in Thomas Finn, "It Happened One Saturday Night: Ritual and Conversion in Augustine's North Africa," *Journal of the American Academy of Religion* 58, no. 4 (1990): 589–616 at 591.

58. Harmless, *Augustine and the Catechumenate*, 111. Harmless is referring to Sermon 24.6.

59. See Miller, *Consuming Religion*, 180–81.

When entering the water, we make profession of the Christian faith in the words of its rule; we bear public testimony that we have renounced the devil, his pomp, and his angels. Well, is it not in connection with idolatry, above all, that you have the devil with his pomp and his angels? . . . If, therefore, it shall be made plain that the entire apparatus of the shows is based upon idolatry, beyond all doubt that will carry with it the conclusion that our renunciatory testimony in the laver of baptism has reference to the shows, which, through their idolatry, have been given over to the devil, and his pomp, and his angels.[60]

Centuries later, however, Chrysostom lamented in one of his baptismal instructions that some of his flock still sought out such entertainment, which he called "Satan's deadly spectacles":

Again there are the chariot races and satanic spectacles in the hippodrome, and our congregation is shrinking . . . . Not only is my grief increased, but so, too, has my discouragement. When a farmer sees that, after all his work and troubles, the earth produces no return for his labors but is no more productive than a stone, he is more hesitant thereafter to work the land because he sees that his work is idle and in vain . . . I look on your laxity as my own personal loss. On this account I consider that my joy is blunted, especially since I understand that this neglect of what I say brings a more serious condemnation on those who are unwilling to derive profit from my series of instructions and who continue in this laxity after I have exhorted them so strongly.[61]

---

60. Tertullian, *On the Shows* 4, in Alexander Roberts and James Donaldson, eds., *Ante-Nicene Fathers The Writings of the Fathers Down to A.D. 325*, vol. 3: *Latin Christianity: Its Founder, Tertullian I. Apologetic; II. Anti-Marcion; III. Ethical* (Peabody, MA: Hendrickson, 2004), 81. Perhaps without too much hyperbole, Tertullian claimed in chapter 24 of this treatise that "the rejection of these amusements is the chief sign to [pagans] that a man has adopted the Christian faith" (89). However, as we will soon see, Tertullian also warned about idolatry that is cloaked and unperceived.

61. John Chrysostom, *Sixth Instruction on Baptism* 1, 4, in Harkins, *St. John Chrysostom*, 93, 94. See also Thomas Finn's commentary on this passage in Thomas Finn, *The Liturgy of Baptism in the Baptismal Instructions of St. John Chrysostom* (Washington, DC: Catholic University of America Press, 1967), 100–101. The phrase "Satan's deadly spectacles" is from *Sixth Instruction on Baptism* 14, in p. 98 of the Harkins text.

In approximately the same era, on at least one occasion Augustine deliberately engaged in extended preaching in order to prevent catechumens, who were to be dismissed just after the conclusion of the homily, from attending a festival going on at the time—in effect forcing them to stay in church until the festival had come to an end.[62]

The division between Christian and pagan was clear in antiquity, yet long before explicit forms of idolatry faded from the scene, Tertullian urged vigilance. He considered idolatry to be the "head of unrighteousness" and warned that Christians should "recognize it not only in its palpable manifestations."[63] Indeed, Tertullian argues that idolatry "subverts the servants of God; and this not only when unperceived, but also when cloaked over."[64] According to the Pauline corpus, greed is a (hidden) form of idolatry (Eph 5:3-5 and Col 3:5). If idolatry is the "head of unrighteousness"— see, for example, the very First Commandment—and if greed is a kind of idolatry, then the baptismal renunciation of false worship is directed at least in part against greed. Indeed, Augustine warned his *competentes* that Paul "very truthfully called [avarice] the service of idols."[65] Chrysostom, for his part, said that he had "oftentimes explained" how "covetousness is said to be idolatry."[66]

Though it quotes neither Ephesians nor Colossians in this connection, the restored Rite of Christian Initiation of Adults does include optional exorcisms against the spirit of greed (or love of money) in paragraph 94 B, C, and D. Here are the relevant excerpts:

---

62. Augustine, *Tractates on John*, 7.24 as quoted in Harmless, *Augustine and the Catechumenate*, 223–24.

63. Tertullian, *On Idolatry* 2, in *Ante-Nicene Fathers* 3:62.

64. Ibid.

65. Augustine, Sermon 216.5 as in Rotelle, ed., *Sermons III/6 (184–229Z)*, 170.

66. John Chrysostom, Homily 8 on Colossians, in Philip Schaff, ed., *Nicene and Post-Nicene Fathers of the Christian Church*, vol. 13: *Saint Chrysostom: Homilies on Galatians, Ephesians, Philippians, Colossians, Thessalonians, Timothy, Titus, and Philemon* (Grand Rapids, MI: Eerdmans, 1988, reprint), 297. In his Homily 65 on John, Chrysostom preached that "more grievous than an evil spirit is the lust of money-loving, and many obey it more than others do idols." Citation from Philip Schaff, ed., *Nicene and Post-Nicene Fathers of the Christian Church*, vol. 14: *Saint Chrysostom: Homilies on the Gospel of John and the Epistle to the Hebrews* (Grand Rapids, MI: Eerdmans, 1989, reprint), 297. See also Homily 20 on Hebrews and Homily 6 on Romans.

B.

In the name of your beloved Son,
our Lord Jesus Christ,
and in the power of the Holy Spirit,
we ask you to remove from these your servants
all unbelief and hesitation in faith,
[the worship of false gods and magic,
witchcraft and dealings with the dead],
the love of money and lawless passions,
enmity and quarreling,
and every manner of evil.

C.

Even when we sinned against you,
you did not abandon us,
but in your wisdom chose to save us
by the incarnation of your Son.
Save these your servants:
free them from evil and the tyranny of the enemy.
Keep far from them the spirit of wickedness, falsehood, and greed.

D.

Help these servants, who hear the word of the Gospel,
and protect them from the spirit of greed, of lust, and of pride.

As indicative as these prayers may be for baptismal resistance to consumerism, it must also be admitted that there are eleven of these minor exorcisms and that the other eight do not mention greed. Furthermore, although the rite specifies in paragraph 93 that the minor exorcisms may be used on more than one occasion, the rite does not mandate more than one minor exorcism. In those RCIA programs where there is only one minor exorcism, there is less than a one-third chance that the exorcism will refer to greed.[67] Finally, although RCIA 90 asserts that the minor exorcisms "draw the attention of the catechumens to the real nature of Christian life, the struggle between flesh and spirit . . . and the unending need

---

67. Of course, whether a given exorcism refers to greed should not be the only criterion when one is making pastoral judgments about which exorcism to use. I am merely stating the odds that one will in fact encounter an exorcism against greed.

for God's help," one can also ask about the degree to which these exorcisms and the renunciation of Satan are experienced with a certain complacence in late-modern culture.[68]

In this connection, we can note Robert Hovda's concern about baptismal renunciations—namely, that for many persons questions of sin and the glamour of evil have been reduced to what he calls "the tiny dimension of sex."[69] James Dunning warns against reducing images of the demonic to the vomiting character in the 1973 movie *The Exorcist*.[70] David Batchelder and Debra Dean Murphy express fear that baptismal renunciations and promises are empty of significance.[71] The title of Batchelder's essay is telling: "Baptismal Renunciations: Making Promises We Do Not Intend to Keep." He voices concern that the "ritual performance at the font is in danger of becoming a scandal of saying what we do not really mean."[72] Murphy, for her part, worries that "because the

---

68. For additional discussion of the practical and cultural obstacles to worthy celebration of minor exorcisms, see David A. Pitt, *"Lex Exorcismi, Lex Vivendi:* The Minor Exorcisms of Adult Initiation and Baptismal Identity," in *A Living Tradition: On the Intersection of Liturgical History and Pastoral Practice*, ed. David A. Pitt, Stefanos Alexapoulos, and Christian McConnell, (Collegeville, MN: Liturgical Press, 2012), 168–71.

69. Robert Hovda, "Renunciation of Evil and Profession of Faith," in *Commentaries on the Rite of Christian Initiation of Adults*, ed. James Wilde (Chicago: Liturgy Training Publications, 1988), 103.

70. James Dunning, "Confronting the Demons: The Social Dimensions of Conversion," in *Conversion and the Catechumenate*, 24–25. On these same pages, Dunning also warns against reducing Satan to "cute little red devils perched on Flip Wilson's shoulder ('The devil made me do it!')."

71. David Batchelder, "Baptismal Renunciations: Making Promises We Do Not Intend to Keep," *Worship* 81, no. 5 (2007): 409–25; Murphy, "Identity Politics," 5–10. See also Christian Scharen, "Baptismal Practices and the Formation of Christians: A Critical Liturgical Ethics," *Worship* 76, no. 1 (2002): 43–66. The baptism scene in the movie *The Godfather* is a classic illustration of making promises one does not intend to keep.

72. Batchelder, "Baptismal Renunciations," 411. Batchelder elaborates: "I worry that our communities have learned to practice a way of speaking ritually that not only permits false witness at the font, but establishes it as the norm. We make claims concerning sin and evil but often live as if we have not really considered the implications. Sometimes I wonder whether the church believes there are any serious implications at all. Ritual practice can give the appearance that accountability is fulfilled simply by one's participation in the rites with the moral

subversive, political nature of Baptism is rarely communicated in the ritual act itself or in preaching and teaching about the rite, baptismal practice is often in danger of becoming a parody."[73]

In antiquity, exorcisms and the renunciation of Satan were no understated affairs. Chrysostom, for example, instructs his hearers in these words: "Then the priest has you say: 'I renounce thee,' Satan, thy pomps, thy service, and thy works. The words are few but their power is great. The angels who are standing by and the invisible powers rejoice at your conversion, receive the words from your tongues, and carry them up to the common Master of all things. There they are inscribed in the books of heaven."[74] Augustine encouraged his *competentes* to see in their exorcisms the real stadium, the real wrestling grounds, the real racetracks of their lives—as opposed to the shows and spectacles of the empire.[75] Thomas Finn observes that for Augustine and his assembly "a contest of Olympic proportions was at hand: a cosmic struggle between the world embodied in the competents and the world

---

weight residing in the rhetoric. Or to say it another way, the ethical responsibility of baptismal vows seems more associated with using strong ritual language that, paradoxically, absolves the community *from* the cross rather than obligates it to the cross."

73. Murphy, "Identity Politics," 8. Writing with an eye toward the blending of American nationalism and Christian faith in the wake of the terrorist attacks of September 2001, Murphy adds: "If the operative assumption, implicit or explicit, is that the church gives form and expression to the politics of modernity (privatized morality, the priority of the individual, the identification of Christianity and nationalism) rather than to the politics of the cross (suffering love, resistance to all other powers and authorities), then Baptism can unwittingly serve to initiate persons into a 'loose confederation of individuals who take no responsibility for the conversion and nurture of others, who do not act as if they really believe that the promises of Baptism are true, and who lack confidence in their ability, by God's grace, to "make disciples."'" Murphy is quoting from John Westerhoff and William H. Willimon, *Liturgy and Learning Through the Life Cycle*, rev. ed. (Akron: OSL, 1994), 13.

See also the homily excerpt quoted in n. 32 of the present chapter, taken from the same page in the Murphy essay. The homilist cautions that cuteness and sentimentality can obscure the gravity of baptism.

74. John Chrysostom, *Second Instruction on Baptism* 20, in Harkins, *St. John Chrysostom*, 51.

75. Augustine, Sermon 216.6 in Rotelle, ed., *Sermons III/6 (184–229Z)*, 170.

embodied in the exorcist."[76] Finn points out that those being exorcised in preparation for baptism were likely naked, hungry, sleepless, and unbathed as they stood or kneeled in the presence of the assembly.[77] Such circumstances might indeed make for high drama and effectively underscore the significance of the rites, but as Christopher Scharen observes in an essay on the weaknesses of contemporary baptismal liturgies, "to suggest a simple revival of such bizarre rituals in the church today would cause laughter at best, and probably scorn. Yet, maintaining the renunciation within the baptismal liturgy without any previous practice in which this rejection is explicated results in a formula empty of contemporary meaning."[78]

If Batchelder, Murphy, and Scharen are all correct in their judgments, what can late-modern liturgical assemblies do to recover a sense of the scope of exorcisms and the renunciation of Satan, especially as these might relate to resisting consumerism? The RCIA itself states in 33/8 (repeated in 224) that the formulary for renouncing false worship that is used during the rite of acceptance into the order of catechumens may be adapted to local circumstances at the discretion of the national conference of bishops. In 33/8, the RCIA for use in the United States adds the following: "The National Conference of Catholic Bishops has established as the norm in the dioceses of the United States that the formularies of renunciation should not be adapted. But for those cases where certain catechumens may be from cultures in which false worship is widespread it has approved leaving to the discretion of the diocesan bishop this matter of making more specific and detailed the formularies of renunciation in the rite of acceptance into the order of catechumens and in the celebration of baptism."[79] Commenting on this passage, David Batchelder offers this assessment:

---

76. Finn, "It Happened One Saturday Night," 601.

77. Ibid. The rite also involved standing and kneeling on a rug of goat hair, emblematic of one's subjection to the power of Satan. Recall that it is the goats who are dismissed from the kingdom in Matt 25.

78. Scharen, "Baptismal Practices and the Formation of Christians," 61.

79. See also OBC 24/3 for a parallel directive, which is explicit in comparison with RBC 24/3.

Sections 32 to 34 in the Roman Catholic RCIA outline those places and conditions where the catechumenate (and its rites) can be adapted. The rubrics in paragraph 224 give discretion for the bishop to make the renunciations more detailed and specific as circumstances require. Such adaptation may be made "where certain catechumens are from cultures in which false worship is widespread." What the church had in mind was the experience of African churches where candidates often participated in "false worship" and "magical arts." Even in the catechumens' first rite (the Rite of Acceptance), a presider may ask: "Are you determined never to abandon [Christ Jesus] and never to seek out soothsayers, magicians, or witch doctors?"

Though it may come as a surprise, research by Jamie Lara demonstrates that such adaptation of the adult catechumenate took place much earlier in Mexico in the 16th century where candidates were led into the middle of the church and instructed to "avoid the traps of death" and "reject the horrors of idolatry." I wonder if we are not making too little use of this invitation to adaptation. Are "false worship" and the "horrors of idolatry" restricted to the continent of Africa and sixteenth-century Mexico?[80]

In a similar vein—and echoing Tertullian's admonition about hidden forms of idolatry—William Reiser argues that "questions such as 'Do you reject sin?' or 'Do you reject the glamour of evil?' need to be spelled out so that people have a firm idea about what exactly they are being asked to reject."[81]

80. Batchelder, "Baptismal Renunciations," 421. The citation concerning widespread false worship is taken from RCIA 33/8. The citation concerning soothsayers is taken from RCIA 72B. The citations concerning Mexico are taken from Jamie Lara, " 'Precious Green Jade Water': A Sixteenth-Century Adult Catechumenate in the New World," *Worship* 71, no. 5 (1997): 415–28.

Batchelder continues on p. 421: "Rabbi James Rudin, in his book *The Baptizing of America*, tells of an airplane sky writer in Florida who was seen tracing the words, 'JESUS LOVES US—JESUS IS THE USA.' What would we call much of American patriotism, if not 'false worship'?" Batchelder is quoting from Rabbi James Rudin, *The Baptizing of America: The Religious Right's Plans for the Rest of Us* (New York: Thunder's Mouth, 2006), 1.

81. William Reiser, "Baptismal Promises: Making the Words Bite," *America* 154, no. 7 (February 22, 1996): 134, quoted in Eileen Crowley, "Making More Visible Our Invisible Baptismal Promises," in *Proceedings: North American Academy of*

Batchelder and Reiser each offer suggestions for revisions of the renunciations and promises. Both writers explicitly name consumerism. First, Batchelder: "Do you renounce all attempts to equate the Gospel of Christ with the American dream? Do you renounce the power of the economy to define human value by what you consume and produce?"[82] Next, Reiser: "Do you commit yourself to that spirit of poverty and detachment that Jesus enjoined on His disciples, and to resisting that spirit of consumerism and materialism that is so strong in our culture?"[83] Drawing upon the Robert Hovda essay cited above, Eileen Crowley suggests that use of visual images depicting the evils one renounces verbally may be a useful tactic.[84]

Liturgy Annual Meeting, San Francisco, January 6–9, 2011, (Notre Dame, IN: North American Academy of Liturgy), 94. Drawing in part on the work of one of her students (Brian Michalski, "Reflecting on the Renewal of Baptismal Promises," unpublished paper for the Catholic Theological Union course W4200 Sacraments I: Initiation and Reconciliation [May 2010]), Crowley discusses revised baptismal promises at a parish in Chicago. See also Reiser, *Renewing the Baptismal Promises* (New York: Pueblo, 1988) for a book-length treatment of issues related to baptismal promises and renunciations.

82. Batchelder, "Baptismal Renunciations," 422. Among the other proposed renunciations offered by Batchelder, some refer to national security, homophobia, sexism, racism, and a "xenophobia that exploits immigrants and deprives them of justice."

83. Reiser, "Baptismal Promises: Making the Words Bite," 134, quoted in Crowley, "Making More Visible Our Invisible Baptismal Promises," 94. Among the other affirmations that Reiser proposes, some refer to being attentive to the poor and to trying to please God in one's daily living. Along with the suggestions offered by Batchelder and Reiser, one can also note the baptismal practice of the Episcopal Church, which, since the implementation of the 1979 *Book of Common Prayer*, includes a baptismal covenant of five questions addressing commitments to ongoing formation in faith and discipleship, to ongoing conversion from sin, to proclamation of the Gospel, to service of others, and to justice and peace. See *The Book of Common Prayer and Administration of the Other Rites and Ceremonies of the Church* (New York: Church Publishing, 2007), 304–5. For discussion of the baptismal covenant, see Fredrica Harris Thompsett, "Baptism: Liberating Sacrament of Identity and Justice," in *Seeing God in Each Other*, ed. Sheryl Kujawa-Holbrook (Harrisburg: Morehouse, 2006), 15–27.

84. See Crowley, "Making More Visible Our Invisible Baptismal Promises," 98–99. On these pages, Crowley quotes Hovda, "Renunciation of Evil and Profes-

Crowley and Hovda both acknowledge that the introduction of projected images into the rite would require care and delicacy in order that the images themselves not become the center of attention. Additionally, the prospect of revising or expanding the formulae for exorcisms and/or the renunciation of Satan raises the prospect of politicizing the liturgy. Mark Searle, for example, observes that the attempt to make liturgy "relevant" runs the risk of watering down the teaching of the church.[85] Louis-Marie Chauvet and Aidan Kavanagh both warn about making liturgy excessively didactic.[86] Acknowledging these risks, Batchelder nevertheless makes a strong case:

> We must always remain cautious about the naming of some sins over others. Nevertheless, such naming for the sake of repentance and renewal is necessary as the epistles to the churches in the New Testament make clear. The more local and pastoral, the more helpful such a practice can be because it is contextual to the community in which persons are being formed in baptismal faith. The dangers invariably come as soon as we try to generalize and suggest a ranking of sin. . . . Nevertheless, it does us no pastoral good to leave the renunciation of sin and evil to generalities. The baptized and baptizing community has never left discerning sin to the privacy of individuals. Its practice is communal. We cannot renounce what we have not unmasked.
>
> Renunciation means naming names. Discerning idols, whether national, cultural, ecclesial, or personal, and how they work their power is absolutely necessary to renunciation. If we do not place under scrutiny our many cultural addictions, we will be unable to see their messianic pretensions for what they are.[87]

---

sion of Faith," 103. The idols of money and property are among the other idols that Hovda specifically mentions in the passage that Crowley cites.

85. See Searle, "Faith and Sacraments in the Conversion Process," 64.

86. Louis-Marie Chauvet, "Rites et symboles," *Masses Ouvrières* 409 (1986): 47–69 at 49–50; Chauvet, *Symbol and Sacrament*, trans. Patrick Madigan and Madeleine Beaumont (Collegeville, MN: Liturgical Press, 1995), 336; Kavanagh, *On Liturgical Theology*, 82, 110. See also Michael Marchal, "Scrutinies: Words That Cut," *Catechumenate* 15, no. 1 (January 1993): 20–26 at 20–21.

87. Batchelder, "Baptismal Renunciations," 417–18.

Writing elsewhere, Batchelder argues that baptismal renunciations should be associated with the practice of hesitation in an environment flooded with consumer goods clamoring for our attention. "Remembering baptism involves a cultivated sensitivity to proceed with caution. In a culture that fosters and rewards impulsiveness, we need to learn how to resist momentary decision-making. Instead, we must take time to consider. Baptismal remembrance takes account of the fact that we cannot say yes to everything made available to us."[88] Chrysostom, too, urged those preparing for baptism to bear in mind the significance of their renunciation of Satan: "Suppose you recall these words you utter when you are being initiated: 'I renounce thee, Satan, thy pomps and thy service.' The madness to be adorned with pearls is one of Satan's pomps."[89] To be sure, Chrysostom addressed this warning particularly to female candidates for baptism, but surely we can ask ourselves what "pearls" we seek to collect today and whether those who gather those pearls behind the veil of the commodity are treated justly.

IX. Ecological and Economic Meaning of the Sacramental Symbol of Water

Under this heading, I will examine the privatization and commodification of water and the pollution of water. When water is privatized or commodified what effect is there on the symbolic function of water in baptism? For most of us, the closest we encounter the privatization of water is when we see ads for and/or consume bottled water. However, in many places around the world, the privatization of water extends to the private ownership of water supply infrastructure. *Fortune* magazine observed in 2000 that "from Buenos Aires to Atlanta to Jakarta, the liquid everybody needs—and will need a lot more of in the future—is going private, creating one of the world's great business opportunities. . . .

88. David Batchelder, "Living Wet: Baptismal Remembrance and Life at the Edge of Dawn," *Liturgy* 21, no. 4 (2006): 11–17 at 15.

89. John Chrysostom, *Twelfth Instruction on Baptism* 48, in Harkins, *St. John Chrysostom*, 188.

Water promises to be to the 21st century what oil was to the 20th century: the precious commodity that determines the wealth of nations."[90] For just one example of the potential consequences of privatization, we can turn to John Hart, who describes what happened in South Africa: "Several cities [in South Africa] privatized water systems in the mid-1990s [and the country] suffered the worst cholera outbreak in its history from 2000 to 2002. People who could not afford to pay for water had resorted to drinking from and bathing in contaminated rivers and water holes."[91]

With respect to the sacramental symbolic quality of water, Hart contends: "The sacramentality [of creation] is obscured . . . by the privatization of water. When an individual, corporation or government . . . removes water from the common domain, reserves water for their own purposes, and allocates or withholds water to control people . . . or otherwise to enhance coercive power or augment profits, these individuals [and groups] are seizing part of God's world and preventing it from fulfilling its purpose in the web of creation: to be a sign and mediation of the Spirit's immanence and solicitous care for the living, and to be the immediate provider of sustenance for all life."[92] All of creation is a gift to humanity, but especially those aspects of creation that are absolutely essential for human life and flourishing. Water is a gift to which all have a right since it is given to all by God.[93]

90. Shawn Tully, "Water, Water Everywhere," *Fortune* (May 15, 2000): 343–54 at 344.

91. John Hart, *Sacramental Commons: Christian Ecological Ethics* (Lanham, MD: Rowman & Littlefield, 2006), 82. Maude Barlow and Tony Clarke detail some of the consequences of privatization in *Blue Gold: The Fight to Stop the Corporate Theft of the World's Water* (New York: New Press, 2002).

92. Hart, "Living Water: Sacramental Commons," address given at National Catholic Rural Life Conference (February 8, 2003) in Washington, DC.

93. In a 2003 statement, the Vatican put it this way: "Water by its very nature cannot be treated as a mere commodity among other commodities. Catholic social thought has always stressed that the defense and preservation of certain common goods, such as the natural and human environments, cannot be safeguarded simply by market forces, since they touch on fundamental human needs which escape market logic (cf. *Centesimus Annus*, 40)." See "Note Prepared by the Pontifical Council for Justice and Peace: A Contribution of the Delegation of the Holy See on the Occasion of the Third World Water Forum" (March

Now, if my experience of water is that of a commodity available only to those able to pay for it, then I experience a disconnect when it comes to baptism, where water is an effective symbol of God's free, gracious, and unmerited love for human beings. The Catholic Church teaches that even "if water distribution is entrusted to the private sector it should still be considered a public good."[94] I submit that there are ethical reasons for such a stand that are grounded in the sacramental practice of the church. In Hart's words, "Water would not be a sign of God's providence . . . and God's freely given grace . . . if its use were dependent on private whim."[95] For his part, Kevin Irwin claims that "one of the purposes of liturgy and sacraments is to articulate how God is experienced as savior in and through the liturgy and how this same God is discoverable and discovered in the rest of life."[96] How well does this happen in a world of privatized water? How much do we contribute to this privatization when we obtain our water in bottled form instead of being content with tap water? I submit that apart from cases of necessity such as natural disasters, the sacramental symbolic implications of using bottled water are not in the least beneficial to the Christian understanding of baptism. Returning to the notion of the veil of the commodity, one can wonder about the expenditure of energy and natural resources to bring bottled water to the grocer's shelf when, in the United

2003). In statements issued in 2004 and again in 2006, the Vatican reaffirmed that everyone has a right to water. See John Paul II, "Message to the Bishops of Brazil," *L'Osservatore Romano* (March 11–17, 2004): 3, and Pontifical Council for Justice and Peace, A Contribution of the Holy See to the Fourth World Water Forum (Mexico City, March 16–22, 2006): "Water, An Essential Element for Life."

94. Pontifical Council for Justice and Peace, *Compendium of the Social Doctrine of the Church*, 485, http://www.vatican.va/roman_curia/pontifical_councils/justpeace/documents/rc_pc_justpeace_doc_20060526_compendio-dott-soc_en.html.

95. Hart, *Sacramental Commons*, 90. See also Timothy O'Malley, "Catholic Ecology and Eucharist: A Practice Approach," *Liturgical Ministry* 20, no. 2 (Spring 2011): 68–78.

96. Kevin Irwin, "The Sacramentality of Creation and the Role of Creation in Liturgy and Sacraments," in *"And God Saw That It Was Good": Catholic Theology and the Environment*, ed. Drew Christiansen and Walter Grazer (Washington, DC: United States Catholic Conference, 1996), 110.

States and many other nations, access to potable water is available at the turn of a faucet.

Concerning the cleanliness of the water to be used in the rite of baptism, the General Introduction to Christian Initiation declares that "the water used for baptism should be true water and, both for the sake of authentic sacramental symbolism and for hygienic reasons should be pure and clean."[97] Here, I want to connect the purity of baptismal water to the purity and cleanliness of *all* water. To accomplish this goal, we must start with water as a symbol, indeed a "rich symbol" according to the blessing of the water at the Easter Vigil.[98] The *Catechism of the Catholic Church* establishes a context for the use of this rich symbol when it teaches that "the liturgy of the Church presupposes, integrates and sanctifies elements from creation and human culture, conferring on them the dignity of signs of grace, of the new creation in Jesus Christ."[99] Furthermore, "the sacraments of the Church do not abolish but purify and integrate all the richness of the signs and symbols of the cosmos and of social life."[100] In other words, the use of material elements in the liturgical life of the church presupposes a kind of symbolism already inherent in those elements. In baptism, the use of water presupposes that water has the inherent symbolism of life, death, and cleansing. Along these lines, Daniel Stevick suggests that being baptized is like taking a shower, only more so: "When we take a shower after particularly strenuous work or play, we often say, 'I feel like a new person!' We are . . . using language of continuity and radical newness, of transformation that is yet restoration. It is the same I and yet a new I; it is the new I and yet the same I, newly enabled to fulfill its intended purposes. Such language is an analogue of the gospel of forgiveness and fresh beginning that we enact in baptism."[101] Stevick's remarks would

97. General Introduction to Christian Initiation, 18. In para. 19, the document further specifies that "the baptismal font . . . should be spotlessly clean."

98. RCIA 222A.

99. *Catechism of the Catholic Church*, 1149.

100. Ibid., 1152. The basic principle at work here is the Thomistic axiom that grace perfects nature. See *Summa theologiae*, I, q. 62, a. 5, resp.

101. Daniel Stevick, "The Water of Life," *Liturgy* 7, no. 1 (1987): 47–53 at 52.

not make sense to a person whose only experience of water is of a fouled and gritty liquid. Taking up the theme of how the church makes use of symbols in its liturgy, Stevick writes: "Water is capable of being used in this expressive ritual [of baptism] because water is a meaning-bearer. It can be a sign because it signifies. *A convincing, authoritative [ritual] does not impose alien meanings on its materials*; rather, it uncovers, selects, uses or heightens meanings that are given in the materials themselves."[102] If my experience of water outside of baptism is that of gritty, foul-smelling and discolored water, then the water ritual of baptism will be a disconnect for me. The life-giving and cleansing symbolism of baptism will have become an "alien meaning" that is imposed on the water. To grasp what is at stake here, we must grasp the distinction Paul Philibert makes between what is "symbolic" and what is "diabolic." Philibert writes: "Both *symbolic* and *diabolic* are compound terms formed from the same Greek root (*bolein*) meaning to throw or cast. However, one begins with the prefix *sym*, which means together, while the other begins with *dia*, which means apart. A symbol throws things together. A diabolic force casts them apart."[103] When my basic experience of water used in baptism is my only experience of clean water, then all my other experiences of water have a diabolic aspect to them. They are diabolic when my experience of these waters is apart *from* and not a part *of* my experience of baptism. To be apart *from* is diabolic. To be a part *of* is symbolic. John Hart makes this point clear: "Water is . . . losing its ability to be a sacramental symbol . . . [and] poisoning of waters . . . has altered the life-giving nature of water. . . . No longer might people celebrate water as a sign of God's creative work. . . . The waters are less sacramental, less a revelatory sign of God's Presence and creativity, and more detrimental, more signs of human ignorance, carelessness, indifference and greed."[104]

102. Ibid., 48 (emphasis added).
103. Paul J. Philibert, *The Priesthood of the Faithful: Key to a Living Church* (Collegeville, MN: Liturgical Press, 2005), 133.
104. John Hart, "Living Water: Sacramental Commons." See also John Hart, *Sacramental Commons*, 91. The Hindu practice of bathing in the Ganges River offers an interesting test case of Hart's claims. On the one hand, the filth and

We can rephrase Hart's text to drive the point home: "The waters are less sacramental, less a revelatory sign of God's Presence and creativity, and more diabolic." Respect for the integrity of water as a sacramental symbol is thus connected to concern about the integrity of water in the natural environment.

X. Conclusion

After first discussing the concept of the veil of the commodity, this chapter turned to an analysis of the paschal mystery as the context of production of the sacrament of baptism. I noted how the cross of Christ is present in both word and gesture in the rite of baptism. I raised concern about the degree to which the sentimentality associated with infant baptism can obscure the life-and-death significance of the rite and also about the degree to which the passivity of the infant could suggest that sacramental engagement requires nothing more than the effortlessness with which consumer goods are to deliver on their promise to the consumer. The chapter next turned attention to the public quality of the ancient and restored catechumenate. In a consumer culture that fosters a sense of nearly atomistic individualism, the status of the catechumen as a public person is a clear counterpoint. The ancient catechumenate, going back to instructions given to would-be Christians in the first century, emphasized the practice of almsgiving. Especially in view of

---

pollution of that river have not prevented innumerable Hindus from using the water for their ablutions. On the other hand, in 2007 some Hindu leaders threatened to boycott their ritual bathing unless the government took action to clean up the river. On this subject, see "Three Worlds, One Planet: Indian River Gods Are Cesspools that Kill Thousands," *The Globe and Mail* (October 10, 1989), n. p.; Emma Tomalin, "Bio-Divinity and Biodiversity: Perspectives on Religion and Environmental Conservation in India," *Numen* 51 (2004): 265–95; "Holy Men Protest over Polluted Ganges," *The Irish Times* (January 9, 2007), 11; "Filthy Ganges Is the Biggest Sin, Say Hindu Worshippers," *Times of London* (January 9, 2007), 30; "Filthy Ganges Won't Wash for Holy Men," *The Australian* (January 10, 2007), 8; "5M Hindus Plunge into Polluted Ganges," *Daily Telegraph* [United Kingdom] (January 16, 2007), 18. It should be noted, however, that the Catholic sensibility that the use of natural elements in religious rites builds on and enhances the qualities inherent in those elements may not be shared across all religions.

the way in which Alexander Schmemann regards consumerism as being at the root of the sin of the first humans, there is something eloquent about the resistance to consumerism embodied in alms-giving. Figures such as St. Augustine and St. John Chrysostom also emphasized that the baptisms about to be conferred on their *competentes* were not a matter simply between God and the person to be baptized but rather placed those baptized in relationship to other persons, believers and non-believers. That relationship entailed a willingness to let one's conduct draw others to Christ for the sake of those others and for the glory of God. The chapter examined the ritual practice of exorcisms and the renunciation of Satan in their ancient context and in the context of late-modern culture. I argued that, due care being taken, revising or expanding the formulae for these rites to include reference to consumerism is one way to enhance baptism's sacramental resistance to consum-erism. Finally, the chapter argued that the water used in baptism, clean and free, can serve as a sacramental-symbolic launching point for action to preserve the purity of water in nature and to resist its commodification.

The present study raises questions for future consideration and examination. There is the matter of undertaking a more com-prehensive and statistically reliable survey of how and whether Roman Catholic parishes communicate about stipends and finan-cial considerations associated with baptism. The fourteen parishes that responded to my questions provide interesting but merely anecdotal evidence. There is the question, too, of assessing how RCIA programs address the issues of baptismal promises and re-nunciations. Writing nearly forty years ago, Orthodox theologian Alexander Schmemann was particularly critical about baptismal catechesis. Schmemann argued that in late-modern culture, the meaning of the renunciation of Satan has become all but lost:

> When this type of renunciation came into existence, its mean-ing was self-evident to the catechumens as well as to the entire Christian community. They lived within a pagan world whose life was permeated with the *pompa diaboli*, i.e., the worship of idols, participation in the cult of the Emperor, adoration of mat-ter, etc. He not only knew what he was renouncing; he was also

fully aware to what a "narrow way," to what a difficult life—truly "non-conformist" and radically opposed to the "way of life" of the people around him—this renunciation obliged him.

It is when the world became "Christian" and identified itself with Christian faith and Christian cult that the meaning of this renunciation began to be progressively lost so as to be viewed today as an archaic and anachronistic rite, as a curiosity not to be taken seriously . . . The very idea that a Christian has to *renounce* something and that this "something" is not a few obviously sinful and immoral acts, but above all a certain vision of life, a "set of priorities," a fundamental attitude towards the world; the idea that Christian life is always a "narrow path" and a fight: all this has been virtually given up and is no longer at the heart of our Christian worldview.

The terrible truth is that the overwhelming majority of Christians simply do not see the presence and action of Satan in the world and, therefore, feel no need to renounce "his works and his service."[105]

Schmemann argued that Christians today are simply unable to grasp "the fact that the 'demonic' consists primarily in falsification and counterfeit, in deviating even positive values from their true meaning."[106]

Certainly, pagan gods are not named as such very often in the late-modern West but even if the demonic is less explicitly identified, opposition to the alien spirits of materialism and greed is not absent from formation in the Christian faith. It is worth noting a story that appeared a few years ago in the journal *Canadian Mennonite*. It contains an account of a man who sought baptism and who brought his wallet with him into the font. He claimed that he was aware of his sinful use of money, and he wanted to have his

105. Schmemann, *Of Water and the Spirit*, 28–29.

106. Ibid., 29. For additional treatment of how consumerism counterfeits Christian virtues, see Sam van Enam, *On Earth As It Is in Advertising?* (Grand Rapids: Brazos, 2005); Burt Fulmer, "Augustine's Theology as a Solution to the Problem of Identity in Consumer Society," *Augustinian Studies* 37, no. 1 (2006): 111–29; Miller, *Consuming Religion*, 7.

priorities reorganized by his baptism.[107] Certainly, he was aware that the rite of baptism has something to say about the use of money and about what we do and do not consume. Perhaps the ancients can teach us something about how to communicate that message with greater effectiveness.

107. Anonymous, "A Converted—and Baptized—Wallet," *Canadian Mennonite* 10 (January 9, 2006): 6. The story comes from John B. Toews, *A Pilgrimage of Faith: The Mennonite Brethren Church in Russia and North America, 1860–1990* (Hillsboro, KS: Kindred Press, 1993). The journal article does not provide page numbers for the reference.

Chapter Two

CONFIRMATION AND CONSUMER CULTURE

I. Introduction

Recent commentators have drawn attention to confirmation as a sacrament that is lost, irrelevant, confusing or without meaning for Christians.[1] I suggest that this confusion about confirmation makes it especially susceptible to distortion in a culture saturated with consumerism. In this chapter, I will analyze proposals for understanding confirmation and the ways in which these proposals, rather than promoting a livelier understanding of the sacrament, instead contribute to the commodification of the sacrament. The proposals are: (a) confirmation is a sacrament of personal commitment to one's Christian faith (and to the defense of that faith); (b) one must demonstrate command of Christian doctrine before one may be confirmed; (c) confirmation is a sacrament

---

1. See for example Virgil Michel, "Confirmation: Our Apathy," *Orate Fratres* 2, no. 6 (1928): 167–71 at 167–68; James R. Gillis, "The Case for Confirmation," *The Thomist* 10 (1947): 159–84 at 159; Joseph Cunningham, *Confirmation: Pastoral Concerns* (Collegeville, MN: Liturgical Press, 1973), 56; LaVerne Haas, *Personal Pentecost: The Meaning of Confirmation* (St. Meinrad, IN: Abbey Press, 1973), 7; William Levada, "Reflections on the Age of Confirmation," *Theological Studies* 57, no. 2 (1996): 302–12 at 309–10; Paul Turner, *Ages of Initiation: The First Two Christian Millennia* (Collegeville, MN: Liturgical Press, 2000), 59; Turner, *Confirmation: The Baby in Solomon's Court*, rev. ed. (Chicago: Liturgy Training Publications, 2006), xi, 91; Joseph Martos, *Doors to the Sacred: A Historical Introduction to Sacraments in the Catholic Church*, rev. ed. (Liguori, MO: Liguori, 2014), 229–36.

of Christian maturity; (d) confirmation is more important than the Eucharist. In an important sense, each of these themes is bound up with the others but distinguishing them from one another will allow for greater precision in the discussion that follows.

II. Consumer Culture

Before turning to confirmation itself, I must address the nature of consumerism. Drawing on a number of authors,[2] I argued in chapter 1 that consumerism involves the commodification of goods, that is, the isolation of goods from their native contexts of meaning and production, repackaging and rebranding those goods to appeal to consumers, and an idealized sense of the ease with which those goods are to be enjoyed.[3] This consumerist decontextualization goes hand-in-hand with a kind of social fragmentation. Following Daniele Hervieu-Léger, Timothy Gabrielli argues: "The coherence of a religious tradition is brought into a space where individuals 'construct meaning' on their own, look-

2. I have in mind here especially Vincent Miller, *Consuming Religion: Christian Faith and Practice in a Consumer Culture* (New York: Continuum, 2005), but see also Christopher Kiesling, "Liturgy and Consumerism," *Worship* 52, no. 4 (1978): 359–68; Louis-Marie Chauvet, *Du symbolique au symbole* (Paris: Cerf, 1979), esp. 253–300; M. Francis Mannion, "Liturgy and the Present Crisis of Culture," *Worship* 62, no. 2 (1988): 98–122; John F. Kavanaugh, *Following Christ in a Consumer Society* (Maryknoll: Orbis Books, 1991), esp. 131–63; Richard Gaillardetz, "Doing Liturgy in a Technological Age," *Worship* 71, no. 5 (1997): 429–51; Walter Brueggemann, "The Liturgy of Abundance, the Myth of Scarcity," *Christian Century* 116 (1999): 342–47; Rodney Clapp, "At the Intersection of Eucharist and Capital," in *Proceedings: North American Academy of Liturgy Annual Meeting*, Tampa, January 2–5, 2000 (Valparaiso, IN: North American Academy of Liturgy), 94; William Cavanaugh, *Theopolitical Imagination: Discovering the Liturgy as a Political Act in an Age of Global Consumerism* (New York: T & T Clark, 2002); Nathan Mitchell, "Consuming Liturgy," *Worship* 79, no. 2 (2005): 168–79; Vincent Miller, "The Liturgy and Popular Culture," *Liturgical Ministry* 15 (2006): 161–70. Of allied interest is James K. A. Smith, *Desiring the Kingdom: Worship, Worldview and Cultural Formation* (Grand Rapids, MI: Baker, 2009).

3. See also my "Consumer Culture and the Body: Chauvet's Perspective," *Worship* 82, no. 4 (2008): 290–310; and "Consumerism and the Liturgical Act of Worship," *Horizons* 38, no. 1 (Spring 2011): 54–74.

ing only for a type of social confirmation from a group. When this happens, the whole enterprise of deep identity is defeated because modernity creates a desire for tradition *on our own terms*, rendering participation in a thick non-voluntarist tradition impossible."[4]

It is also worth noting that consumerist shopping is associated with possessiveness. I plunk down my cash and I am entitled to ownership of the good (or use of the service) in question. Consumerism is governed by the rights and obligations of commercial exchange. The controlling metaphor of commercial exchange, however, runs counter to the notion of grace as gift, a notion that is fundamental to the Christian tradition.

III. Confirmation as Strengthening for Combat and Personal Commitment

Analyzing texts such as the *Apostolic Tradition* and the Gelasian Sacramentary, J. D. C. Fisher concludes that "it is quite clear what confirmation originally was not—it had nothing to do with personal confession of the faith by those who had been too young to do this at their baptism: it was not an act of self-commitment."[5] *The* sacrament of commitment was baptism. As we saw in chapter 1, baptism marked one's conversion from paganism to the God of Jesus Christ. Baptism was quickly regarded as necessary for salvation; confirmation was never regarded with that kind of gravity.

---

4. Timothy R. Gabrielli, "Chauvet in Space: Louis-Marie Chauvet's Sacramental Account of Christian Identity and the Challenges of a Global Consumer Culture," in *Religion, Economics, and Culture in Conflict and Conversation*, The Annual Publication of the College Theology Society 56, ed. Laurie Cassidy and Maureen O'Connell (Maryknoll: Orbis Books, 2011), 143. Gabrielli here acknowledges his indebtedness to Danièle Hervieu-Léger, *Religion as a Chain of Memory*, trans. Simon Lee (New Brunswick, NJ: Rutgers University Press, 2000), 94.

5. J. D. C. Fisher, *Confirmation Then and Now* (Chicago: Hillenbrand Books, 2005; originally published as part of the Alcuin Club Collection 60 [London: SPCK, 1978]), 137. The *Apostolic Tradition* is a church order going back approximately to the third century but scholarly debate about its dating is ongoing. See John Baldovin, "Hippolytus and the *Apostolic Tradition*: Recent Research and Commentary," *Theological Studies* 64, no. 3 (2003): 520–42. The Gelasian Sacramentary dates to the late seventh century.

The subsequent story in the West is well-known. After Constantine, the ranks of Christians swelled. In the Latin West bishops reserved to themselves the capacity to administer confirmation. Simple arithmetic meant that fewer Christian babies and adult converts could be baptized and confirmed as part of the same ritual. Since celebration of confirmation was not regarded as a prerequisite for reception of the Eucharist,[6] and since it was not regarded as necessary for salvation, its separation from baptism gave rise to ambiguity about its meaning. Not for the last time in liturgical history, a change in practice led to a change in theory: in fifth-century Gaul, Bishop Faustus of Rietz advised his flock that confirmation involved being strengthened for the battle of a Christian moral life: "We are reborn in baptism for life, and we are confirmed after baptism for the strife. In baptism we are washed; after baptism we are strengthened. . . . Confirmation arms and supplies those needing to be preserved for the struggles and battles of this world."[7]

In the ninth century, enterprising French clerics crafted a number of statements defending the prerogatives of the church against local nobles and attributed these statements to popes and other ecclesiastics of preceding centuries. To give their documents an air of legitimacy, these clerics included several statements that had in fact been made by church leaders. Faustus' attempt to persuade his flock to seek confirmation was attributed to a Pope Melchiades. The collection assembled by the clerics carried the day and hence Faustus' words concerning preparation for battle were invested with papal authority by those who were taken in by these False Decretals.

---

6. "In the age of the Fathers . . . the altar was not fenced against any baptized persons, unless they were under ecclesiastical discipline." Fisher, *Confirmation Then and Now*, 138–39.

7. Paul Turner, *Sources of Confirmation: From the Fathers through the Reformers* (Collegeville, MN: Liturgical Press, 1993), 35–36. Turner points out that some historians attribute this passage to the seventh-century figure Eusebius Gallicanus. In any event, the line of reasoning being put forward here represents an adaptation to a changed practice. Some earlier texts had discussed the anointing associated with baptism as a matter of providing strength to the one anointed (e.g., Cyril of Jerusalem, *Mystagogical Catecheses*, III, 4; the *Euchologion* of Serapion) but Faustus invokes this sense of strengthening with respect to a ritual now distant in time from baptism.

Military imagery was taken up by Bishop William Durandus of France who added to the ritual of confirmation a slap on the cheek in the thirteenth century.[8] His approximate contemporary Thomas Aquinas repeated that confirmation is given for strength in combat.[9] Picking up a theme first raised by Rabanus Maurus in the ninth century, Thomas also argued that confirmation confers the grace to profess one's faith publicly.[10] Neither of these themes is adumbrated by the sixteenth-century Council of Trent, but in its section on the sacrament of confirmation, the *Roman Catechism* issued after the council's conclusion uses military imagery ("a perfect soldier of Christ") and it cites "Pope Melchiades" with reference to being "equipped for battle."[11] Up through the twentieth century, confirmation continued to be associated with being strengthened for battle. Associating the notion of strengthening with the importance of proclaiming one's faith, the Dogmatic Constitution on the Church promulgated by the Second Vatican Council holds that those who are confirmed "are more perfectly bound to the church and are endowed with the special strength of the holy Spirit. Hence, as true witnesses of Christ, they are more strictly obliged both to spread and to defend the faith by word and deed."[12] In 1966, Pope Paul VI also invoked images of militancy.[13] Since this same pope oversaw the promulgation of the reformed rite in 1971, one is not surprised to find an emphasis on "strength"

8. For the ritual of Durandus, see Paul Turner, *The Meaning and Practice of Confirmation: Perspectives from a Sixteenth-Century Controversy* (New York: Peter Lang, 1987), 290. See also Durandus' *Explanation of the Divine Offices* 6:84, 1.6.8 in the companion CD for Turner, *Ages of Initiation*, section 8.10.

9. See *Summa Theologiae* III, q. 72, a. 4, ad. 3; III, 72, q. 5, resp.; III, q. 72, a. 9, ad. 1; see also the soldier imagery in III, q. 72, a. 10, ad. 2. Thomas refers to "Pope Melchiades" six times in III, 72: twice in article 1, once in article 7, twice in article 8, and once in article 9.

10. *Summa Theologiae* III, q. 72, a. 5, ad. 2. For Rabanus' teaching, see the citation of his *On the Institution of Clerics* 1.30, in Turner, *Sources of Confirmation*, 36.

11. *Catechism of the Council of Trent for Parish Priests*, trans. John McHugh and Charles Callan (Rockford, IL: Tan Books, 1982), 201, 199. The section on confirmation cites Melchiades by name four times.

12. *Lumen Gentium* 11.

13. See the Memorandum quoted in Annibale Bugnini, *The Reform of the Liturgy 1948–1975*, trans. Matthew J. O'Connell (Collegeville, MN: Liturgical Press, 1990), 615n5.

in the revised rite itself.[14] The 1994 *Catechism of the Catholic Church* associates the sacrament of confirmation with "strengthening" in six places.[15] Clearly, since the time of Faustus, confirmation has been associated with the idea of personal commitment to being a soldier for Christ.

This development is problematic from at least three perspectives. First, theologically, confirmation ought to be understood as a sacrament that occupies the middle ground between being indistinct from baptism and utterly distinct from baptism. In his discussion of this question, Kenan Osborne suggests that to talk of confirmation as granting "a special strength to spread and defend the faith" implies that baptism offers no such special strength.[16]

Second, with reference to a culture of consumerism, it is important to note that the choice involved in this personal commitment to be a solider of Christ all too easily becomes just one more "choice" among many consumer "choices."[17] In other words, there is a risk that the sacrament of confirmation will play a role in what I have elsewhere described as the consumerist chronic reinvention of the self.[18] If I choose to be a person who is more appealing in bed, I can go buy a pill that will allow me to reinvent myself as a more pleasing partner. If I choose to be more a part of the "in" crowd, I can reinvent myself as "in" by buying the latest model iPhone. More and more, a consumer culture defines one

14. See especially the (1971) Rite of Confirmation 2. The (2016) Order of Confirmation 2 likewise mentions being strengthened. All citations of the 2016 Order of Confirmation will be from The *Order of Confirmation for Use in the Dioceses of the United States of America* (Washington, DC: USCCB, 2016).

15. *Catechism of the Catholic Church* 1285, 1289, 1303, 1308, 1310, and 1312. The *Catechism* uses military imagery in 1295.

16. Kenan Osborne, *Sacramental Guidelines: A Companion to the New Catechism for Religious Educators* (New York: Paulist, 1995), 63. Osborne warns: "Confirmation does not make people 'super Christians,' and our language describing confirmation should not foster such a view."

17. See the discussion of choice in Timothy Gabrielli, *Confirmation: How a Sacrament of God's Grace Became All about Us* (Collegeville, MN: Liturgical Press, 2013), 53–64. Gabrielli's work pointed the present author to the works of Virgil Michel, Francis Buckley, James Gillis, Mary Charles Bryce, Gerard Fourez and Marian Bohen.

18. See my "Consumerism and the Liturgical Act of Worship."

by the consumer choices one has made—a phenomenon Zygmunt Bauman refers to as the "transformation of consumers into commodities."[19] Bauman observes that consumerism is associated with the idea of being born again: "Into one abominably short visit on earth, a visit not that long ago bewailed for its loathsome brevity and not radically lengthened since, humans-turned-consumers are now offered the chance to cram many lives: an endless series of new beginnings."[20]

I doubt that there are catechetical programs for confirmation that speak of the sacrament as a product that one can choose to acquire for the purpose of one more "new beginning" in an endless series of new beginnings. Nevertheless, in a culture marked by deterioration in the permanency of the self, is there not a risk that confirmation will be understood as just one more reinvention of the self the more one emphasizes the element of personal commitment?

In the same vein, problems can arise if confirmation is too strongly presented as a "once and for all" choice. Again, Gabrielli offers an important consideration: "It seems that wedding one's choice for Catholicism to a designated time unwittingly encourages drifting away after the choice is made because, in the perception of the young person, the choice has been made and therefore the hard work has been done."[21] In a document published in 2004, the United States Conference of Catholic Bishops Committee on Pastoral Practices addressed the nature of the commitment expressed in the confirmation of young people of high school age: "Recommitment is not a once-in-a-lifetime event, but Confirmation is a once-in-a-lifetime event."[22] Catechesis concerning confirmation must find the middle way between viewing the

19. Zygmunt Bauman, *Consuming Life* (Malden, MA: Polity, 2007), 12. He refers to the "unending effort" of the human subject "to itself become, and remain, a sellable commodity."

20. Ibid., 101.

21. Gabrielli, *Confirmation*, 60–61.

22. United States Conference of Catholic Bishops Committee on Pastoral Practices, *Receive the Gift, The Age of Confirmation: A Resource Guide for Bishops* (Washington, DC: USCCB, 2004), 14.

sacrament as just another in a series of reinventions of the self and viewing the sacrament as the definitive moment of commitment to one's Christian faith.

The third perspective I wish to address is the consumerist notion of choice as autonomous. Think of how many families of four have two or more television sets so that each member of the family can watch a favorite show without having to consider what others may want to watch. Each member of the family is empowered to make an independent choice. Consumer choices are "my" choices. According to this logic, the choice to make a personal commitment to be a soldier of Christ is likewise "my" choice. Theologically, however, any understanding of choice and free will must take into account God's grace, which is the prerequisite for the making of any choice that is conducive to the good. Thus, one's choice to seek the sacrament of confirmation is a choice already borne up and sustained by God's grace—and, as we shall point out below, the grace of the sacrament is precisely grace/gift, and not a reward that is earned.

IV. Command of Christian Doctrine as Prerequisite for Confirmation

It is clear that adult initiation into the Christian faith was always preceded at the very least by preaching of the gospel. Tracing the full history of the evolution of the catechumenate is a task well beyond the scope of this book. The point at issue is that immediate exposure and assent to basic articles of faith developed into a period—sometimes years long—of preparation for initiation.[23] Up until the fourth century or so the catechumenate preceded baptism itself and thus also confirmation. As noted above, after the fourth century one sees a sharp rise in the number of infant baptisms, the decline of the catechumenate, and the eventual separation of baptism from confirmation in the West. What does one do with those who are initiated into Christian faith and life by baptism but who have been neither catechized nor confirmed?

---

23. See section V of chapter 1, p. 13.

Clearly, catechesis will now follow baptism and in the case of those Christians baptized in infancy eventually the degree of mastery of Christian doctrine becomes a matter of some import for celebration of confirmation.

The rise of martial imagery in connection with the sacrament of confirmation and the attendant need to "defend" the faith goes hand-in-hand with the idea that one must be reasonably knowledgeable about the faith before one may be confirmed. According to Paul Turner, it was Wulfstan II, archbishop of York in the early eleventh century, who first established a catechetical requirement for confirmation.[24] Perhaps the most significant impetus for associating confirmation with command of doctrine was the sixteenth-century Protestant Reformation and its ensuing Catholic response. A first point to make is that prior to the rise of Protestant-Catholic polemics, Western Christendom was in basic agreement about the status of confirmation as a sacrament; it had been listed among the seven sacraments at the Second Council of Lyons in 1274. Now, with respect to confirmation and many other points of worship and doctrine, there were rival understandings of what was proper and true. In each camp it became important to train youth not to succumb to the false views of the other camp. Catechesis into a "true" Christian life could no longer be as easily taken for granted.

A second point to make is that while Reformers denied that confirmation was a sacrament, they saw value in it precisely as a moment during which youth could demonstrate their facility with church doctrine. Among the first to argue this case was Philip Melanchthon in 1521, who claimed that being tested on doctrinal matters was a practice with ancient roots.[25] Martin Luther and Jean Calvin expressed similar views. Preaching in 1523, Luther said

24. Wulfstan held that those to be confirmed must know the Lord's Prayer and the Creed. See Wulfstan II "Canons Written under King Edgar" 22, quoted in the companion CD for Turner, *Ages of Initiation*, section 7.6.

25. See Carolus Gottlieb Bretschneider and Henricus Ernestus Bindsell, eds., *Corporus reformatorum. Philippi Melanchthonis, opera quae supersunt omnia*, vol. 21 (Halis Saxonum: C. A. Schwetschke et filium, 1834–1860; reprint New York: Johnson Reprint, 1963), 853, quoted in Turner, *The Meaning and Practice of Confirmation*, 23.

that "Confirmation should not be bothered with as the [Catholic] bishops desire, but nevertheless we do not find fault with this: Any pastor might investigate the faith from children and, if it is good and sincere, he may impose hands and confirm."[26]

Responding to these views, Trent sought to avoid reducing the sacrament of confirmation to an examination of candidates' faith and command of doctrine;[27] nevertheless, the Roman Church in 1742 for the first time universalized basic catechetical requirements for the celebration of confirmation. Pope Benedict XIV wrote: "The bishop should admonish pastors and strictly order them that none of them should administer the holy sacrament of the Eucharist and hand over the confirmation 'sheet' (as they say) to those who do not know the most important matters of faith, the main points of doctrine, and the excellence and power of the sacrament."[28] As if Protestant-Roman Catholic polemics were not sufficient motive to promote catechesis among young people, David O'Brien points out that the secularizing effects of the French Revolution in the late eighteenth century stirred the pot even more: "From that point on children and youth became objects of political struggle as contending groups sought to win the allegiance of young men, and to a lesser degree young women, who now had real choices available to them."[29] The subsequent fortress mentality of nineteenth-century Roman Catholicism continued into the twentieth century.

This brief rehearsal of the history of doctrinal mastery as a prerequisite for confirmation brings us to the present day. Whatever good motives there may be for requiring basic command of Chris-

---

26. Martin Luther, "Sermon on Laetare Sunday Afternoon" (1523), quoted in the companion CD for Turner, *Ages of Initiation*, section 9.7. For the nearly identical perspective of Jean Calvin, see Jean Calvin, *Institutes of the Christian Religion*, 4.19.4.

27. See Trent's first canon on the sacrament of confirmation. Text in Norman Tanner, ed., *Decrees of the Ecumenical Councils*, vol. 2: *Trent to Vatican II*, (Washington, DC: Georgetown University Press, 1990), 686.

28. Benedict XIV, *Etsi minime* 9, quoted in the companion CD for Turner, *Ages of Initiation*, section 10.4.

29. David O'Brien, "Catholic Youth: The Presumed Become the Pursued," in *The Catholic Church in the Twentieth Century: Renewing and Reimaging the City of God*, ed. John Deedy (Collegeville, MN: Liturgical Press, 2000), 90.

tian doctrine before the celebration of confirmation, key problems arise in a culture permeated by consumerism. Here, I will direct attention to the issue of presenting the sacrament of confirmation as a reward.

The notion that grace of any kind is offered to human beings as a kind of reward for their accomplishments was rejected as long ago as the fifth century when Augustine disputed the question with Pelagius. For the purpose of the present chapter, it is instructive to turn to Pope Pius X. His decision in 1910 to lower the age for First Communion while saying nothing about the age for confirmation contributed to the confusion about the place of confirmation in the Roman Catholic Church. However, it is the reasoning for lowering the age for First Communion that is important here. Concerning the practice of denying the Eucharist to children—even dying children—the relevant curial decree stated that "such is the injury caused by those who insist on extraordinary preparations for First Communion, beyond what is reasonable; and they doubtless do not realize that such precautions proceed from the errors of the Jansenists who contended that the Most Holy Eucharist is a reward rather than a remedy for human frailty."[30] The decree makes explicit that one must be judicious about setting the catechetical bar too high. A child may receive Holy Communion when "the child knows the difference between the Eucharistic Bread and ordinary, material bread, and can therefore approach the altar with proper devotion. Perfect knowledge of the things of faith, therefore, is not required, for an elementary knowledge suffices."[31]

The cultural phenomenon of consumerism was not yet in full swing when Pius X promulgated this teaching in 1910. Nevertheless, despite Pius' attempt to prevent the notion of a reward given to the deserving from deepening its grasp on Communion, less than thirty years after Pius' decree, Matthias Laros had this to say about confirmation:

30. Sacred Congregation of the Discipline of the Sacraments, *Quam Singulari* (August 8, 1910). Text in James J. McGivern, ed., *Worship and Liturgy* (Wilmington, NC: McGrath, 1978), 36.

31. *Quam Singulari.*

Since Confirmation is nowadays usually administered quite soon after First Communion, that is to say at a very early age, the advisability of changing and amplifying the preparation for this Sacrament might be considered; for at present only children at school are at all likely to receive the methodical instruction which should precede Confirmation. The National Movements in Germany and elsewhere has shown that one can perfectly well enroll children for political purposes, and that these are proud and eager to fulfil the tasks and responsibilities which such enrolment brings. Why should not the same sort of thing be done by bringing children together for dedication to the service of God? . . . We are bound by the teaching of the Church not to receive any Sacrament, until we are fully prepared for it.[32]

Quite apart from the disturbingly ambiguous approbation of the Hitler Youth (another dimension of the martial imagery associated with confirmation) this passage's emphasis on being "fully prepared" for confirmation runs counter to the emphasis Pius X had placed on what we might call being "adequately prepared." For Laros, confirmation is given to the deserving.

Seeking to defend catechetical requirements for confirmation while at the same time rebutting charges of Jansenism, Francis Buckley wrote in 1966: "Jansenism may have been partly responsible for postponing confirmation and the Eucharist, presenting the sacraments as rewards for being good. There was also a tendency to regard these sacraments as a reward for attending catechism class. But these abuses were not as important or basic as was the desire to lead the child to a genuine interior profession of faith, so that the reception of the sacraments would be a truly human act for him."[33] The emphasis on a "truly human act" is a manifestation of the turn to the subject that characterized much of mid-twentieth-century Christian theology. In itself, this emphasis is laudable, but even if the motive for significant catechetical preparation is pure, the cultural context within which that preparation takes place cannot be ignored. In a culture marked by consumer-

32. Matthias Laros, *Confirmation in the Modern World*, trans. George Sayer (New York: Sheed and Ward, 1938), 8–9.

33. Francis Buckley, "What Age for Confirmation?" *Theological Studies* 27, no. 4 (December 1966): 655–66 at 658.

ism and my "right" to obtain things that I have worked for, it is not enough for confirmation preparation to be non-reward oriented. It must be *seen* to be non-reward oriented.

For this reason, it is essential to lay stress on the gift quality of confirmation. The revised sacramental formula, "Be sealed with the gift of the Holy Spirit," is important in this regard.[34] The US bishops emphasize the point: "At whatever age a person celebrates Confirmation, the sacrament remains the gift of the Holy Spirit."[35] Yet the bishops acknowledge that often enough, the sacrament is in fact experienced as a reward.[36] Besides encouraging reflection on the traditional seven gifts of the Holy Spirit, formation programs seeking to oppose "reward" thinking could ask those preparing for confirmation to engage lines from the Bible that stress the primacy of God's initiative (e.g., 1 Cor 4:7; 1 John 4:7-12).

V. Confirmation and Maturity

Thomas Aquinas offers two passages that have had significant impact on the theory and practice of confirmation. He writes: "Man receive[s] spiritual life in Baptism, which is a spiritual regeneration: while in Confirmation man arrives at the perfect age, as it were, of the spiritual life."[37] Later, he adds: "In this sacrament [=confirmation] the fulness of the Holy Ghost is given for the spiritual strength which belongs to the perfect age. Now when man comes to perfect age he begins at once to have intercourse with others; whereas until then he lives an individual life, as it were,

---

34. Paul Turner writes: "Drawing on the image of the traditional gifts of the Holy Spirit, this word [=gift] almost warned against making too much of preparation for Confirmation. Seven-year-olds [are] eligible for the sacrament, and it comes not as reward, but as gift." Turner, "That the Intimate Connection of Confirmation with the Whole of Christian Initiation May Stand Out More Clearly," *National Bulletin on Liturgy* 36, no. 174 (Fall 2003): 150–54 at 151.

35. United States Conference of Catholic Bishops Committee on Pastoral Practices, *Receive the Gift*, 2.

36. See ibid., 9, 14.

37. *Summa Theologiae* III, q. 72, a. 1, resp. I am using the text in *Summa Theologica*, vol. 2, trans. Fathers of the English Dominican Province (New York: Benziger, 1947), 2424.

confined to himself."[38] Although Thomas makes it quite clear that the "perfect age" he has in mind is a matter of a spiritual age and not a chronological age,[39] twentieth-century writers sometimes talked about confirmation as a sacrament that effects spiritual maturity but also requires chronological maturity.

Virgil Michel and Matthias Laros refer to confirmation as a ceremony marking a spiritual "coming of age," and Laros specifically adds that the sacrament "does not merely celebrate the attainment of maturity; it actually effects it."[40] Echoing Thomas, Michel writes: "Whereas baptism therefore gives one the priestly power to do chiefly what is necessary for one's own salvation Confirmation gives one the power to do battle publicly against the enemies of faith and to profess one's faith openly. . . . A child may be concerned only with its own well-being; but the adult citizen is duty bound to work for the good of the community."[41] According to Francis Buckley in 1966, "The coming of the Spirit at confirmation is not so much for the sake of the recipient as for others."[42] Buckley also argues that the spiritual maturity associated with the coming of the Holy Spirit "presupposes a biological and psychological maturity."[43] This last point about biological and psychological maturity has also been a part of postconciliar arguments in favor of postponing confirmation until adolescence.[44]

At least two problems arise with this emphasis on maturity. First, a consumer culture stresses the right to obtain commodities once the prerequisites have been fulfilled (i.e., once I have put down my cash). Second, this emphasis on maturity associ-

---

38. *Summa Theologiae*, III, q. 72, a. 2, resp. I am using the text in *Summa Theologica*, vol. 2, 2425.

39. See *Summa Theologiae*, III, q. 72, a. 8, ad 2 in *Summa Theologica*, vol. 2, 2430.

40. Michel, "Confirmation: Our Apathy," 169; Laros, *Confirmation in the Modern World*, 21.

41. Michel, *Our Life in Christ*, 135. Damasus Winzen writes in a similar vein. See Winzen, "Anointed with the Spirit (II)," *Orate Fratres* 20, no. 9 (1946): 389–97 at 390.

42. Buckley, "What Age for Confirmation?" 660–61.

43. Ibid., 656.

44. See, for example, Kieran Sawyer, "A Case for Adolescent Confirmation," in *Confirming the Faith of Adolescents: An Alternative Future for Confirmation*, ed. Arthur Kubick (New York: Paulist, 1991), 39.

ated with confirmation devalues baptism. Earlier in this chapter, I directed attention to the problem of earning or being rewarded with one's confirmation in exchange for demonstrating mastery of Christian belief. Here, the issue is not mastery of belief but "maturity," especially when this term is understood in the sense employed by Buckley—namely, "biological and psychological maturity." Instead of (or perhaps in addition to) passing exams on Christian faith, those to be confirmed must be biologically and psychologically mature. It is worth noting that Buckley took issue with the age of seven specified in the 1917 *Code of Canon Law*, which was in force at the time of his article. The age of seven, however, is typically associated with the "age of discretion" in Catholic thought and the 1983 *Code* uses the latter phrase when addressing the proper age for reception of confirmation.[45] The phrase "age of discretion" is also well-known for its appearance in *Quam singulari*, which lowered the age for First Communion. Hence, as far as Catholic liturgical law is concerned, the minimum base requirements for First Communion and reception of confirmation are not significantly different.[46] This general similarity underscores the notion that both sacraments are gifts,[47] a point that cannot be overstressed in a consumer culture.

The second problem concerns the devaluation of baptism. We have already seen Kenan Osborne's concern in this regard. Marian

45. See can. 891 of the 1983 *Code of Canon Law*. Additionally, *Catechism of the Catholic Church* 1308 maintains that "although Confirmation is sometimes called the 'sacrament of Christian maturity,' we must not confuse adult faith with the adult age of natural growth, nor forget that the baptismal grace is a grace of free, unmerited election and does not need 'ratification' to become effective." Paragraph 1308 then cites *Summa Theologiae*, III, q. 72, a. 8, ad 2.

46. Writing after Vatican II, Richard P. Moudry makes the same observation: "There is no difference between the personal readiness required of a candidate for confirmation and that of a first communicant. The idea that confirmation presupposes a need for greater maturity in the candidate than do baptism or first communion is without support in Vatican II." Richard P. Moudry, "The Initiation of Children: The Path One Parish Took," in *When Should We Confirm?* ed. James A. Wilde (Chicago: Liturgy Training Publications, 1989), 78.

47. In this connection, see Linda Gaupin, "Now Confirmation Needs Its Own *Quam Singulari*," in *When Should We Confirm?*, 85–93.

Bohen argued in the same vein at the time that Vatican II was held: "The completion effected by confirmation does not consist in the 'socializing' of an individualistic child of God, nor in the imposition of the obligation to think about and concern oneself with others: 'A *Christian* [baptized] is one who is charged with the salvation of his fellow men.' "[48] Those who are baptized are always to be concerned about others but very young children are to do so in the manner of very young children. Older children are to do so in the manner of older children and so forth. Connecting altruism and responsibility too narrowly to the sacrament of confirmation does a disservice to both baptism and confirmation.

VI. Confirmation and Eucharist

I turn now to the fourth and final theme identified at the outset, namely, the problem of viewing confirmation as more important than Eucharist. Gerard Austin puts it well: "Our major sacraments are baptism and eucharist. . . . Currently, many pay more attention to confirmation than to baptism, and often more preparation is demanded for confirmation than for eucharist itself. We forget that eucharist is the summit of the spiritual life and the goal of all the sacraments."[49] To the degree that confirmation is played up as a singular spectacle (alongside other singular spectacles in consumer-driven entertainment culture), the holiness of ordinary Christian existence can be overshadowed or even ignored. Vincent Miller points out that Christian liturgies "face competition from glitzy theme parks, the sensory overload of dance clubs, the thrilling promise of shopping malls, the drama of *American Idol* and the

48. Marian Bohen, *The Mystery of Confirmation* (New York: Herder & Herder, 1963), 39.

49. Gerard Austin, "Eucharist and the Confirmation Debate," in *Confirmed as Children, Affirmed as Teens*, ed. James Wilde (Chicago: Liturgy Training Publications, 1990), 23. As early as the False Decretals, Christian figures had argued that confirmation was more important than baptism on the grounds that confirmation required an ecclesiastic (i.e., a bishop) of greater rank and dignity than baptism. The Ad Hoc Committee on the Age of Confirmation in the Diocese of Lafayette (Louisiana) raised similar concerns. See the "Final Report and Recommendations to the Council of Priests of the Diocese of Lafayette" (April 21, 2005), 37–38.

NFL playoffs."[50] Yet in *Lumen Gentium* 34, Vatican II holds that it is the holiness of the everyday that is celebrated in the Eucharist: "For all [the works of the laity], if accomplished in the Spirit, become spiritual sacrifices acceptable to God through Jesus Christ: their prayers and apostolic undertakings, family and married life, daily work, relaxation of mind and body, even the hardships of life if patiently borne (see 1 Pet 2:5). In the celebration of the Eucharist, these are offered to the Father in all piety along with the body of the Lord." In this connection, it is important to note that the 1971 Rite of Confirmation specifies that "Confirmation takes place as a rule within Mass."[51] This directive overturns the practice of celebrating confirmation apart from a eucharistic setting, a common feature of US Catholic experience prior to Vatican II.[52] The relationship between confirmation and Eucharist comes to the fore when the former is celebrated in the context of Mass. As important as confirmation is, confirmation *points to the Table*. The "Amen" repeated at each eucharistic celebration constitutes one's ongoing commitment to the Christian faith,[53] a faith to be lived out in the daily and often unspectacular pursuit of holiness.

VII. Conclusion

In this chapter addressing the challenges of celebrating the sacrament of confirmation in a culture saturated with consumerism, I have addressed four major points: confirmation as a sacrament of personal commitment to one's Christian faith, the requirement that one demonstrate command of Christian doctrine before one may be confirmed, confirmation as a sacrament of maturity, and

---

50. Miller, "The Liturgy and Popular Culture," 161.

51. 1971 Rite of Confirmation 13. This directive is retained in the 2016 Order of Confirmation 13.

52. See Mary Charles Bryce, OSB, "Confirmation: Being and Becoming Christian," *Worship* 41, no. 5 (May 1967): 284–98 at 287.

53. A point made by Mary Charles Bryce and by Gerard Austin. See Bryce, "Confirmation: Being and Becoming Christian," 298, and Austin, "Eucharist and the Confirmation Debate," 23–24. On the Eucharistic "Amen," see also Sermon 272 of St. Augustine.

confirmation as more important than Eucharist. Is there a way forward?

I think that several of the problems identified in this chapter can be resolved by restoring the sequence of baptism-confirmation-Eucharist as a matter of general practice. At present only a handful of Roman Catholic dioceses in the United States observe this sequence,[54] but one can make a strong case that this sequence is the preference of the universal Catholic Church. Paul Turner notes that the phrase "sacraments of initiation" (with reference to baptism, confirmation, and Eucharist) makes important appearances in the documents of Vatican II, indicating an inter-connection among these sacraments.[55] The phrase recurs in the 1971 Rite of Confirmation and the 1972 Rite of Christian Initiation of Adults.[56] Turner adds that all the relevant "major documents, including the *Code of Canon Law* and the *Catechism,* treated the sacraments in the order baptism-confirmation-Eucharist. But when the Sacred Congregation for Divine Worship published the revised Rite of Confirmation in 1971, its opening decree said that confirmation completed initiation into the Christian life, implying that Com-

54. As of this writing these dioceses are Denver, CO; Fargo, ND; Gallup, NM; Gaylord, MI; Great Falls-Billings, MT; Honolulu, HI; Manchester, NH; Phoenix, AZ; Portland, ME; Saginaw, MI; Spokane, WA; Springfield, IL; Tyler, TX. In recent years, some dioceses (Greensburg, PA; Marquette, MI; Sacramento, CA) that had this sequence in place have returned to baptism-Eucharist-confirmation.

55. See the companion CD for Paul Turner, *Ages of Initiation,* section 12.8. *Ad Gentes* (Decree on Missionary Activity) 14 uses the phrase "sacraments of initiation" and discusses the three sacraments in the order baptism-confirmation-Eucharist. Paragraph 36 of the same document presents that sequence but without the phrase "sacraments of initiation." *Presbyterorum Ordinis* (Decree on the Ministry and Life of Priests) 2 uses the phrase but without any discussion of sequence. See also *Sacrosanctum Concilium* 71. None of these documents, however, mandates the sequence baptism-confirmation-Eucharist.

56. See the companion CD for Paul Turner, *Ages of Initiation,* section 12.8. The opening paragraph and the ninth paragraph of the 1971 apostolic constitution on the sacrament of confirmation use the phrase and present the three sacraments in the order baptism-confirmation-Eucharist. The phrase appears in the Rite of Christian Initiation of Adults 6, and of course the entire RCIA is designed around the sequence baptism-confirmation-Eucharist. For the apostolic constitution, see *The Rites of the Catholic Church as Revised by the Second Vatican Council,* 1:472, 474.

munion preceded."[57] In his 2007 *Sacramentum Caritatis*, Pope Benedict XVI addressed the issue of different sequences, noting that "it must never be forgotten that our reception of Baptism and Confirmation is ordered to the Eucharist. Accordingly, our pastoral practice should reflect a more unitary understanding of the process of Christian initiation. . . . It needs to be seen which practice better enables the faithful to put the sacrament of the Eucharist at the center, as the goal of the whole process of initiation."[58] With respect to the woes of the sacrament of confirmation, there is no more urgent priority than the assessment encouraged by Benedict.

If no change in sequence is forthcoming soon, I suggest that the church consider the practice of fasting. Both Peter Lombard (d. 1164) and Hugh of St. Victor (d. 1141) taught that confirmation should be administered only by those who fast to those who fast.[59] Saying nothing about the minister of the sacrament, regional councils in Constance (1300) and Cologne (1536), taught that those to receive confirmation should fast.[60] The *Roman Catechism*

57. Companion CD for Paul Turner, *Ages of Initiation*, section 12.8. Paragraph 3 of the 1971 Rite of Confirmation advises that "Pastors have the special responsibility to see that all the baptized reach the completion of Christian initiation and therefore that they are prepared with the utmost care for Confirmation." One need not infer that "completion of Christian initiation" and "confirmation" are synonymous, but the text is open to such a reading. The 2016 rite contains similar language about "completion." See Order of Confirmation 3.

58. Pope Benedict XVI, Post-Synodal Apostolic Exhortation on the Eucharist (*Sacramentum Caritatis*, February 22, 2007) 17–18, https://w2.vatican.va/content /benedict-xvi/en/apost_exhortations/documents/hf_ben-xvi_exh_20070222 _sacramentum-caritatis.html. I am grateful to Bernadette Gasslein for pointing me to this passage. Note, too, that *Sacrosanctum Concilium* 71 holds that the rite of confirmation was to be revised in order to bring out the connection it has with the entire complex of Christian initiation. However, this paragraph does not explicitly mandate a change in the sequence of the sacraments of initiation.

59. See Lombard's *Sentences* 4:7, 3–4, and Hugh of St. Victor, *On the Sacraments*, 2:7, 5. These texts may be found in Turner, *Sources of Confirmation*, 40; 50–51. The same teaching was promulgated by the regional Council of Arles in 1260; text in the companion CD for Turner, *Ages of Initiation*, section 8.11.

60. The conciliar text for Constance is available in the companion CD-ROM for Turner, *Ages of Initiation*, section 8.11; the text for Cologne is available in section 9.6 of the same CD-ROM.

(1566) urged pastors to recommend fasting to those about to be confirmed.[61] The Roman Curia repeated this recommendation in 1774.[62] Clearly, there is precedent for recommending that one fast prior to reception of confirmation.[63] Fasting is precisely a non-consumerist stance.

Four recent catechetical documents, however, rarely mention fasting or mention it only in passing. The Vatican published the second edition of the *Catechism of the Catholic Church* in 1994. It discusses fasting eight times, but three of those references address the importance of not fasting for show.[64] The *General Directory for Catechesis*, issued by the Vatican in 1997, never refers to fasting.[65] The United States Conference of Catholic Bishops published *Our Hearts Were Burning within Us* in 1999.[66] Like the *General Directory*, it has not one reference to fasting. The Conference published its *National Directory for Catechesis* in 2005; it gives one reference each to the Lenten fast and to the fast observed before receiving communion.[67]

On the other hand, OHWB is marked by consistent encouragement of lifelong faith formation, including awareness of the ascetical tradition of the church.[68] The NDC, for its part, urges that

61. *Catechism of the Council of Trent for Parish Priests*, 208.

62. See Sacred Congregation for the Propagation of the Faith, "Instruction" (May 4, 1774). The text is available in the companion CD for Turner, *Ages of Initiation*, section 11.3.

63. Fasting (and almsgiving) also have an extensive association with preparation for initiation in the ancient catechumenate. See the discussion of almsgiving in chapter 1, section VI, p. 14.

64. The *Catechism of the Catholic Church* mentions fasting in 575, 1387, 1430, 1434, 1438, 1755, 1969, and 2043. Paragraphs 575, 1430, and 1755 concern not engaging in fasting or other penitential works in order to draw attention to oneself. Unlike the first edition of the Catechism, this edition makes no mention of fasting with reference to confirmation.

65. Congregation for the Clergy, *General Directory for Catechesis*, http://www.vatican.va/roman_curia/congregations/cclergy/documents/rc_con_ccatheduc_doc_17041998_directory-for-catechesis_en.html .

66. United States Conference of Catholic Bishops, *Our Hearts Were Burning within Us* (Washington, DC: USCCB, 1999). Henceforth OHWB.

67. United States Conference of Catholic Bishops, *National Directory for Catechesis* (Washington, DC: USCCB, 2005), 126; 107. Henceforth NDC.

68. See OHWB 94.

"catechesis has to find a way to break the 'buy, use, buy again, use again' cycle of consumerism,"[69] and it holds that good confirmation programs are those that ensure that "parents and sponsors are involved in the catechetical preparation of the children for Confirmation."[70] The NDC further states that "within [good] family-centered catechetical programs are opportunities for parents to catechize their children directly, for spouses to catechize each other, and for children to catechize one another and their parents."[71]

One way of approaching a fast before receiving confirmation would be to pattern it on the fast recommended for catechumens on Holy Saturday (RCIA 185) rather than as a full-fledged seasonal fast (such as the Lenten practice). In a consumer culture, however, it might be more effective instead to use as a model the practice of fasting from consumer purchases on Black Friday, the day after Thanksgiving, and to expand the practice beyond a single day. Imagine the impact on consumer habits if those to be confirmed, their families, and their sponsors refrain from consumer purchases (electronic gadgets, books, movie tickets, concert tickets, stylish clothes, etc.) for a week before celebrating the sacrament.[72] Imagine the even greater impact if entire parishes were to take up this practice in solidarity with those in their midst who are to be confirmed so that the already-confirmed and those to be confirmed provide a mutual witness to each other. I have in mind here the kind of mutual witnessing that takes place during the RCIA process, as newcomers and the already baptized find encouragement and inspiration in each other.[73]

69. NDC 16.

70. Ibid. 123.

71. Ibid. 259.

72. The 1287 Synod of Exeter directed parents to have their children confirmed by the age of three. If the parents neglected this duty, then the parents were to fast on bread and water every Friday until their children were confirmed. The text from the synod is in CD for Turner, *Ages of Initiation*, section 8.11. This directive indicates that fasting can be associated with confirmation beyond the fast of the minister and the recipient. Although the fasting of parents here has a punitive character, it indicates a (co)responsibility for celebration of the sacrament, which is what I have in mind vis-à-vis abstaining from consumer purchases.

73. See Aidan Kavanagh, *The Shape of Baptism: The Rite of Christian Initiation* (Collegeville, MN: Liturgical Press, 1978), 130.

This kind of fast can be taken up into the kind of fasting God desires in Isa 58:6-7 (NRSV):

> Is not this the fast that I choose:
>   to loose the bonds of injustice,
>   to undo the thongs of the yoke,
> to let the oppressed go free,
>   and to break every yoke?
> Is it not to share your bread with the hungry,
>   and bring the homeless poor into your house;
> when you see the naked, to cover them,
>   and not to hide yourself from your own kin?[74]

One must be careful not to allow this consumer fast and its associated work for economic justice to become just one more hoop to complete before getting the "reward" of confirmation but to the extent that these practices become routinized in parishes, they can spread beyond preparation for confirmation. They can work change in how believers situate themselves in and respond to a culture of consumerism.

---

74. See also Pope Leo the Great, *Sermon on Lent 40: On Lent II*, 4.

Chapter Three

EUCHARIST
AND CONSUMER CULTURE

I. Introduction

*Q*uia sine dominico non possumus: "because we cannot exist without the day of the Lord!"[1] So said the martyrs of Abitine facing persecution under the third-century Roman Emperor Diocletian when asked why they would rather face death than refrain from celebration of the Eucharist. These martyrs phrase in sharp and moving language a primary dictum of the Catholic mindset, namely, that the Eucharist is at the center of Christian existence.[2] It stands to reason, then, that the health and vitality of eucharistic celebrations is directly connected to the health and vitality of the church and that whatever threatens the health and vitality of those celebrations also challenges the

---

1. *Acta SS Saturnini et aliorum plurimorum martyrum*, 9: PL 8,709. See also John Paul II, apostolic letter *Dies Domini* (May 31, 1998), 46; Darío Castrillón Hoyos (prefect of the Congregation for the Clergy), Speech on the Occasion of the Fourth Video-Conference "Sacramentarian Theology from the Second Vatican Council to Our Times" (December 15, 2001); Benedict XVI, *Sacramentum Caritatis* (February 22, 2007) 95.

2. For recent magisterial statements on this subject, see Vatican II, Decree on the Ministry and Life of Priests (*Presbyterorum Ordinis*, December 7, 1965) 6; Sacred Congregation of Rites, Instruction on Eucharistic Worship (*Eucharisticum Mysterium*, May 25, 1967) 1; *General Instruction of the Roman Missal* (1975) 1 and the corresponding passage in *General Instruction of the Roman Missal* (2002) 16; *Catechism of the Catholic Church* (1994) 1327; John Paul II, Encyclical Letter on the Eucharist (*Ecclesia de Eucharistia*, April 17, 2003) 3; Benedict XVI, *Sacramentum Caritatis* 15.

well-being of the church as a whole. I want to examine here the challenges that present-day consumer culture poses to the vitality of eucharistic celebrations. I will do so by discussing three dyads: individualism and community; passivity and participation; commodification and gift. The astute reader will observe that the first term in each pair is drawn from an aspect of consumer culture and the second term is drawn from an aspect of eucharistic liturgical theology. Following this discussion, I will turn briefly to a treatment of celebration of First Communion. I will then offer some concluding remarks and suggestions.

II. Individualism and Community

"Consumerism," writes William Cavanaugh, "supports an essentially individualistic view of the human person in which each consumer is a sovereign chooser."[3] Bruce Rittenhouse extends Cavanaugh's analysis: "Persons who construct their identity primarily in terms of economic consumption tend to view their decisions in the explicitly religious sphere as free sovereign acts, in the same manner as their consumer decisions."[4] The Mass, then, is not grasped as a unitary act of corporate worship but rather as the juxtaposition of a number of individual acts of worship. Apart from any specific analysis of consumer culture, the Second Vatican Council had already sought to counteract the tradition of worshipers praying their own individual devotions at Mass (e.g., the rosary) by, among other things, permitting the use of vernacular languages in Catholic liturgy thus rendering the prayers of the Mass comprehensible.[5] In the almost sixty years since the close of the council, the relentless onslaught of consumerist advertising has worked to erode the corporate quality of worship.[6] In the words of

3. William Cavanaugh, *Being Consumed: Economics and Christian Desire* (Grand Rapids, MI: Eerdmans, 2008), 53.

4. Bruce Rittenhouse, *Shopping for Meaningful Lives: The Religious Motive of Consumerism* (Eugene, OR: Cascade Books, 2013), 39.

5. See *Sacrosanctum Concilium* 36.

6. Cavanaugh observes: "Virtually everywhere we look or listen—television, radio, web sites, newspapers, magazines, billboards, junk mail, movies, videos, t-shirts, buses, hats, cups, pens, pencils, gas-pump handles, walls of public restrooms—is saturated with advertising." Cavanaugh, *Being Consumed*, 19.

Michael Warren: "Pay attention to commercial imagery concocted to bring endlessly before consciousness the next set of products to purchase, and one's spirit becomes preoccupied with having and consuming, and even one's ordinary speech becomes littered with commercial imagery. One may eventually approach worship or catechesis as a commercial product, evaluated by whether it does or does not satisfy, that is, enlarge the self or comfort the self."[7]

One way to get this point across is to turn attention to habits surrounding family meals. In paragraph 1149, the *Catechism of the Catholic Church* points out that "the liturgy of the Church presupposes, integrates and sanctifies elements from creation and human culture, conferring on them the dignity of signs of grace, of the new creation in Jesus Christ." Part of the sign-function of the Eucharist, then, is drawn from ordinary meals, an element of human culture. As more and more family members eat independently of each other, the sign-function of eucharistic dining breaks down. When families eat in food courts at malls (each choosing his or her own style of food because, after all, each one is encouraged by advertising to be a sovereign chooser) and in fast-food restaurants in general (with thirty-minute limits on seating), the link between dining together at Eucharist and dining outside of eucharistic celebration becomes frayed. Kevin Irwin identifies shared preparation of food and coming together for a meal as elements of the sacramentality of ordinary meals. He adds: "For Americans, Thanksgiving Day is probably the single commonly shared example of this sacramental presumption (specifically work expended to prepare and relationships deepened because the food is taken together in a ritual way). But that kind of experience may itself be understood as unique because it occurs once a year and is not a 'daily and domestic thing.'"[8] In a similar vein, Benjamin Barber writes: "Dining cannot be hurried without impeaching its integrity as dining: Mama Napoli's sweet sausages cannot be consumed like hotdogs in a face-stuffing contest and keep

7. Michael Warren, *Faith, Culture and the Worshiping Community* (New York: Paulist, 1989), 76–77.

8. Kevin Irwin, *Models of the Eucharist* (New York: Paulist, 1995), 51. The phrase "daily and domestic thing" is drawn from David Power, *Unsearchable Riches: The Symbolic Nature of Liturgy* (Eugene, OR: Wipf & Stock, 2008; Collegeville, MN: Liturgical Press, 1984), 96.

their character as Mama's sweet sausages meant to evoke an evening family's dinner on Mulberry Street. Thanksgiving at Wendy's isn't possible, even if Wendy's hires out a four-star chef and puts turkey, sweet potatoes, and cranberry sauce on real crockery—unless you have two or three hours and an extended family at the ready, in which case why would you be at Wendy's?"[9] Celebrating the eucharistic meal in a consumer culture characterized by truncated meals is analogous to celebrating baptisms in a region where local bodies of water are fouled by pollution or industrial waste. Just as the cleansing sign-function of the baptismal water is undercut by the way in which (polluted) water is experienced apart from the baptismal ritual,[10] so too is the sign-function of the eucharistic meal weakened when other meals are not marked by shared food and shared conversation.

If the capacity of the Eucharist to be an effective sign of the unity of the Christian community is connected to the ways in which family meals in that community are indeed times of unity, it is connected also to the ways in which the life of a parish is as a whole marked by a communitarian spirit. In an *Angelus* address in 2011, Pope Benedict XVI remarked that "in an ever more individualistic culture, such as the one in which we are immersed in western society and which tends to spread throughout the world, the Eucharist constitutes a sort of 'antidote' that works in the minds and hearts of believers and continually sows in them the logic of communion, service and sharing."[11] This important insight needs to be counterbalanced by a point made by Aidan Kavanagh:

9. Benjamin Barber, *Consumed: How Markets Corrupt Children, Infantilize Adults, and Swallow Citizens Whole* (New York: Norton, 2007), 104. On the question of dining vs. merely scarfing food, see also Jan Michael Joncas, "Tasting the Kingdom of God: The Meal Ministry of Jesus and Its Implications for Contemporary Worship and Life," *Worship* 74, no. 4 (July 2000): 329–65 at 330, 359; Laura Hartman, *The Christian Consumer: Living Faithfully in a Fragile World* (New York: Oxford University Press, 2011), 161.

10. See section IX of chapter 1, p. 32.

11. Pope Benedict XVI, Angelus (St. Peter's, June 26, 2011), http://www.vatican.va/holy_father/benedict_xvi/angelus/2011/documents/hf_ben-xvi_ang_20110626_en.html.

A harvest festival will not make crop failure go away. Here, the problem lies not on the festal table but in the fields and among those who work them.

The moral in this for liturgical celebration is as hard as it is unavoidable. The celebration may well be impossible because repentance has not been undertaken, penance done, or conversion consummated. These endeavors, which are acts of worship in their own way, represent the sort of effort in faith which makes all festal celebration, liturgical or otherwise, possible.[12]

The work of celebrating the Eucharist fruitfully (which is always the work of Christ in which the church participates[13]) requires the work of building and maintaining community, and vice versa. Transposed to a consumerist key, this work involves resisting what James K. A. Smith calls the "strange configuration of sociality"[14] of the shopping mall. This configuration entices shoppers to compare themselves and their appearances (and the appearances of others) to the many posters in store windows of "attractive" people wearing the latest fashions. Christian shoppers who embrace this configuration see in others not the image of God but people with whom they do or do not wish to associate based on standards of fashion and appearance promoted in advertising.

Those who assemble to celebrate Eucharist do so in a configuration of sociality that is not to be grounded in an appearance-driven competition. Indeed, the *General Instruction of the Roman Missal* directs Christians at Eucharist "to shun any appearance of individualism or division, keeping before their eyes that they have only one Father in heaven and accordingly are all brothers and sisters to each other."[15] Hence, the model for eucharistic dining is not cliques at the mall but the table fellowship of Jesus. Jan Michael Joncas draws attention to the unity-in-diversity that characterized

12. Aidan Kavanagh, *Elements of Rite* (New York: Pueblo, 1982), 30. See also John Paul II, *Ecclesia de Eucharistia* 35.

13. See *Sacrosanctum Concilium* 7.

14. James K.A. Smith, *Desiring the Kingdom: Worship, Worldview, and Cultural Formation* (Grand Rapids, MI: Baker, 2009), 96, 98.

15. *General Instruction of the Roman Missal* (2002) 95. See also the corresponding passage in the *General Instruction of the Roman Missal* (1975) 62.

Jesus' meals: "Among the disciples who share Jesus' table are at least four members of the *am ha-aretz* (Peter, Andrew, James, John), a tax collector collaborating with the hated Roman occupying force (Matthew/Levi), and Zealots (Simon, Judas Iscariot)—all Jews who would normally never share a common meal."[16] A strange configuration of sociality indeed!

In a culture shaped by consumerist individualism, celebration of Eucharist can be misinterpreted to bolster individualism. Back in 1935, Virgil Michel had already sounded a warning: "When we receive Communion we may be inclined to think of it as Christ coming into our hearts and becoming our own exclusive possession, and we think with gratitude of the infinite Christ confining Himself within the limits of our small heart. When twenty persons receive Communion at Mass and go back to their separate pews, this would almost imply that there were now twenty Christs among the pews."[17] Writers have also drawn attention to the ways in which consumerist individualism is a sign and cause of fractured personal identity.[18] Whereas once people felt rooted in their clan, tribe, or village, and rooted also in their work and religious worldview, in recent times social and geographical mobility, instability in employment, and the rise of skepticism about religious claims have undermined this sense of rootedness and permanence. Bruce Rittenhouse argues that "consumerism is uniquely attractive as an existential strategy in the contemporary world situation precisely because so many other existential strategies have been marginalized in this context, including those

16. Joncas, "Tasting the Kingdom of God," 348.

17. Virgil Michel, "The Liturgy: The Basis of Social Regeneration," *Orate Fratres* 9, no. 12 (1935): 536–45 at 542. Michel immediately adds: "We know, of course, that this is not the Catholic doctrine. When twenty or more individuals receive Communion they have all been intimately united to one and the same sacramental Christ." Pope Benedict XVI makes a similar point in his encyclical letter *Deus Caritas Est* (December 25, 2005) 14.

18. See Richard Elliot and Kritsadarat Wattanasuwan, "Brands as Symbolic Resources for the Construction of Identity," *International Journal of Advertising* 17, no. 2 (1998): 2–10; David Burns and Jeffrey Fawcett, "The Role of Brands in a Consumer Culture: Can Strong Brands Serve as a Substitute for a Relationship with God?" *Journal of Biblical Integration in Business* 15 (Fall 2012): 28–42.

grounded in work, nation, heteronomous religion—i.e., religion that demands subjection to clerical authority—and the various ideologies of progress."[19] The issue of subjection to authority comes into play, for example, with the "Sunday obligation" for Catholics to attend Mass.

Timothy O'Malley and Louis-Marie Chauvet have important insights to offer on the question of individualism and authority. O'Malley's contribution comes in the context of comments he makes about the Eucharistic Prayer: "This narrative of divine love [in the institution narrative of the Eucharistic Prayer] remains for us *the* instituting narrative, one that radically forms the identity of Christians; we who seek to imitate the radical self-gift of Christ in the unfolding of our lives in time and space. There are other narratives. Often, they disfigure our identities."[20] Again and again, the Eucharistic Prayer reminds those assembled that authentic human living necessarily involves gift of self after the pattern of the Master who offered up his very life. Self-assertion over against any and all forms of authority is ruled out when one seeks to live a Christoform life. Chauvet makes a similar point: "Receiving Christ is possible only under the mode of 'receiving oneself from him.'"[21] Indeed, in the eucharistic celebration of praise and thanksgiving, we recognize that "all that we have and all that we are, and even our very act of thanksgiving, is a gift from God."[22] Christians, then, can seek to forge identities in and through consumer purchases with brand names. That attempt, however, is not compatible with the God-given identity renewed each week when the Body of Christ assembles for eucharistic celebration.

19. Rittenhouse, *Shopping for Meaningful Lives*, 32–33.

20. Timothy P. O'Malley, *Liturgy and the New Evangelization: Practicing the Art of Self-Giving Love* (Collegeville, MN: Liturgical Press, 2014), 97.

21. Louis-Marie Chauvet, "Le sacramentologue aux prises avec l'Eucharistie," *La Maison-Dieu* 137 (1979): 49–72 at 61. My translation.

22. Louis-Marie Chauvet, "Le sacrifice de la messe: Un statut chrétien du sacrifice," *Lumière et vie* 146 (1980): 85–106 at 97. My translation. This point is brought home in Common Preface IV of the Roman Missal: "For, although you have no need of our praise, yet our thanksgiving is itself your gift, since our praises add nothing to your greatness but profit us for salvation." *The Roman Missal, Third Typical Edition* (Collegeville, MN: Liturgical Press, 2011), 616.

III. Passivity and Participation

Movies and sporting events are important expressions of consumer culture. Theatre-goers plunk down their cash and then settle into a seat to be entertained for a few hours. Fans pay the price of admission and behold the athletic spectacle before them— if they don't just pay for cable television and watch the game from home—and indeed consumerist passivity is best symbolized by the hours each day that Americans typically sit in front of a television. As Vatican II reminds us, however, liturgy (including eucharistic liturgy) calls for the assembly to take "that full, conscious, and active part in liturgical celebrations which is demanded by the very nature of the liturgy."[23] Here I wish to examine eucharistic participation as over against consumerist passivity.[24]

An important aspect of participation in eucharistic liturgy is that such participation is meant to be grounded in a much wider practice. I have already drawn attention to the problem of a harvest festival without a harvest. Anne Koester frames the issue positively: "As the baptized, we also practice our liturgical dispositions between Sundays *by living our lives!*"[25] I will address below the nature of those dispositions; here it is important to note that liturgical participation takes place as part of a continuum that spans all of human activity. Eucharistic liturgy and all of life are meant to inform each other; one is not to be abstracted from the other. Bruce Rittenhouse considers the contrasting mindset associated with consumerism and postmodernism: "[Another] point of compatibility between consumerism and postmodernism is their

23. *Sacrosanctum Concilium* 14. The text adds that this active part in liturgy is something to which Christians "have a right and to which they are bound by reason of their Baptism."

24. Lawrence Madden warns: "Some attend church with a consumer mentality. The minister produces and the person in the pew either rejects the product or accepts it for consumption. To bring about full participation, we must also contend with the passivity of 'entertainment' models of participation. Here the assembly is viewed as an audience and the ministers as performers. This attitude is not restricted to the people in the assembly." Lawrence Madden, "A New Liturgical Movement," *America* 171, no. 6 (September 10, 1994): 16–19 at 18.

25. Anne Koester, "To Live and Learn: What Does Liturgy Teach?" *Liturgical Ministry* 14 (Fall 2005): 180–88 at 182.

disintegration of the modern understanding of a unitary personal identity. In consumerism, personal identity is spatially and temporally discontinuous. The institutions that formerly provided continuity to identity have faded in significance. Meaning exists in discrete acts of consumption and discrete acts of recognition by other persons."[26] Active participation in eucharistic celebration involves assenting to a Christian meaning of life that undergirds all of life. In the words of Mark Searle: "Active participation is nothing more nor less than the realization and activation of the common life of Christ into which we are initiated by baptism."[27] Active participation involves assenting to and effecting the requirement of self-offering love at the service of the neighbor.

Catholic liturgical theology looks to the presentation of bread and wine at eucharistic celebrations as a paradigmatic expression of the self-offering disposition of the assembly. The "spiritual meaning" of this rite, contends Adolf Adam, "consists in the fact that the faithful intend to offer themselves together with their gifts in the eucharistic celebration. Their faith and inner surrender of themselves is in harmony with the self-giving of the Lord, who sacrifices himself for us."[28] Writers such as Catherine Vincie and Barry Harvey emphasize that the gifts of bread and wine are not gifts from nature as such but are precisely gifts in which human labor and culture are implicated.[29] Yet Stephen Wilbricht and Paul Bradshaw raise pointed questions about whether assemblies do

---

26. Rittenhouse, *Shopping for Meaningful Lives*, 44. See also Michael Warren, *At This Time, In This Place: The Spirit Embodied in the Local Assembly* (Harrisburg, PA: Trinity Press International, 1999), 9. On the consumerist chronic reinvention of the self, see my "Consumerism and the Liturgical Act of Worship," *Horizons* 38, no. 1 (2011): 54–74 at 57–64.

27. Mark Searle, "Active Participation," *Assembly* 6, no. 2 (September 1979): 65–72 at 72.

28. Adolf Adam, *The Eucharistic Celebration: Source and Summit of Faith*, trans. Robert C. Schultz (Collegeville, MN: Liturgical Press, 1994), 55.

29. Catherine Vincie, "The Preparation of the Gifts: The Mystagogical Implications," in *A Commentary on the Order of Mass of* The Roman Missal, ed. Edward Foley, John Baldovin, Mary Collins, and Joanne Pierce (Collegeville, MN: Liturgical Press, 2011), 222; Barry Harvey, "The Eucharistic Idiom of the Gospel," *Pro Ecclesia* 9, no. 3 (2000): 297–318 at 303–4.

in fact regard the bread and wine along the lines of Adam, Vincie, and Harvey. First, Wilbricht:

> Is the sacrificial nature of the bread and wine, in and of themselves, truly comprehended by our worshiping communities today? Most likely the answer is "no." The bread and wine presented at the altar usually neither comes from the fields of those assembled, nor does the assembly have any sense of the work that is invested in producing bread out of wheat and wine out of crushed grapes. When we "see" the bread and wine processed gracefully and lovingly to the altar, held carefully and with dignity in the hands of the priest, and placed gently upon the table, do we "see" the struggle that is paradigmatic of our own struggle to "eucharistize" all of life, giving so that others might live?[30]

There is a risk, then, that eucharistic assemblies may be in a sense alienated from the bread and wine brought forward. They may engage with these symbols in a truncated and shallow fashion, which is how consumerism engages symbols generally. In antiquity, as Paul Bradshaw notes, the presentation of bread and wine was much more richly contextualized:

> The twentieth-century Liturgical Movement, which introduced this custom as one of its principal expressions, . . . informed people that they were thus "doing what the early church did" and that the action symbolized the offering to God of themselves, their souls and bodies, their work and life, through the ministry of their representatives. Unfortunately, many members of congregations have failed to visualize those carrying the gifts as being their representatives because they themselves did not elect or appoint them to this task, and in most cases every member of a congregation does not eventually get to take a turn at doing this, but it tends instead to be restricted to a relatively small

---

30. Stephen Wilbricht, *Rehearsing God's Just Kingdom: The Eucharistic Vision of Mark Searle* (Collegeville, MN: Liturgical Press, 2013), 128–29. Wilbricht here acknowledges dependence on the work of Daniel Groody, "Fruit of the Vine and Work of Human Hands: Immigration and the Eucharist," *Worship* 80, no. 5 (September 2006): 386–402.

number of people who can be counted on to be present when needed and to be willing to do it without too much persuasion. Moreover, what was usually omitted in the description of "what the early church did" was that in those distant days people did not simply carry things from one place to another in the building. Just as they had formerly done when the Eucharist was a complete meal, they continued to bring their contributions of bread and wine from home themselves. What they presented was truly their own offering, not something thrust into their hands by others.[31]

Bradshaw points out that among the very earliest generations of Christians, members of the eucharistic assembly would bring foodstuffs to share as part of a full meal. This food was "a practical and not just a symbolic expression of the sacrificial love for one another that was meant to characterize the new movement. Many believers lived in such poverty that the food provided on these occasions by wealthier members of the community and also given to them to take home afterward to consume during the week was vital to their physical well-being."[32] Here, the connection between presentation of gifts and self-offering love of neighbor was direct and practically immediate. Those assembled *participated* in the meaning of eucharistic celebration.

I would add that consumer culture does not prepare people to participate in acts of sacrificial self-offering love. In a study of the place of sacrifice in present-day American Catholic culture, Thomas Landy notes that "one element that has helped undermine the logic of sacrifice is the spread of consumer culture, an element of late capitalism. . . . The logic of capitalism demands that individuals 'sacrifice' themselves and many of their needs in order to find a place for themselves in that system, but capitalism rarely rewards altruism, and it is wary of forms of sacrifice that benefit other social entities to the extent that they come at a true cost to

---

31. Paul Bradshaw, "The Relationship between Historical Research and Modern Liturgical Practice," in *A Living Tradition: On the Intersection of Liturgical History and Pastoral Practice*, ed. David Pitt, Stefanos Alexopoulos, and Christian McConnell (Collegeville, MN: Liturgical Press, 2012), 9.

32. Ibid., 14.

the enterprise."[33] In a culture of acquisition, it can be difficult to sustain a disposition of self-offering love. That acquisitiveness and self-sacrifice do not mix may perhaps be self-evident but the effect of consumer culture on the disposition of self-offering love so central to eucharistic participation involves more than just a conflict between greed and generosity. Recall Rittenhouse's observation about consumer culture and temporal/spatial discontinuity of identity. Rightly, I think, Landy contends that a disposition of sacrificial self-offering is properly situated only in something more permanent: "The notion of sacrifice—certainly in its religious origins—would seem inherently to concern some connection to a larger, even cosmic order."[34]

For Christians, a key component of this larger, cosmic order is the paschal mystery. The *Catechism of the Catholic Church*, for example, teaches that "the Paschal mystery of Christ's cross and Resurrection stands at the center of the Good News that the apostles, and the church following them, are to proclaim to the world"[35] and that "in the liturgy of the Church, it is principally his own Paschal mystery that Christ signifies and makes present."[36] For additional insight on participation and the paschal mystery, I turn once again to Timothy O'Malley, who writes that full active and conscious participation

> includes immersion of our imagination, our very bodies, into the salvation history that liturgical prayer unfolds; it is a participation that culminates in our being taken up into the paschal mystery of Christ, one in which as we give our humanity over to the Father, we become divine; it is a participation in the church, a community that finds its source not in its own ideas, its own theories, but in the efficacious love of God healing the wounded heart of individual and society alike; it is a participation in sacred signs,

33. Thomas Michael Landy, "The Place of Sacrifice: Contemporary American Catholics and Changing Religious Beliefs," (PhD diss., Boston University, 2001), 219.

34. Ibid., 211. See also Katherine Turpin, "Consumer Capitalism and Adolescent Vocational Imagination: An Exploration of the Pedagogical Dynamics of Ongoing Conversion," (PhD diss., Emory University, 2004), 144–45.

35. *Catechism of the Catholic Church* 571.

36. *Catechism of the Catholic Church* 1085.

which serve as concrete ways that our humanity slowly practices the art of self-giving love through the glorification of God.[37]

Whereas active participation in consumerism typically involves making what William Cavanaugh has called "sovereign" choices, active participation in eucharistic celebration, on the other hand, involves consenting to *being chosen* by God. Even the act of assembling for worship is essentially a *response* to the call of God and not merely a set of simultaneous decisions by like-minded individuals.[38] Eucharistic Prayer III is instructive here. Shortly after the *Sanctus* this prayer says of the Father that "you never cease to gather a people to yourself, so that from the rising of the sun to its setting a pure sacrifice may be offered to your name."[39] Essential to this sacrifice is the assembly itself, for the prayer asks that the Spirit "make of us an eternal offering to you." Note that the offering is "eternal," that is, without interruption and without end. The self-offering of the assembly in response to God's gift of salvation in Christ is without the discontinuities associated with the consumerist postmodern fragmentation of the self. The sacrificial disposition fits into the cosmic order of the paschal mystery and indeed into the life of the Trinity itself. Roc O'Connor writes:

> The paschal mystery threatens the security, ambition, need for control, and prideful pretense of every Christian who enters into the eucharistic liturgy . . . .
> Don't most of us struggle with being the center, the source, the one worthy of all worship and glory? "It's about *me*, not about you!" is our battle cry. What follows? Competition, envy,

37. O'Malley, *Liturgy and the New Evangelization*, 32–33.

38. On assembling as a response to divine initiative see Judith Kubicki, *The Presence of Christ in the Gathered Assembly* (New York: Continuum, 2006), 34–37; Catherine Vincie, *Celebrating Divine Mystery: A Primer in Liturgical Theology*, (Collegeville, MN: Liturgical Press, 2009), 52–58; Paul Janowiak, *Standing Together in the Community of God: Liturgical Spirituality and the Presence of Christ* (Collegeville, MN: Liturgical Press, 2011), 36; Kevin Irwin, *What We Have Done, What We Have Failed to Do* (New York: Paulist, 2013), 165; Warren, *Faith, Culture and the Worshiping Community*, 196–97.

39. Later in this prayer the language is more forceful: "Listen graciously to the prayers of this family, whom you have *summoned* before you" (emphasis added).

independence, rivalry, grudges, feuds, strife, and wars—you know, daily life. So, we see that *one aspect of the Church's entry into the self-offering that is characteristic of the Trinity threatens our sovereignty.* Doesn't it make sense, then, that resistance to the primacy of God arises in the proclamation of, indeed the very *entering into,* the sacrifice of praise when we consider it as an address that needs to be answered at a personal level? Of course. Such resistance appears because we are merely human beings who would rather command our own destinies than surrender by entering the flow of the life of the Trinity.[40]

Eucharistic celebration of the paschal mystery supposes participation in an entire lifeworld of self-offering and a surrender of sovereignty. Mark Searle cautions that active participation is not simply a matter of "getting everyone to join the responses and the singing and the moving about,"[41] and though there is certainly something to be said for taking part in songs and responses or in sharing a sign of peace, fundamentally, as Searle also contends, "full, conscious, and active participation in the liturgy of the Church means nothing less than full, conscious, active participation in the life of grace, lived and manifested individually and collectively, as union with God and communion with all of humanity."[42] In Robert Hovda's words, at liturgy "the Church has no consumers, no body of mere clients or patients, no passive membership."[43]

IV. Commodification and Gift

I have already referred to the "strange configuration of sociality" of the shopping mall. This phrase from James K. A. Smith

40. Roc O'Connor, "The Threat of the Paschal Mystery," *Liturgical Ministry* 12 (Winter 2003): 52–56 at 52, 54. I have emphasized the phrase that begins with "one aspect." Other phrases are emphasized in the original.

41. Mark Searle, *Called to Participate: Theological, Ritual, and Social Perspectives*, eds. Barbara Searle and Anne Y. Koester (Collegeville, MN: Liturgical Press, 2006), 16.

42. Ibid., 38.

43. Robert Hovda, "Liturgy Forming Us in the Christian Life," in *Liturgy and Spirituality in Context: Perspectives on Prayer and Culture,* ed. Eleanor Bernstein (Collegeville, MN: Liturgical Press, 1990), 136–51 at 149.

is just one part of his overall discussion of the "liturgies of mall and market . . . that shape our imaginations and how we orient ourselves to the world."[44] One feature of these liturgies is waiting in lines. Consumers wait in line when they buy clothes, food and other items. Typically, these clothes and foods are commodified, that is, they are uprooted from the social contexts in which they were produced and then placed under the sovereign authority of the consumer who determines their meaning and/or the use to which the goods will be put.[45] Christians gathered for eucharistic celebration wait in line when they are in the communion procession. How might waiting in line at the supermarket orient a person to a communion procession? Do we wait in the communion line to get what is ours? Do Christians treat Eucharist in a commodified fashion, shorn of its intrinsic connection to the self-offering of Christ in which those who communicate implicate themselves?[46] Benedict XVI rightly holds that "in the Eucharist Jesus does not give us a 'thing,' but himself; he offers his own body and pours out his own blood. He thus gives us the totality of his life."[47]

The Eucharist is a gift, not a commodity. If I purchase a can of black beans at the supermarket, it will not matter to the store manager if I eat those beans or toss the unopened can in the garbage. The can of beans is a commodity. If I receive a crystal flower vase from a friend as a gift, it *will* matter to that friend if I deliberately drop the vase or use it to hold flowers on a mantel. Even if the vase were made of the cheapest pottery, giver and recipient are implicated in a relationship in which intentions and actions matter.[48] As gift, the Eucharist is part of what James K. A. Smith calls

44. Smith, *Desiring the Kingdom*, 25. His fuller treatment of these liturgies appears on pp. 96–101.

45. See Vincent Miller's discussion of supermarkets in *Consuming Religion: Christian Faith and Practice in a Consumer Culture* (New York: Continuum, 2003), 38; see also the discussion of Tibetan prayer flags on p. 4.

46. See Kevin Seasoltz, *A Virtuous Church: Catholic Theology, Ethics, and Liturgy for the 21st Century* (Maryknoll, NY: Orbis Books, 2012), 180.

47. Benedict XVI, *Sacramentum Caritatis* 7.

48. Hence, Louis-Marie Chauvet writes: "The symbolic essence of the gift is precisely characterized not by the worth of the object offered–this can be practically nothing in terms of usefulness or commercial value, and yet the 'nothing'

the "alternative economy" of Christian worship.[49] "The Eucharist," argues William Cavanaugh, "undercuts the primacy of contract and exchange in modern social relations."[50] John Paul II drives this point home:

> We cannot, even for a moment, forget that the Eucharist is a special possession belonging to the whole Church. It is the greatest gift in the order of grace and of sacrament that the divine Spouse has offered and unceasingly offers to His spouse. And precisely because it is such a gift, all of us should in a spirit of profound faith let ourselves be guided by a sense of truly Christian responsibility. A gift obliges us ever more profoundly because it speaks to us not so much with the force of a strict right as with the force of personal confidence, and thus—without legal obligations—it calls for trust and gratitude. The Eucharist is just such a gift and such a possession. We should remain faithful in every detail to what it expresses in itself and to what it asks of us, namely, thanksgiving.[51]

The one who gives a gift exercises the capacity to be self-offering, for gifts are precisely things that are not owed. In the exercise of this capacity to be self-offering, the giver of the gift recognizes the capacity of the recipient likewise to engage in behavior that is not owed in the sense of *legal* obligation but in the sense of what Louis-Marie Chauvet has called "obligatory generosity."[52] What is involved here is not contractual obligation, the mutual fulfillment of agreed upon terms. What is at stake is the mutual recognition of giver and recipient as subjects capable of self-offering (and thus beings who can enter relationship). Obligatory generosity applies

---

offered is received as a true gift–but by the *relationship of [covenant]*, friendship, affection, recognition, gratitude it creates or recreates between the partners." Chauvet, *Symbol and Sacrament*, trans. Patrick Madigan and Madeleine Beaumont (Collegeville, MN: Liturgical Press, 1995), 107.

49. Smith, *Desiring the Kingdom*, 204.

50. William Cavanaugh, *Theopolitical Imagination: Discovering the Liturgy as a Political Act in an Age of Global Consumerism* (New York: Continuum, 2002), 47.

51. John Paul II, Letter on the Mystery and Worship of the Eucharist (*Dominicae Cenae*, February 24, 1980) 12, https://w2.vatican.va/content/john-paul-ii/en/letters/1980/documents/hf_jp-ii_let_19800224_dominicae-cenae.html.

52. Chauvet, *Symbol and Sacrament*, 100–101.

not only to cases of material gifts but even to words themselves. Chauvet offers the case in which I offer a greeting to someone: "By the simple fact of its enunciation, it effects a mutual recognition and seals a contract between the two partners, whose status is *ipso facto* modified by their mutual relation with the other partner. The worst insult that one can give to someone sometimes consists precisely in not responding to him when he addresses a word to us: it is a kind of 'killing,' by way of denying his presence: hence the violent response of the speaker: 'You could at least answer me!' "[53] The words I offer to another invite relationship. The Word the Father sends into the world invites relationship. The gift of Eucharist invites relationship. The Eucharist is not a brute thing but the very subjectivity, the very being, of the Risen Lord. It calls for a response.

As we have seen above, this response involves forming one's life and the life of one's community into an "eternal offering." Here I would like to draw particular attention to how the gift quality of Eucharist helps to shape that eternal offering for, as Alexander Schmemann puts it, worship "is the epiphany of the world."[54] Eucharistic worship in particular is an effective demonstration— a sacrament—of how Christians are to use the material of this world. Rowan Williams offers an apt summary: "The objects of the world, seen in the perspective of the eucharist, cannot be proper material for the defence of one ego or group-ego against another, cannot properly be tools of power, because they are signs of a creativity working by the renunciation of control, and signs of the possibility of communion, covenanted trust and the recognition of shared need and shared hope."[55] Mark Searle makes a strikingly similar point: "Creation, groaning to be redeemed from the homicidal perversions to which our sinful use has subjected it, finds its liberation when it is used as it is used in the liturgy: to acknowledge and express the justice of God in the midst of the people, who are being bonded into a community by their common and respectful use of material things. Over against that stand

53. Chauvet, *Du symbolique au symbole* (Paris: Cerf, 1979), 65. My translation.

54. Alexander Schmemann, *For the Life of the World* (Crestwood, NY: St. Vladimir's Seminary, 1963), 121. See also Smith, *Desiring the Kingdom*, 143.

55. Rowan Williams, *On Christian Theology* (Oxford: Blackwell, 2000), 218.

all forms of selfish appropriation and misuse of created realities, an appropriation and abuse that seem inseparable from unjust relationships between people."[56] Eucharistic worship is the world done right, so to speak. Those who assemble use the gifts of creation and human labor to sustain and nourish one another on their collective journey to *theosis*, to union with God. That journey is a matter of both soul and body. That journey is shared. Along these lines, Goffredo Boselli echoes Benedict's point about eucharistic gift and adds a communal dimension: "[The sacramental body of Jesus] is not simply *body* but is in essence *body-for-you*, body given; the gift-nature of Jesus' body is not added in a second moment but belongs to it from the start . . . . The *body-for-you* negates every individualistic logic."[57] The body of Christ on the cross is offered for all. So, too, the eucharistic body is not merely for "you" but essentially for "you" in the plural. Everything we have said about obligatory generosity above applies to individual Christians and to those Christians as members of communities. In the end, the themes of community, participation, and gift interpenetrate.

V. First Communion

It is not my intention here to rehearse the entire history of First Communion practices. I will note simply that the first evidence we have for special celebration of First Communion for groups of children dates back only to about 1593 in France.[58] As early as 1864, people were sounding warnings about misplaced priorities

---

56. Mark Searle, "Serving the Lord with Justice," in *Vision: The Scholarly Contributions of Mark Searle to Liturgical Renewal*, ed. Anne Koester and Barbara Searle (Collegeville, MN: Liturgical Press, 2004), 15–16. Writing on the Eucharist in a similar vein, Alexander Schmemann contends: "In Christ our earthly food . . . becomes that for which it was created—participation in the divine life." Schmemann, *The Eucharist: Sacrament of the Kingdom* (Crestwood, NY: St. Vladimir's Seminary, 1987), 110.

57. Goffredo Boselli, *The Spiritual Meaning of the Liturgy*, trans. Barry Hudock (Collegeville, MN: Liturgical Press, 2014), 199.

58. Paul Turner, *Ages of Initiation: The First Two Christian Millennia* (Collegeville, MN: Liturgical Press, 2000), 37. Turner adds on p. 39: "The idea for Catholic First Communion rituals began in parishes. The elaborate ceremonies caught on within fifty years of the earliest records. Gradually, dioceses and religious

associated with these celebrations. In that year, a letter writer to the British journal *The Queen* observed of a First Communion in France that "no one can have been a witness to that ceremony without feeling that with all its beauty and gracefulness it was calculated rather to instil feelings of vanity and love of adornment into the minds of children than to fulfil its apparent object of inculcating mortification and self-denial."[59] Anthea Jarvis observes that in its article on First Communion for children, the *Catholic Encyclopedia* advised that "no effort should be spared to fix the occasion indelibly on the mind of the young communicant. For this purpose the Mass at which it is received should be celebrated with special solemnity, boys and girls being suitably attired."[60] Reflecting on more recent developments in England, Jarvis writes:

> After a selective trawl through the archive of the *Catholic Pictorial*, a weekly (now monthly) newspaper published in Liverpool starting in 1962, I have concluded that the first signs of "fantasy dressing" occurred in the mid-1970s, when full-length dresses were reintroduced, worn with bridal headdresses, and miniature tuxedo suits, worn with big bow ties, began to be seen on boys. By the early 1990s pearl and diamanté embroideries and crinoline petticoats had arrived, dresses with "shepherdess" overskirts looped up with posies of white rosebuds were standard, and outfits had to be accessorised with white lace parasols, gloves, and of course matching bags. Stories were current in Liverpool in the late 1990s about a battery-powered tiara worn by a little girl that lit up at the moment she received the Sacred Host, and of the family of a little boy who hired a Rolls Royce and a red carpet for his arrival at the church.[61]

---

communities began to regulate First Communions, but Rome never authorized a rite of First Communion."

59. Letter from reader J. H. in *The Queen* (January 30, 1864), 97, quoted in Anthea Jarvis, "The Dress Must Be White, and Perfectly Plain and Simple: Confirmation and First Communion Dresses, 1850–2000," *Costume: The Journal of the Costume Society* 1234, no. 41 (May 2007): 83–98 at 85.

60. Patrick Morrisroe, "Communion of Children," in *The Catholic Encyclopedia* (New York: The Encyclopedia Press, 1913) 4: 170–71 at 171, quoted in Anthea Jarvis, "The Dress Must Be White," 90.

61. Jarvis, "The Dress Must Be White," 95.

In her 2007 study of the impact of consumer culture on celebration of First Communion, Jo-Ann Metzdorff reports feedback from Roman Catholic pastors in Nassau County, New York. These pastors noted the following:

> Competition with regard to clothing and other "trappings," and the pressure to keep up with or outdo other families. This pressure is more evident among the girls; there is an increasing need among the girls not to have the same dress as another child.
>
> An increase in the use of limousines to take children and families to and from the church. Some parishes resorted to banning their use.
>
> Extravagant parties costing tens of thousands of dollars held in catering halls.
>
> Young girls being treated like brides (hair, nails, make-up, elaborate headpieces, expensive dresses).
>
> Photography and video distracting from the liturgy. Many parishes have banned the use of cameras and videos or have hired photographers to take pictures of the children. It has been noted that this rule of no pictures is often ignored, especially now with camera phones.
>
> The event itself is commodified. It is not a celebration of a sacrament but of a "rite of passage," with no real connection to the faith beyond that of a family tradition.
>
> The emphasis on monetary or extravagant gifts for the children.[62]

Forbes reports that Nassau County ranks among the twelve wealthiest counties in the United States by median household income,[63]

---

62. Jo-Ann Metzdorff, "The Consumer Culture and Family Faith Formation, Practice and Preparation for First Holy Communion," (DMin thesis, Seminary of the Immaculate Conception, 2007), 62. For a parallel analysis, see Peter McGrail, *First Communion: Ritual, Church and Popular Religious Identity* (Burlington, VT: Ashgate, 2007), esp. 151–67.

63. See Tom Van Riper, "America's Most Affluent Neighborhoods," *Forbes* (February 13, 2012), http://www.forbes.com/sites/tomvanriper/2012/02/13 /americas-most-affluent-neighborhoods/. For a report on costs associated with First Communion in Ireland, see Charlie Weston, "Parents Spending 17pc Less on Child's Holy Communion," http://www.independent.ie/irish-news/parents -spending-17pc-less-on-childs-holy-communion-26742545.html. Apart from Nassau County, I was unable to find reports on First Communion costs in the United States.

so the experience of these pastors (e.g., chartering limousines) cannot be called typical of First Communion in the United States. Nevertheless, their accounts provide disturbing indicators of the influence of consumerism on First Communion practices.

We can revisit the pairings of individualism and community, passivity and participation, and commodification and gift to assess these disturbing indicators. Certainly, when families try to outdo each other with respect to dress we have the strange configuration of sociality about which James K. A. Smith writes. Such competition flies in the face of the warning in the *General Instruction* against displays of individualism. When First Communion is associated merely with family tradition and not with participation in the eternal self-offering of Christ, we see realized Bruce Rittenhouse's comments about meaning and discrete acts of consumption. Eucharist is split from its intrinsic connection to building up the community and attached, for example, to lavish receptions which, as lavish as they may be, come to an end. When emphasis shifts from the gift of Christ in the consecrated species to the cash one receives after the liturgy, the meaning of the event becomes monetized. One may experience gratitude for the cash but by and large in a consumer culture cash is used for the purchase of commodities. The meaning of Eucharist as involving a gift of *self* to the other is obscured when one receives cash to spend *on* oneself. Nor is the situation helped when parishes sponsor First Communion "boutiques" at which parents can purchase gifts for their children.[64]

VI. Conclusion

There is no question that consumerism has had and is having a corrosive effect on eucharistic celebration and that this effect is especially evident in celebrations of First Communion. Before turning to discussion of how eucharistic celebrations can have corrosive effects on consumer culture, I think it is first important to place this discussion of consumerism in context. It was not my intent to provide a detailed history of First Communion practices

---

64. See Metzdorff, "The Consumer Culture and Family Faith Formation," 100.

above, and it is not my intent now to provide a detailed history of eucharistic practices in general. It *is* important, however, to draw attention to several key developments in the history of the Eucharist, which was never free of problems of one sort or another.

We can begin with the Last Supper itself. As Joncas has observed, the table fellowship of Jesus saw Jews from quite different orbits coming together to dine—and the Last Supper included the man who would hand Jesus over to the religious authorities later that evening. We can turn to Paul's sharp criticism of eucharistic practice in Corinth: when you ignore the needs of those around you, it is not really the Lord's Supper that you celebrate (1 Cor 11:20). Clearly all was not well at the Last Supper or in Corinth. Nor was all well in the late fourth century, when John Chrysostom had to plead for those assembled to partake of the Eucharist.[65] The Fourth Lateran Council in 1215 had to mandate that Christians receive Eucharist at least once a year.[66] The Roman Missal of 1570, the first universal guideline for the celebration of Mass, contained no directives for the assembly; all of its instructions were for the clergy. The history of eucharistic worship is replete with causes for concern. Concern about the impact of consumerism is well-founded but it should not induce a false sense that all had been well until the rise of consumer culture.

Returning to the three pairings that have framed this chapter, let us begin with individualism and community. Virgil Michel had warned about giving the impression of "twenty Christs" when members of the assembly return to their pews after communion. A subtle but important countermeasure is available, namely, providing to the assembly only bread consecrated at the Mass they are attending. As Adolf Adam points out, liturgical directives supporting this practice have a long history:

> It is not just recently that the Church has placed great value on all the communicants' receiving only hosts that have been conse-

65. In his third Homily on Ephesians, Chrysostom complains that "in vain do we stand before the altar; there is no one to partake." Citation taken from John Chrysostom, *Homilies on Ephesians* 3, in Philip Schaff, ed., *Nicene and Post-Nicene Fathers of the Christian Church*, vol. 13: *Saint Chrysostom: Homilies on Galatians, Ephesians, Philippians, Colossians, Thessalonians, Timothy, Titus, and Philemon* (Grand Rapids, MI: Eerdmans, 1988, reprint), 64.

66. DS 812.

crated in that particular celebration of the Mass. The explicit wish that this would happen was expressed by Vatican II's Constitution on the Liturgy (SC 55), the General Instruction (GIRM 1975, no. 56h), and in other postconciliar documents. Before that, it was the wish of Pius XII who cites Benedict XIV (1740–58) as an authority. The original purpose of storing consecrated hosts in the tabernacle was to have them available at all times for Viaticum to the critically ill. It is as surprising as it is deplorable that many parishes simply ignore this meaningful recommendation of several popes and continue to consecrate in order to "stock up ahead of time."[67]

One point in avoiding recourse to the tabernacle is to emphasize that each person receiving communion does so not from just any source but from the bread consecrated in *their* presence by virtue of God's grace and *their* prayer said aloud by the presider.[68] This point is all the more reinforced if there is one bread to be consecrated, either in the form of a loaf or in the form of a single host large enough to be broken into pieces so that all my communicate from it. As St. Paul put it, the one bread declares the unity of the assembly.[69] In the fraction rite, the practical is inseparable from the symbolic.[70]

67. Adam, *The Eucharistic Celebration*, 103–4. The directive from the *General Instruction of the Roman Missal* (1975) 56/H is found also in the *General Instruction of the Roman Missal* (2002) 13, 85. Adam refers to Pius X, Encyclical Letter on the Sacred Liturgy (*Mediator Dei*, November 20, 1947) 118, which in turn draws on Benedict XIV, Letter to the Bishops of Italy (*Certiores Effecti*, November 13, 1742). The warning against stocking up ahead of time is taken from Emil J. Lengeling, *Die neue Ordnung der Eucharstiefeier* (Münster: Regensberg, 1970), 246.

68. Another point of partaking in the bread consecrated at the Mass one attends is to highlight the necessary theological interconnection between the meal dimension of the Mass and the sacrificial dimension of the Mass, but the task of addressing that topic is for another time. See Margaret Mary Kelleher, "Preamble," in *A Commentary on the* General Instruction of the Roman Missal, 92–93. See also my "A Holy and Living Sacrifice," *Liturgical Ministry* 18 (Spring 2009): 59–67.

69. See 1 Cor 10:17.

70. On this subject, see Louis-Marie Chauvet, *Thèmes de réflexion sur l'eucharistie* (Lourdes: Congrès Eucharistique International, 1981), 25; Chauvet, *Symbol and Sacrament*, 406–8. It should be noted, however, that the *General Instruction of the Roman Missal* (2002) cautions in 83 that the fraction rite "should not be unnecessarily prolonged." That directive, which has no antecedent in the *Instruction* of 1975, appears to be at odds with eucharistic emphasis on unity.

With respect to the question of participation and passivity, I noted the concerns of Stephen Wilbricht and Paul Bradshaw about the assembly being alienated from the presentation of bread and wine. One approach to address this alienation would be to have members of the assembly prepare and bake the bread to be consecrated or even to produce the wine. Though this approach has been used in a number of parishes, it may not be practical in many cases. Mat Verghese has offered another suggestion, namely, familiarizing assemblies with the work that goes into making bread and wine. Parishes can arrange for farmers and vintners to give presentations or even for parish delegations to visit wheat farms and vineyards.[71] Even if parishioners are not directly involved in the production of the materials used in eucharistic celebrations, becoming more aware of the wider social web they inhabit can assist parishioners to grasp the wider dimensions of eucharistic offering.[72] Parishes can also investigate acquiring bread and wine made from wheat and grapes that were tended and harvested by people paid a just wage under just working conditions.

Concerning commodification and gift, we can turn to a line from the *General Instruction of the Roman Missal* (2002) which, when it addresses communion in the hand, states: "The faithful are not permitted to take the consecrated bread or the sacred chalice by themselves."[73] In their commentary on this text, Martin Connell and Sharon McMillan observe that "the prescription that the faithful are not to take the eucharistic elements by themselves . . . is an affirmation of a foundational sacramental principle that *the sacraments are signs of God's grace and pure gifts which are accepted*

---

71. Mat Verghese, " 'Fruit of the Earth and Work of Human Hands': Celebration of the Eucharist as a Site of Ecological Conversion," (MA thesis, Villanova University, 2015), 47. See also Michael J. Wood, *Cultivating Soil and Soul: Twentieth-Century Catholic Agrarians Embrace the Liturgical Movement* (Collegeville, MN: Liturgical Press, 2009); Marc Boucher-Colbert, "Eating the Body of the Lord: Eucharist and Community-Supported Farming," in *Embracing Earth: Catholic Approaches to Ecology*, ed. Albert J. LaChance and John E. Carroll (Maryknoll, NY: Orbis Books, 1994), 115–28.

72. On the wider social web, see Harvey, "The Eucharistic Idiom of the Gospel," 303–4.

73. *General Instruction of the Roman Missal* (2002) 160.

or received, not taken."[74] At the mall, one takes home what one has purchased. At Mass, one receives what one was given. If assemblies are taught to take this point to heart, note again that the practical and the symbolic will be interwoven.

On the subject of First Communion, Josef Jungmann raises a relevant theological question: "Is it right for Christians to extol First Communion day as something extraordinary . . . ? It is, after all, our 'daily bread.' "[75] Parishes might consider moving away from separate Masses for First Communion and incorporating First Communion into the regular weekend schedule of Masses.[76] In order to avoid an atmosphere of competing fashions, parishes might require all children to wear a simple white robe for their First Communion. As Jo-Ann Metzdorff points out, the use of white garments has the bonus of referring back to the white garments at baptism.[77]

I do not pretend that any of the suggestions that I have offered here are in any sense a comprehensive response to the challenge that consumerism poses to eucharistic celebration in the twenty-first century. Yet I share Vincent Miller's belief that the principle of sacramentality offers grounds for countering consumerism and commodification: "By hallowing physical things, it endows them with importance. As mediations of the divine, they matter."[78] Hallowing physical things is a Christian practice preeminent in eucharistic celebrations. Though Christians consume these hallowed things, Benedict XVI points out that

---

74. Martin Connell and Sharon McMillan, "The Different Forms of Celebrating Mass," in *A Commentary on the Order of Mass of* The Roman Missal, 257 (emphasis added).

75. Josef Jungmann, *Handing on the Faith*, trans. A. N. Fuerst (New York: Herder & Herder, 1964), 325.

76. See Metzdorff, "The Consumer Culture and Family Faith Formation," 99.

77. Ibid., 100. Even albs, of course, are subject to degrees of extravagance. Use of albs for First Communion is common in Poland and websites such as https://www.holyart.pl/specjalne-okazje/pierwsza-komunia-swieta/stroje-do-pierwszej-komunii?sorter_id=2&sort=20a offer selections ranging from simple to elaborate. I am indebted to my Villanova University colleague Jerry Beyer for pointing this out to me.

78. Miller, *Consuming Religion*, 189.

by receiving the body and blood of Jesus Christ we become sharers in the divine life in an ever more adult and conscious way. . . . We can apply Saint Augustine's words, in his *Confessions*, about the eternal *Logos* as the food of our souls. Stressing the mysterious nature of this food, Augustine imagines the Lord saying to him: "I am the food of grown men; grow, and you shall feed upon me; nor shall you change me, like the food of your flesh, into yourself, but you shall be changed into me." It is not the eucharistic food that is changed into us, but rather we who are mysteriously transformed by it. Christ nourishes us by uniting us to himself; "he draws us into himself."[79]

79. Benedict XVI, *Sacramentum Caritatis* 70. Benedict is quoting from Augustine's *Confessions*, 7.10.16. The second quotation in this excerpt is taken from Benedict XVI, Homily at Marienfeld Esplanade (August 21, 2005): *Acta Apostolicae Sedis* 97 (2005): 892.

Chapter Four

RECONCILIATION
AND CONSUMER CULTURE

I. Introduction

In his 1984 Post-Synodal Apostolic Exhortation on Reconciliation and Penance (*Reconciliatio et Paenitentia*), John Paul II observed that "the sacrament of penance is in crisis."[1] In remarks he offered to US bishops on their *ad limina* visit to Rome in 1988, John Paul sought to tamp down apprehension about the sacrament, saying that "these statements [about penance in crisis] are neither negative expressions of pessimism nor causes for alarm; they are rather expressions of a pastoral realism that requires positive pastoral reflection, planning and action."[2] While it might not be appropriate to panic at the steep drop in the number of

---

1. John Paul II, Post-Synodal Apostolic Exhortation on Reconciliation and Penance (*Reconciliatio et Paenitentia*, December 2, 1984) 28. James Dallen comments that the "crisis" was palpable already in 1973 when the postconciliar rite of penance was promulgated: "By the time the Rite of Penance was published, the crisis of penance was a major concern. Initial evaluations of the new ritual were cautiously optimistic, but a sharp decline in confessions was apparent. Some observers saw this decline as regression, signaling the loss of the sense of sin and penance, and a few even blamed the liturgical changes initiated by Vatican II. Others, however, saw the decline as the correction of a previous overemphasis." James Dallen, *The Reconciling Community* (Collegeville, MN: Liturgical Press, 1986), 222.

2. Pope John Paul II, *Ad Limina Address to US Bishops* (May 31, 1988) 7, http://w2.vatican.va/content/john-paul-ii/en/speeches/1988/may/documents/hf_jp-ii_spe_19880531_usa-ad-limina.html.

Catholics seeking the sacrament of reconciliation, it is worthwhile to turn to those numbers briefly before addressing the central concern of this chapter—namely, the ways in which a cultural context marked by consumerist individualism affects Catholics' understanding and practice of the sacrament of reconciliation. Following the presentation of statistics, I will discuss possible reasons for the decline before zeroing in on the influence of consumer culture. After remarks on consumer culture, I will address the ways in which I think postconciliar theology of the sacrament can respond to consumer challenges. I will conclude with some remarks about the resituation of the sacrament in the early years of the twenty-first century.

II. Statistics and Reasons

Historian James O'Toole provides evidence of decline in recourse to reconciliation: "In 1900 . . . Sacred Heart Parish in Newton, Massachusetts, a middle-class suburb of Boston, set a pattern that would remain in place for several decades: four priests heard confessions from 3:30 to 6:00 p.m. and again from 7:00 to 9:30, a total of five hours, every Saturday. . . . By 1972, the regularly scheduled time had been reduced from five to three hours each Saturday . . . and by 1991 that was cut to only an hour and a half."[3] A study conducted in 1990 by the National Conference of Catholic Bishops found that the average time per parish was 1.8 hours a week, not far off from the numbers at Sacred Heart.[4] The same study indicated that 4 percent of Catholics celebrated the sacrament weekly, 5 percent celebrated monthly, 17 percent every two or three months, 55 percent once or twice a year, and 19

3. James O'Toole, "In the Court of Conscience: American Catholics and Confession, 1900–1975," in *Habits of Devotion: Catholic Religious Practice in Twentieth-Century America*, ed. James O'Toole (Ithaca, NY: Cornell University Press, 2004), 169–70. On these pages, O'Toole provides accounts of two other Boston-area parishes that scaled back significantly their scheduled hours for confession and data about parishes in Milwaukee in the 1960s.

4. National Conference of Catholic Bishops Committee for Pastoral Research and Practices, "Sacrament of Penance Study," *Origins* 19, no. 38 (February 22, 1990): 613–24 at 615.

percent never.[5] More recently, the Center for Applied Research in the Apostolate (CARA) conducted studies in 2005 and again in 2008. To the question "how often, if ever, do you participate in the Sacrament of Reconciliation or Confession," respondents answered as follows:[6]

	2005	2008
Once a month or more	2%	2%
Several times a year	10%	12%
Once a year	14%	12%
Less than once a year	32%	30%
Never	42%	45%

Without parsing the methods and survey instruments used by the bishops and by CARA, the numbers are fairly straightforward, and they are falling. Nearly half of Catholics in the 2008 study never participate in the sacrament of reconciliation.

Given the confidentiality associated with the celebration of this sacrament[7] and the understandably personal/private reasons persons may have for not seeking it out, determining why the numbers have fallen is no easy task.[8] I do not intend to attempt here an exhaustive inventory, but a number of factors have in various ways contributed to the decline. One such factor is the decline in the number of ordained ministers relative to the size of the Catholic population in the United States. CARA reports that in 1965 the total number of diocesan and religious priests was

5. Ibid., 617.

6. Chart taken from Center for Applied Research in the Apostolate (CARA), *Sacraments Today: Belief and Practice among U.S. Catholics* (Washington, DC: Georgetown University Press, 2008), 57.

7. See can. 983 of the 1983 *Code of Canon Law* for the seal of the confessional.

8. In an email sent to this writer on August 2, 2015, Mary Gautier, senior research associate at CARA, indicated that she was not aware of any surveys addressing why Catholics choose not to seek the sacrament of reconciliation.

58,632; that number fell to 38,275 in 2014. Over the same period, the size of the Catholic population grew from 46.3 million to 66.6 million.[9] As a matter of arithmetic, access to priests is not what it once was. A second factor is the widespread negative reaction to Pope Paul VI's *Humanae Vitae* in 1968, which reaffirmed the Catholic prohibition on artificial means of birth control.[10] Catholics who used such methods in good conscience and who judged that they could no longer turn to the church as a moral guide in sexual ethics expanded that judgment more generally. A third and more recent factor is the searing scandal of clerical sexual abuse in the Catholic Church. Bishops themselves have acknowledged the impact of abuse on the sacrament of reconciliation.[11] Addressing the Catholics of Ireland with respect to abuse in that country, Pope Benedict XVI admitted that "I know some of you find it difficult even to enter the doors of a church after all that has occurred."[12] A fourth factor is that Catholics are finding other means of addressing guilt and alienation. One such means is the postconciliar Mass with its penitential rite (which includes what the Roman Missal itself calls an absolution) and the recitation of "only say the word and my soul shall be healed" that precedes the rite of

9. All statistics on priests and total number of Catholics are taken from "Frequently Requested Church Statistics," Center for Applied Research in the Apostolate (CARA), http://cara.georgetown.edu/frequently-requested-church-statistics/. The figures for the Catholic population reflect Catholics actively affiliated with a parish.

10. See James Dallen, "The Confession Crisis: Decline or Evolution?" *Church* 4, no. 2 (Summer 1988): 13–17 at 13; David Coffey, *The Sacrament of Reconciliation* (Collegeville, MN: Liturgical Press, 2001), 95; Annemarie S. Kidder, *Making Confession, Hearing Confession: A History of the Cure of Souls* (Collegeville, MN: Liturgical Press, 2010), 235.

11. See George Lucas, "Pastoral Letter on Reconciliation" (February 10, 2008); Timothy Dolan, "The Altar and the Confessional: Pastoral Letter on the Sacrament of Penance" (March 17, 2011). Lucas headed the Diocese of Springfield, IL, and Dolan is currently archbishop of New York City. The release in 2018 of the Pennsylvania Grand Jury Report has drawn new attention to the problem of abuse and cover-up.

12. Pope Benedict XVI, Letter to the Church of Ireland (March 19, 2010) 6, https://w2.vatican.va/content/benedict-xvi/en/letters/2010/documents/hf_ben-xvi_let_20100319_church-ireland.html.

communion.[13] In addition, there has been a growing acceptance among Catholics of therapy, counseling, and support groups. Whereas once there was suspicion of forms of psychotherapy indebted to Sigmund Freud,[14] there has emerged instead a sense that professional psychologists and counselors have more formal training in their field than did parish priests.[15] In her 2010 study of confession and repentance, Annemarie Kidder theorizes that the fact that the sacrament of reconciliation is free of charge can actually work against the perceived value of the sacrament in a consumer culture in which value is attached to dollars: "From the health-care profession people know that health comes at a price; and it is assumed that the higher the cost, the more valuable the service."[16] In light of Kidder's remarks, we turn now to a discussion of aspects of consumer culture that affect the understanding and practice of the sacrament of reconciliation.

III. Consumer Culture and Reconciliation

The rise of consumerism is associated with the rise of free-market individualism and with the replacement of traditional modes of identity construction/repair (family, religion, social class) with identity construction/repair by way of purchases and consumption. I will address these notions and then one of the paradoxes of consumer culture—that to show weakness or admit fault in our culture is to lose face, and yet marketers are all too eager to indicate and exploit the ways in which individuals fail to hit the mark.

13. These two parts of the Mass are addressed by O'Toole, "In the Court of Conscience," 174–75. For the reference to "absolution" in the Missal, see the Order of Mass 4 in *The Roman Missal*, 515.

14. See O'Toole, "In the Court of Conscience," 175–76.

15. O'Toole offers this telling vignette: " 'My priest never had the training that my psychiatrist has,' [a] woman observed . . . explaining why she was more disposed to seek the latter's aid. 'I go to him out of an awareness that I want to change, to grow. My priest never allowed me to do that.' " O'Toole, "In the Court of Conscience," 177.

16. Kidder, *Making Confession, Hearing Confession*, 234. Of course, in contexts where health care is less expensive, the force of Kidder's argument is diminished.

The Enlightenment, with its radical questioning of traditional modes of authority and its trust in individual reason, included an emphasis on pushing the practice of religion out of the public sphere and into the private realm of the individual's relationship with the divine.[17] As a child of the Enlightenment, American culture is characterized by this individualism. A companion document to the already referenced 1990 study of the US bishops puts it this way:

> Individualism is considered to be one of the chief characteristics of American culture and society by most analysts today. Nowhere are its effects more evident than in the notions of liberty and freedom, which are often so much a part of the very fabric of our culture that we are not aware of the various ways in which they affect important religious dimensions of Catholic life. . . . We live in a cultural matrix within which self-identity and value are most often measured by an ethos of self-determination.
>
> This ethos has shaped the structures of our government and our economic system.[18]

According to this ethos, the economic common good of the people is nothing other than the aggregate of individual, discrete economic transactions. In parallel fashion, the quality of the moral life of the people is an aggregate of strictly individual actions. In the words of Barry Harvey, "forgiveness and reconciliation have been reconfigured as 'an individual transaction between God and a particular person, largely devoid of its eschatological context and with virtually no consequences for either Christian community or social and political life.' "[19]

---

17. See the accent on the individual in William James, *The Varieties of Religious Experience* (New York: Mentor, 1958); Alfred North Whitehead, *Religion in the Making* (New York: Meridian Books, 1965).

18. National Conference of Catholic Bishops Committee for Pastoral Research and Practices, *Reflections on the Sacrament of Penance in Catholic Life Today: A Study Document* (Washington, DC: United States Catholic Conference, 1990), 13.

19. Barry Harvey, "The Eucharistic Idiom of the Gospel," *Pro Ecclesia* 9, no. 3 (2000): 297–318 at 309. Harvey is quoting L. Gregory Jones, *Embodying Forgiveness: A Theological Analysis* (Grand Rapids, MI: Eerdmans, 1995), 38.

The word "reconfigured" is important here. Initially, of course, in the era of canonical penance, forgiveness and reconciliation for sinners was quite public, at least for serious sinners. Repentant Christians who had committed grave sins such as adultery, murder, or apostasy were enrolled in the order of penitents, formally excluded in varying degrees from the eucharistic assembly, and had to engage in practices such as fasting and almsgiving as effective symbols of their sorrow for sin and their desire to rejoin the assembly. The reconciliation extended to the penitent at the conclusion of their penance (in some cases years long) was a once in a lifetime opportunity. For several reasons, including the sometimes severe character of penitential practices (e.g., abstinence for life from marital relations even after reconciliation) and the fact that most Christians did not engage in such serious sins, most Christians never sought pardon from the church in this way. An additional disincentive was that the public nature of the process, intended to be a means by which the community could pray for sinners and grieve their sins with them, all too often became a source of public humiliation for sinners. The rise of a repeatable—and private—form of ecclesial pardon in Ireland in the fifth century hastened the decline of the canonical form when the Irish form spread to continental Europe starting in the sixth century. Lateran IV clearly vindicated the repeatable form of the sacrament in 1215; this council declared that "all of the faithful of either sex, after they have reached the age of discernment, should individually confess all their sins in a faithful manner to their own priest at least once a year."[20] This private and repeatable form meant that more Christians sought ecclesial pardon more often, but it also undermined the properly *ecclesial* and communal nature of sacramental pardon. The trend toward the individualization of sin and forgiveness thus preceded the onset of consumerism

20. The citation from chapter 21 of Lateran IV (DS 812) is taken from Norman Tanner, ed., *Decrees of the Ecumenical Councils*, vol. 1: *Nicaea I to Lateran V* (Washington, DC: Georgetown University Press, 1990), 245. Standard treatments of the history of reconciliation are available in Dallen, *The Reconciling Community*, esp. 56–138; Joseph Martos, *Doors to the Sacred: A Historical Introduction to Sacraments in the Catholic Church*, rev. ed. (Liguori, MO: Liguori, 2014), 317–74.

by centuries but, given this already existing trend, the rise of Enlightenment individualism and, later, free market individualism, catalyzed this trend, morphing it into a mindset wherein people who once sought forgiveness through the mediation of the church now sought it directly from God.

In the Christian tradition a classic understanding of sin includes alienation from self, others, and God. One's being—one's identity—is twisted out of shape by sin. If a believer is to flourish, this identity must be reformed. For the ancient church as indeed for the Catholic Church today the primary means of re-formation is baptism. In the words of the *Catechism of the Catholic Church*: "baptism not only purifies from all sins, but also makes the neophyte a 'new creature.' "[21] For serious postbaptismal sin, *metanoia* or the reconstruction and repair of one's way of being, thinking, and acting, is associated with the sacrament of reconciliation.[22] With the rise of the Irish system the social process of reconstruction undertaken in canonical penance gave way to private forms. While the Irish form helped to set the stage for profoundly individualized understandings of sin and forgiveness, another element of the Irish form deserves examination. If we are going to talk about the ways in which a consumer culture mediates identity construction via the purchase of commodities, we must also talk about the tariffs involved in repentance in the Irish system of forgiveness and the later appearance of indulgences and stipend Masses.

In a passage worth quoting at length, Peter Fink offers a sharply critical assessment of the tariff system, which involved the drafting and use of manuals ("penitentials") to gauge the gravity of sin and assign correspondingly light or severe penances:

> The Irish penitentials are notorious for assigning specific penances for an unimaginable range of human flaws, with the only distinguishing note among them being the duration or extent of

21. *Catechism of the Catholic Church* 1265.

22. As early as the third century, Tertullian was referring to ecclesial reconciliation as a "plank" after the shipwreck of post-baptismal sin. See his *On Repentance*, 4, 2. Text available in Alexander Roberts and James Donaldson, eds., *Ante-Nicene Fathers The Writings of the Fathers Down to A.D. 325*, vol. 3: *Latin Christianity: Its Founder, Tertullian I. Apologetic; II. Anti-Marcion; III. Ethical* (Peabody, MA: Hendrickson, 2004), 659.

the penance itself. Sin is accounted in varying degrees of seriousness, not by the specifics of the act nor even by the specifics of the effect but by the amount of penance that is assigned to it. A debt is incurred, and a debt must be paid for forgiveness to ensue. The only variable is the amount to be paid.

The development of this "economic," "quid pro quo" relationship between sin and forgiveness was indeed most unfortunate, for it separated totally both sin and its undoing from their own proper human processes. The payment of debt was the thing, and that was regulated by the code which prescribed it. Certainly this is the farthest from either the psychological or the theological task of growth and conversion.[23]

Just as humiliation was an unintended side effect of the public nature of canonical penance, the emergence of a sometimes crude "quid pro quo" understanding of the relationship between penitential practices and sin was a side effect of what was originally an attempt simply to standardize penances as a matter of fairness to sinners who committed more or less the same sin in different regions so that they may repair their lives and their identities along somewhat similar paths. As Fink notes, almsgiving was associated with canonical penance. Indeed the practice was associated with forgiveness of sins in the Bible.[24] Engaging in a bit of patristic era hyperbole, John Chrysostom urged his hearers to "purchase salvation through almsgiving."[25] Originally, such alms were given to the poor directly but eventually financial offerings were at times provided to the church for the care of the poor—or for the upkeep of ecclesial properties and the support of the clergy. Alms given to the church could quite easily be seen as payment for ecclesial pardon. Further complicating matters is that, in the canonical form, absolution took place at the completion of one's penance but in the Irish form, absolution typically preceded the

23. Peter Fink, "Reconciliation and Forgiveness: A Theological Reflection," in *Alternative Futures for Worship*, vol. 4: *Reconciliation*, ed. Peter Fink (Collegeville, MN: Liturgical Press, 1987), 81–82.

24. See Sir 3:30; 1 Pet 4:8.

25. John Chrysostom, Homily 7.6.22, in *On Repentance and Almsgiving*, trans. Gus George Christo (Washington, DC: Catholic University of America Press, 1998), 104. See the discussion of alms in chapter 1, section VI, p. 14.

start of one's penance. This sequence led Annemarie Kidder to observe that "since absolution immediately followed the act of confession, penances were considered largely debts owed to the church for the service of bestowing forgiveness, thus shortchanging the former extensive penitential process and turning it into what could be perceived as a brief business transaction."[26]

Although some penances under the canonical form extended beyond the moment of reconciliation with the church, generally speaking a sinner who underwent the canonical form, was reconciled, and died without again committing serious sin could be reasonably sure that all the punishment incurred by the one serious sin was lifted by the penitential practices and reconciliation with the church. When absolution preceded penitential practices, however, the understanding of sin and punishment changed. Sacramental absolution was understood to apply to the *eternal* punishment for sin (i.e., the risk of damnation) but it did not necessarily apply to the *temporal* punishment. Penitential practices, including the giving of alms, were seen as applying to the temporal punishment for sin. As Trent put it, "let [confessors] rather bear in mind that the satisfaction they impose should not only be aimed at protecting the new life and at being a remedy against weakness, but also be for the atonement and punishment of past sins."[27] All is well if a person completes his or her penance be-

---

26. Kidder, *Making Confession, Hearing Confession*, 58.

27. Council of Trent, Session 14, chap. 8 (DS 1692). I am using the translation in Norman Tanner, ed., *Decrees of the Ecumenical Councils*, vol. 2: *Trent to Vatican II*, (Washington, DC: Georgetown University Press, 1990), 709. The *Catechism of the Council of Trent* underlined this point by teaching: "Such being the nature of satisfaction, it will not be difficult to convince the faithful of the necessity imposed on the penitent of performing works of satisfaction. They are to be taught that sin carries in its train two evils, the stain and the punishment. Whenever the stain is effaced, the punishment of eternal death is forgiven with the guilt to which it was due; yet, as the Council of Trent declares, the remains of sin and the temporal punishment are not always remitted." *Catechism of the Council of Trent for Parish Priests*, ed. John McHugh and Charles Callan (Rockford, IL: TAN Books, 1982), 298. Small wonder, then, that David Coffey observes that "a common misunderstanding, reinforced by the catechesis that has come down to us from the Council of Trent (that is, in both the conciliar documents and the *Rituale Romanum* of 1614), is that the penance is a punishment for the sins confessed." Coffey, *The Sacrament of Reconciliation*, 118.

fore dying, but under a repeatable form of reconciliation, each visit to the confessor would bring a new set of penances. In an era with generally low life expectancy and high mortality rates resulting from injuries and sickness, sinners might not be able to see their penance through to completion. For such people there is purgatory, conceived of as a means by which dead sinners whose eternal punishment has been lifted but who have some form of debt yet to pay in the form of temporal punishment may in fact satisfy that remaining temporal punishment. For the loved ones of such deceased sinners, there arose the stipend Mass and the use of indulgences.

The stipend Mass is a practice according to which a donor provides funds to the church in exchange for which a Mass (or a number of Masses) is celebrated with the intention of the donor (a good harvest, a happy marriage, etc.) given special consideration by the priest-celebrant. Stipend Masses allowed loved ones to support the deceased by the eucharistic sacrifice to shorten their time in purgatory. The sale of indulgences involved a donation to the church in exchange for which the church would allot some of the infinite treasury of the merits of Christ's sacrifice to the plight of the donor's loved one in purgatory. We are far, far removed here from the biblical notion of conversion from sin and purity of heart. The reformation of the sinner is reduced here to a financial transaction.[28]

Arthur Miller's 1968 play *The Price* can help us connect these remarks about sin, forgiveness, *metanoia*, and money to consumer culture and the repair of the self. Here the character Solomon speaks to Victor in Act 1: "'What is the key word today? Disposable. The more you can throw it away the more it's beautiful. The

---

28. Trent forbade the sale of such indulgences (see Trent, Session 25, Decree on Indulgences [DS 1835]). Stipend Masses are still permitted in the Roman Catholic Church, however. See Paul VI, *Motu Proprio* on Mass Stipends (*Firma in traditione*, June 13, 1974); *Mos iugitur*, a decree issued by the Congregation for the Clergy (March 23, 1991) with the approval of Pope John Paul II. M. Francis Mannion has argued that "the conclusion cannot be avoided that the Mass stipend in its medieval and modern form is a highly problematic institution." M. Francis Mannion, "Stipends and Eucharistic Praxis," *Worship* 57, no. 3 (1983): 194–214 at 210. See also Edward J. Kilmartin, *The Eucharist in the West: History and Theology*, ed. Robert Daly (Collegeville, MN: Liturgical Press, 1998), 205–37.

car, the furniture, the wife, the children—everything has to be disposable. Because you see the main thing today is—shopping. Years ago a person, he was unhappy, didn't know what to do with himself—he'd go to church, start a revolution—*something*. Today you're unhappy? Can't figure it out? What is the salvation? Go shopping.' "[29] If I am less than I want to be, instead of going to church (and perhaps the sacrament of reconciliation) I can buy Nike shoes to "Be Like Mike." If I am feeling inadequate, promotional material for Axe Signature Intense Body Perfume tells me to "Charge yourself, get ready to make your presence felt. . . . Get set to make a bold statement, tell the world you have arrived with Axe Signature Intense body perfume."[30] The ad says nothing about confessing one's faults. Is your life empty? Sam van Enam has an ad for you: "There is a commercial with a young couple sitting together on a couch, telling the camera why Big Lots department store is important to them. They boast of deals found on chairs and love seats, and snuggle close as if a significant change has occurred in their lives. The girl looks at her boyfriend/husband and then at the camera again. Through joyful tears, she says, 'The world is so full of emptiness. That's why Big Lots has furniture.' "[31] What matters in this ad is one's relationship to *things*. Emptiness is satisfied not by conversion of heart and the abandonment of selfishness but by the acquisition of material items.

No doubt I could identify more such ads and no doubt readers could name similar ads—and that is my point. Taken in isolation, these ad campaigns for Nike, Axe, and Big Lots might generate some chuckles, but these campaigns—the political and military overtones of this word are fitting—in the end boil down to just one campaign waged relentlessly by marketers: You are what you buy; you are what you consume. Note well that you are what *you*

---

29. Arthur Miller, *The Price: A Play* (New York: Viking, 1968), 40–41.

30. Product statement for Axe Signature Intense Body Perfume, https://www.amazon.com/Signature-Intense-Body-Perfume-122ml/dp/B016V5K4TE. Apparently, the scent of "woody extracts, vanilla, and green hazelnut" has something to do with "arriving."

31. Sam van Enam, *On Earth as It Is in Advertising?* (Grand Rapids, MI: Brazos, 2005), 16.

buy. Identity reconstruction in consumerism is *self*-reconstruction along the lines of free-market individualism. In consumerism, conversion is a self-determined process. Konrad Baumgartner argues that the opposite is true in the Christian ambit: "In [Christian] conversion everyone is addressed in a different way, but the question with which we are confronted is always the same: are you prepared to *forgo the self-confident shaping of your own history, and God's history with us?*"[32] And if Arthur Miller provided an opening link to connect religious *metanoia* and consumerism, Walter Brueggemann can supply a closing link:

> The socioreligious environment of consumer culture in the United States makes penitence an urgent topic and, in general, as unwelcome as it is urgent. That environment is dominated by strident moral certitude, by unrestrained polemics toward those who think differently, and by an unashamed self-indulgence toward one's own autonomous way of life. . . . I have been thinking, moreover, that this self-indulgence, including the self-indulgence of moral certitude and rectitude, is not far removed from the "sale of indulgences" that triggered Luther's response in the sixteenth century. The parallel is more than the recurrence of the term "indulgence," for the religious-ethical pretense in both cases is the assumed capacity to purchase [!] well-being, to "purchase" by payment to the church as moral guarantor or as "purchase" to the mall, or to "get purchase" through ideological claim; all such "purchases" subvert the truth of God's rule and distort the true posture of each of us before that holy truth.[33]

32. Konrad Baumgartner, "The Process of Conversion and Its Ministries," in *The Fate of Confession*, ed. Mary Collins and David Power (Edinburgh: T & T Clark, 1987), 41. In light of Baumgartner's comments here, consider paragraph 398 of the *Catechism of the Catholic Church* on the fall of humanity: "In that sin man *preferred* himself to God and by that very act scorned him. He chose himself over and against God, against the requirements of his creaturely status and therefore against his own good. Constituted in a state of holiness, man was destined to be fully 'divinized' by God in glory. Seduced by the devil, he wanted to 'be like God,' but 'without God, before God, and not in accordance with God.' "

33. Walter Brueggemann, "The Summons to New Life: A Reflection," in *Repentance in Christian Theology*, ed. Mark Boda and Gordon T. Smith (Collegeville, MN: Liturgical Press, 2006), 347.

Lurking behind the consumerist notion of self-repair or self-reconstruction is a paradox: to show weakness or admit fault is to lose face—and yet in consumer culture marketers are all too eager to indicate the ways in which individuals fail to hit the mark. In a culture characterized by free market individualism, we are all self-sufficient, self-made people—until we aren't. Advertising points out to us the ways in which we have missed the mark and suggests to us that we need the market's help to correct our appearance, our dress, our very way of being in the world. As Sam van Enam writes, the root experience here is fear, and the end is sought in vain: "Advertisers create a standard that is impossible to meet, and they highlight our inadequacies when we fail. In other words, they confirm that we should be afraid. When we perceive that others meet the standard more than we do, fear propels us to find significance in order to overcome these inadequacies, even if the pursuit is characterized by futility."[34] In a consumerist, competitive culture, weakness is something one dare not show and fault is something one dare not concede. "In a culture that unreasonably expects people ever to achieve success and never to admit fault," asks Paul Turner, "does liturgical forgiveness have something to offer?"[35]

IV. The Second Vatican Council, Reconciliation, and Consumer Culture

The historical overview of the sacrament provided here thus far began with the communally oriented practice of once-in-a-lifetime canonical penance and concluded with Lateran IV's mandate of annual private confession and Trent's understanding of penitential practices as involving "punishment" by means of satisfying the temporal punishment for sin. Yet if Trent likened confessing of one's sins to showing one's wounds to a physician,[36] thus invoking images of care for one's spiritual health, the predominant

34. Van Enam, *On Earth as It Is in Advertising?*, 56.
35. Paul Turner, "Amen Corner: Between Consultation and Faithfulness: Questions That Won't Go Away," *Worship* 89, no. 4 (July 2015): 351–58 at 357–58.
36. See Trent, Session 14, chapter 5 (DS 1680).

mode of thinking was legalistic: sins were crimes. James Dallen offers this observation: "The context within which [personal repentance] was expressed and experienced changed as the ecclesiastical administration of the formal process began to consist of applying impersonal laws to abstract categories of sins and as its supervisors were perceived as legislators and judges. As the ecclesial process of repentance was increasingly regulated by law, more stress was laid on ecclesiastical penalty than on strengthening community and rehabilitating sinners."[37] In a similar vein, Franco Sottocornola writes that "the idea of 'reconciliation' with the Church gives way to the idea of personal purification from sin."[38] Sottocornola served on the commission that produced the revised rite of penance after Vatican II; it is fitting to include his remarks here by way of turning now to the ways in which the revised rite responds and does not respond positively to Paul Turner's question above. I will begin with a discussion of Vatican II's vision of the sacrament. I will turn then to the question of identity construction/repair in the revised rite.

Vatican II's Constitution on the Sacred Liturgy treats the sacrament of penance quite briefly: "The rite and formulas of Penance are to be revised so that they more clearly express both the nature and effect of the sacrament."[39] James Dallen offers an important assessment of this one sentence: "The Constitution on the Liturgy called for a reform to express the sacrament's nature and effect more clearly. A declaration accompanying the final text presented

---

37. Dallen, *The Reconciling Community*, 58. Consider this discussion of penitential practice from the *Catechism of the Council of Trent*: "Penance is a sort of compensation for sin, springing from the free will of the delinquent, and is appointed by God, against whom the offence has been committed. Hence, on the one hand, there is required the willingness to make compensation, in which willingness contrition chiefly consists; while, on the other hand, the penitent must submit himself to the judgment of the priest, who holds God's place, in order to enable him to award a punishment proportioned to the gravity of the sin committed." *Catechism of the Council of Trent for Parish Priests*, 273.

38. Franco Sottocornola, "The Liturgical Experience and Expression of Reconciliation," in *From Alienation to At-one-ness*, ed. Francis Eigo (Villanova, PA: Villanova University Press, 1977), 199.

39. *Sacrosanctum Concilium* 72.

to the council and an official interpretation by Archbishop [Paul] Hallinan indicated that the word 'nature' had been added alongside 'effects' to stress the sacrament's *social and ecclesial character.*"[40] The social and ecclesial character of the postconciliar rite is manifested in the use of Scripture, the revised formula of absolution, and the creation of two new forms of the rite (Form II, the Rite of Reconciliation of Several Penitents with Individual Confession and Absolution and Form III, the Rite for Reconciliation of Several Penitents with General Confession and Absolution) along with Form I, the Rite of Reconciliation of Individual Penitents. I will discuss each of these topics and then turn to a treatment of the revised rite's understanding of penitential practices.

If the Bible is the book of the church,[41] and if, as Vatican II holds, "liturgical services are not private functions but are celebrations of the church,"[42] then liturgical services ought to feature the Bible. The 1614 *Rituale Romanum* says nothing about the use of Scripture during celebration of reconciliation. Sottocornola argues that the postconciliar addition of reading from Scripture "will make one understand that this moment of grace (reconciliation) is connected to all of salvation history."[43] Reading from Scripture is required in Forms II and III of the rite but not in Form I, the Rite of Reconciliation of Individual Penitents.[44] Some observers have expressed regret over the merely optional use of Scripture

40. James Dallen, "Theological Foundations of Reconciliation," in *Reconciliation: The Continuing Agenda*, ed. Robert J. Kennedy (Collegeville, MN: Liturgical Press, 1987), 16 (emphasis added). The declaration to which Dallen refers may be found in *Acta Synodalia Sacrosancti Concilii Oecumenici Vaticani II* 2, pars 2 (Rome: Typis Polyglottis Vaticanis, 1962), 558–59, and the statement from Bishop Hallinan may be found in *Acta Synodalia Sacrosancti Concilii Oecumenici Vaticani II* 2, pars 2 (Rome: Typis Polyglottis Vaticanis, 1962), 567. See also James Dallen, "*Reconciliatio et Paenitentia*: The Postsynodal Apostolic Exhortation," *Worship* 59, no. 2 (1985): 98–116 at 107.

41. On this point see Karl Rahner, *Foundations of Christian Faith: An Introduction to the Idea of Christianity*, trans. William Dych (New York: Crossroad, 1986), 369–78.

42. *Sacrosanctum Concilium* 26.

43. Franco Sottocornola, "Les nouveaux rites de la penitence," *Questions liturgiques* 55 (1997): 89–136 at 97. My translation.

44. The use of Scripture in Form I is optional. See the Rite of Penance 17.

in Form I.[45] One can hope that more bishops will follow the lead of the bishops of Illinois, who in 1989 emphasized that Scripture "should be included in the individual form of the sacrament."[46]

I reproduce here the preconciliar formula of absolution followed by the postconciliar formula.

> May our Lord, Jesus Christ, absolve thee, and by His very authority do I absolve thee from every bond of excommunication, suspension, and interdict, in so far as lies within my power and thou hast need of it. Furthermore, I absolve thee from thy sins in the name of the Father, and of the Son, and of the Holy Spirit.
>
> God, the Father of mercies, through the death and resurrection of his Son has reconciled the world to himself and sent the Holy Spirit among us for the forgiveness of sins; through the ministry of the Church may God give you pardon and peace, and I absolve you from your sins in the name of the Father, and of the Son, and of the Holy Spirit.[47]

As he had argued with respect to use of Scripture, Sottocornola also argues about the revised formula of absolution: "the formula is the summary of all of salvation history,"[48] and it "inserts the reconciliation of the sinner into the history of salvation."[49] Reconciliation is not an individual transaction with God but rather

45. See Kenan Osborne, *Reconciliation and Justification: The Sacrament and Its Theology* (New York: Paulist, 1990), 212; Coffey, *The Sacrament of Reconciliation*, 128.

46. Bishops of Illinois, "The Sacrament of Penance: Guidelines for Illinois Dioceses" (February 2, 1989) 9.

47. The preconciliar formula is taken from *The Roman Ritual*, vol. 1: *The Sacraments and Processions*, ed. and trans. Philip T. Weller (Boonville, NY: Preserving Christian Publications, 2016), 309, 311. The postconciliar formula is found in the Rite of Penance 46 and 55 for Forms I and II. This formula is one of two options for Form III. See the Rite of Penance 62.

48. Sottocornola, "Les nouveaux rites de la penitence," 116. My translation. Note as well that the preconciliar formula never uses the first-person plural whereas the postconciliar formula employs "us."

49. Ibid., 98. My translation. He adds that the reconciliation of the sinner is "a personal moment of the universal reconciliation with the world that, in Christ, God has already put into effect and which now continues visibly in the Church by means of the Holy Spirit."

a manifestation in the penitent's life of a process that God has undertaken vis-à-vis the world. And yet, as with the *optional* use of Scripture in Form I, observers have drawn attention to a lacuna in the postconciliar formula of absolution: none of them mention reconciliation with the church.[50] I will return to this point later.

If the use of Scripture and the revision in the formula of absolution are somewhat subtle expressions of the social and ecclesial character of the sacrament of reconciliation, the same cannot be said for Forms II and III of the sacrament, each of which involves penitents assembling for celebration of the sacrament. The Rite of Penance 22 offers this summary of Form II: "Communal celebration shows more clearly the ecclesial nature of penance. The faithful listen together to the word of God, which as it proclaims his mercy invites them to conversion; at the same time they examine the conformity of their lives with that word of God and help each other through common prayer. After confessing and being absolved individually, all join in praising God together for his wonderful deeds on behalf of the people he has gained for himself through the blood of his Son."[51] Though Form II entails individual confessions, this form is not merely an aggregate of juxtaposed individual confessions. Rather, in Sottocornola's words, it is a matter of "the profoundly ecclesial and communitarian nature of repentance and the liturgy of repentance."[52] In a 1990 pastoral letter on the sacrament, Archbishop Roger Mahony of Los Angeles wrote that "the importance of the Church community and its role

50. See David Coffey, *The Sacrament of Reconciliation*, 114.

51. Commenting on Form II, Annibale Bugnini, a key figure in the entire postconciliar liturgical reform, offers this assessment: "Critiques of the past as well as more recent studies had shown the rather negative side of traditional penance with its excessive individualism, not only ritual but also moral and psychological. It was desirable, therefore, that the penitential rite should bring out more clearly the responsibility which human beings share in good and evil, the collective as well as individual awareness of guilt, and the ecclesial nature of reconciliation.

This new rite [Form II] satisfies these requirements, for it locates individual confession and absolution within a communal preparation and conclusion." Annibale Bugnini, *The Reform of the Liturgy, 1948–1975*, trans. Matthew O'Connell (Collegeville, MN: Liturgical Press, 1990), 680–81.

52. Sottocornola, "Les nouveaux rites de la penitence," 101. My translation. See also Bugnini, *The Reform of the Liturgy, 1948–1975*, 680–81.

in reconciliation is so central to the rationale of the revised Rite of Penance, that the second form of the Sacrament may be viewed as that form which best expresses the nature of the Sacrament as a sign of Christ's forgiveness and reconciliation."[53] Form II is, however, at times beset by two related practical problems. If there are many penitents, ministers might feel pressured to keep confessions (too) brief.[54] Likewise, those who have had their time with a minister might not be willing to stay until all have been absolved. Individuals might leave before the concluding communal praise of God.[55] Yet, this form clearly has the potential to locate the penitent's process of identity construction/repair squarely in the context of a Christian community seeking such repair. Indeed, the bishops of Illinois directed in 1989 that Form II "should not be used when . . . the participants are not particularly disposed to a communal celebration of this sacrament but have only come for the sake of individual confession and absolution."[56]

Franco Sottocornola has hailed Form III, the rite for reconciliation of several penitents with general confession and absolution, as the "most important innovation in the sacrament from the pastoral point of view."[57] For his part, David Coffey argues that "as a totally communal experience of reconciliation, it embodies, more effectively than the other two rites, the wish of Vatican II that as a result of the prescribed reform the 'social and ecclesial

---

53. Archbishop Roger Mahony, *In Praise of God's Mercy: Pastoral Letter on the Sacrament of Penance* (Los Angeles: Lent, 1990), 7. Franco Sottocornola opined that Form II would become the most widely used form for the sacrament. See "Les nouveaux rites de la penitence," 117.

54. This problem was identified in *Reflections on the Sacrament of Penance in Catholic Life Today: A Study Document*, 4–5.

55. David Coffey writes that "one of the weaknesses and disappointments of the rite is that when it is carried out in a normal parish setting, it is well nigh impossible to persuade the people to remain to the end. . . . *Exomologesis* (the confession of the praise and the mercy of God) . . . is an important element of the sacrament, providing the ultimate purpose and context for celebrating it." Coffey, *The Sacrament of Reconciliation*, 149. For additional discussion of leaving early, see Timothy Brunk, "Celebrating Reconciliation in Advent," *PrayTell* (blog), December 14, 2015, http://www.praytellblog.com/index.php/2015/12/14/celebrating-reconciliation-in-advent/.

56. Bishops of Illinois, "The Sacrament of Penance" 17.

57. Sottocornola, "Les nouveaux rites de la penitence," 119. My translation.

character' of the sacrament should be made more evident."[58] Even as this rite was being developed, however, the Congregation for the Doctrine of the Faith issued in 1972 a set of Pastoral Norms clarifying that "individual, complete confession and the receiving of absolution remain the only ordinary way for the faithful to obtain reconciliation with God and the Church, unless physical or moral impossibility excuses them from this manner of confessing" and that "unless there is a good reason preventing it, those who receive pardon for serious sin through general absolution are to go to auricular confession before any further reception of general absolution."[59] At the 1984 synod on reconciliation and penance, some bishops questioned these and other restrictions placed on Form III,[60] but John Paul II's post-synodal exhortation emphasized these restrictions, leading James Dallen to contend that "in contrast with [John Paul's] usual approach to social issues, he speaks cautiously of social sin and the Church's role in society. It is as though sacramental piety requires privacy and isolated individualism, with social action and calls to it only loosely connected. . . . The points that are emphasized are those most prominent in the teaching of Trent: individual confession and the priestly ministry of absolution. Vatican II's focal themes, reconciliation with the Church and the sacrament's social and ecclesial nature and effects, are put into the background."[61] I think

---

58. Coffey, *The Sacrament of Reconciliation*, 146.

59. Sacred Congregation for the Doctrine of the Faith, Pastoral Norms *Sacramentum Paenitentiae* (June 16, 1972), I, VII. Norm III advises that "the procedure is not lawful solely on the basis of a large number of penitents, for example, at some great festival or pilgrimage." There must be a "danger of death" or "other serious need." The Pastoral Norms may be found in International Commission on English in the Liturgy, *Documents on the Liturgy, 1963–1979: Conciliar, Papal, and Curial Texts* (Collegeville, MN: Liturgical Press, 1982), 948–51. The restrictions noted in the norms appear as well in the Rite of Penance 31 and 34. For a brief discussion of the implementation of the reform of the sacrament of reconciliation after Vatican II, see Bugnini, *The Reform of the Liturgy, 1948–1975*, 664–83.

60. See Bishop Francis Lodonu [Keta-Ho, Ghana], "Reconciliation and African Realities," *Origins* 13, no. 20 (October 27, 1983): 349–50 at 350; Archbishop Samuel Carter [Kingston, Jamaica], "Is General Absolution Underutilized?" *Origins* 13, no. 20 (October 27, 1983): 343–44; Archbishop Gabriel Wako [Khartoum, Sudan], "When General Absolution Is Needed," *Origins* 13, no. 21 (November 3, 1983): 368.

61. Dallen, *The Reconciling Community*, 226.

Dallen's analysis of the exhortation is sound and that, in any case, the restrictions in place on Form III mean that most celebrations of reconciliation involve individual confession at some point. We will return to this matter.

Each form of the rite associates identity construction/repair with the communal dimension of faith, whether rather weakly in Form I with its optional use of Scripture or more clearly in the communal shape of Forms II and III. Important for our consideration here is this line from paragraph 7b of the Rite of Penance, which applies to all three forms: "In order that this sacrament of healing may truly achieve its purpose among the faithful, it must take root in their entire life and move them to more fervent service of God and neighbor." Gone is Trent's emphasis on punishment, on righting one's individual ledger of sin and guilt. Rather, identity repair involves here service of God and neighbor—what we might more aptly describe as the promotion of justice and the common good. In fact, the rite of penance never mentions punishment and, even when in paragraph 18 the rite mentions atonement, it couches it in terms of the communal and social: "[The penance] should serve not only as atonement for past sins but also as an aid to a new life and an antidote for weakness. As far as possible, therefore, the penance should correspond to the seriousness and nature of their sins. This act of penance may suitably take the form of prayer, self-denial, and especially service to neighbor and works of mercy. These will underline the fact that sin and its forgiveness have a social aspect." To a greater or lesser extent, the three forms of the postconciliar rite of penance offer a contrast to consumerist individualism and identity construction by individual purchases in the market. However, I think the Catholic Church can and should do more to resituate the sacrament of reconciliation in the twenty-first century, and it is to this topic I now turn.

V. Conclusion

Paul Turner asks whether liturgical forgiveness has something to offer in a culture bent on concealing faults and emphasizing success. I believe the answer to this question is "yes" with an "if." The "if" concerns at least two broad questions: (1) Is this liturgical forgiveness isolated from the rest of a believer's life, or is it connected to and expressed in all the dimensions of that life?; and (2) Is the Christian community to which a person belongs truly a reconciling community that recognizes its own faults as it extends mercy to its members and beyond? Let us examine these questions briefly.

I have noted that James Dallen faults John Paul's 1984 exhortation for an individualistic piety with respect to the sacrament of reconciliation. That same exhortation, however, contains an important line about situating the sacrament in the context of one's life: "If we link penance with the metanoia which the Synoptics refer to, it means the inmost change of heart under the influence of the word of God and in the perspective of the kingdom. But penance also means changing one's life in harmony with the change of heart, and in this sense doing penance is completed by bringing forth fruits worthy of penance: It is one's whole existence that becomes penitential, that is to say, directed toward a continuous striving for what is better."[62] John Paul's argument about the penitential quality of the whole of one's life echoes the Council of Trent and indeed, Martin Luther.[63] Perhaps even more to the point, the notion is biblical. Consider Isaiah 58:4-8 and Romans 12:1. First, Isaiah, from the NRSV:

> Look, you fast only to quarrel and to fight
>   and to strike with a wicked fist.
> Such fasting as you do today
>   will not make your voice heard on high.
> Is such the fast that I choose,
>   a day to humble oneself?
> Is it to bow down the head like a bulrush,
>   and to lie in sackcloth and ashes?
> Will you call this a fast,
>   a day acceptable to the LORD?

---

62. John Paul II, *Reconciliatio et Paenitentia* 4.

63. See Trent, Session 14, foreword to chapters on Extreme Unction (DS 1694), as well as the first of Luther's 95 Theses—e.g., in Heiko A. Oberman, *Luther: Man between God and the Devil*, trans. Eileen Walliser-Schwarzbart (New Haven, CT: Yale University Press, 1989), 164.

Is not this the fast that I choose:
> to loose the bonds of injustice,
> to undo the thongs of the yoke,

to let the oppressed go free,
> and to break every yoke?

Is it not to share your bread with the hungry,
> and bring the homeless poor into your house;

when you see the naked, to cover them,
> and not to hide yourself from your own kin?

Then your light shall break forth like the dawn,
> and your healing shall spring up quickly;

your vindicator shall go before you,
> the glory of the LORD shall be your rear guard.

The message is clear: ritual (in this case the penitential practice of fasting) is insufficient. If however, the ritual flowers forth into the practice of justice then one's life is marked by coherence. One's identity is repaired and sustained in a communal context.

For his part, Paul urges his Roman readers "by the mercies of God, to present your bodies as a living sacrifice, holy and acceptable to God, which is your spiritual worship" (NRSV). By way of response to the reconciling power of God manifest in the death and resurrection of Jesus Christ, Paul argues that Christians ought to hand over their very being as sacrifice—understood here in the sense of self-offering love. Clearly, Paul had no conception of the sacrament of reconciliation as it was later implemented in the church, yet this same mercy of God is effectively made manifest in that sacrament and the same response is indicated. Roger Mahony puts it this way: "Conversion is broader than the celebration of the Sacrament of Penance in its ritual forms. Conversion extends to the whole of the Christian life and involves a myriad of persons and events which lead to and flow from the sacramental encounter."[64] When liturgical forgiveness is understood in this way, perhaps it will have something to offer.

I suggest that something even more is needed. Specifically, catechesis about this sacrament and the rite itself must place greater

64. Archbishop Roger Mahony, *In Praise of God's Mercy*, 17.

emphasis on reconciliation with the church. For its part the community of believers—local and universal—must be and must be seen to be the kind of community to which one would want to be reconciled. Dallen argues that "the Church cannot be a reconciling force in society if it cannot reach out to its own marginal and alienated members. That, it seems, is the real crisis of penance, for those are the essential dimensions of Church ministry in this sacrament."[65] When all of ecclesial life and all aspects of the lives of Christians attend to the importance of being reconciled to one another, then the reconciliation with God that the rite symbolizes and effects will take on a well-grounded meaning—not the shallow reinvention of self associated with the purchase and use of commodities. For this reason, there is warrant to reconsider the restrictions in place on Form III of the sacrament, which presents the gathered ecclesia together calling for God's mercy and grace, a people seeking to serve God in holiness (see *Lumen Gentium* 9).

These suggestions will not be a panacea. The sacraments, as Louis-Marie Chauvet points out, remind us that we are not in the immediate presence of God, which alone heals all hurt, pain, and death.[66] They may, however, help to counter the false narrative of identity construction and repair associated with consumerism.

---

65. James Dallen, *The Reconciling Community*, 355. Dallen points out that this line of thinking was advanced by some bishops at the 1984 synod. Elsewhere, Dallen writes: "If there is a crisis in the sense that something undesirable and even dangerous threatens, it is not that the numbers of confessions are down or that our understanding and experience are changing. The threat is that people are not experiencing the church as a converting and reconciling community. They regard the church, local and universal, as more committed to preservation than transformation, as more interested in excluding than including, as more concerned with injustice in society than in the church, as unwilling to reach out to those alienated from the church to offer them a home. Whether their perceptions are accurate is not the point. What is crucial is that they do not experience the church as a converting and reconciling community." Dallen, "The Confession Crisis," 16–17. See also Nathan Mitchell, "Amen Corner: Gathering as an Act of Reconciliation" *Worship* 85, no. 6 (November 2011): 542–53 at 547–49.

66. See Louis-Marie Chauvet, "L'Église fait l'eucharistie; l'eucharistie fait l'Église" *Catéchèse* 71 (1978): 171–82 at 182.

Chapter Five

ANOINTING OF THE SICK AND CONSUMER CULTURE

I. Introduction

Humans have a longing for the infinite, for the transcendent. Our hearts are restless, as Augustine observed.[1] Reminders that we are limited constitute for Daniel Sulmasy the essence of human suffering. "Finitude," he writes, "is the message, and illness is the messenger."[2] Here I wish to examine the nature of illness in a consumer culture and the pastoral-sacramental response of the church to situations of illness. What does it mean to be ill and to suffer? What does an ecclesial context have to say about illness in the life of a believer? What is the significance of anointing?

This chapter unfolds in three parts. The first offers observations about the meaning of illness in a consumer society. A clear sense of personal identity and an abiding sense of self are difficult to maintain in such a society. That challenge is aggravated when illness restricts one's capacity to interact with others and to *be* oneself. The second section of the chapter examines briefly the history of the sacrament of the anointing of the sick, noting the long detour into a time when the sacrament was used more or less exclusively for the dying. I will also provide statistics about

---

1. Augustine, *Confessions*, 1.1.
2. Daniel Sulmasy, "Suffering, Spirituality and Health Care," in *Good Is the Flesh: Body, Soul, and Christian Faith*, ed. Jean Denton (New York: Morehouse, 2005), 88.

the current practice and understanding of the sacrament. In the third section, I discuss the counter-narrative of illness presented by the sacrament over against ideas abroad in consumer culture.

II. Health and Illness in a Consumer Society

In 1946, the fledgling World Health Organization offered an understanding of health to a world reeling from global war. Health, it said, "is a state of complete physical, mental and social well-being and not merely the absence of disease or infirmity."[3] Some have argued that this standard is simply unrealistic,[4] but because it sets such a high bar, this standard meshes well with the consumerism of recent times. Providers of medical goods and services, economizing and merging in the face of competition, are only too happy to draw attention to their wares on the part of those pursuing this standard of health. As the *New York Times* reported more than twenty-five years ago:

> Insurers, hospitals, doctor groups and new kinds of hybrid health care companies are buying each other out, forging strategic alliances and sometimes engaging in cutthroat price wars as they seek to position themselves for the coming competition.
>
> The object is to gain the best position for signing up insured patients—"money generating biological structures," as Uwe Reinhardt, an economist at Princeton University, says they might be defined today.[5]

---

3. Preamble to the Constitution of the World Health Organization as adopted by the International Health Conference, New York, June 19–22, 1946; signed on July 22, 1946 by the representatives of sixty-one states (Official Records of the World Health Organization, no. 2, 100) and entered into force on April 7, 1948.

4. David B. Morris calls it a "fantasy borrowed from modernist utopian fiction." Morris, *Illness and Culture in the Postmodern Age* (Berkeley, CA: University of California Press, 1998), 241. See the discussion of Morris in Bruce Morrill, *Divine Worship and Human Healing: Liturgical Theology at the Margins of Life and Death* (Collegeville, MN: Liturgical Press, 2009), 37–44.

5. Erick Eckholm, "While Congress Remains Silent, Health Care Transforms Itself," *New York Times* (December 18, 1994), http://www.nytimes.com /1994/12/18/us/healing-process-special-report-while-congress-remains-silent -health-care.html. On the phenomenon of direct to consumer marketing of

Certainly the medical field has seen significant advances in the past several decades, including the curtailing of smallpox and polio and, more recently, progress on a vaccine for the Ebola virus.[6] Yet in the period 2000–2015, the number of cosmetic plastic surgery procedures in the United States more than doubled.[7] Such an increase suggests that surgical intervention is more and more often being applied in cases where desire to alter personal appearance (as opposed to, say, preserving life) is the motive for seeking treatment.

Marketers' appeals to consumers' vanity and insecurity are well-known. One ought to drive a car and dress in keeping with one's socioeconomic standing, for example. One's mouth ought to have very white teeth, and one's head ought to have plenty of hair, which must, of course, be the right color. Here, however, I want to set the question of vanity aside and direct attention instead to the more deeply rooted consumerist phenomenon of abstraction and commodification. Consider the experience of buying a car. As much as each brand tries to maintain a certain mystique, individual cars are also marketed as collections of features: fuel economy, sound system, GPS devices, rear-view cameras, airbags, acceleration, seating capacity, dual climate controls, heated seats and mirrors, cruise control, and so forth. In some ways, choosing among these options is like deciding which toppings to put on a pizza. Now consider the variety of cosmetic procedures: breast augmentation, breast lift, buttock lift, calf augmentation, chin

---

prescription drugs, see Elisabeth Rosenthal, "Ask Your Doctor if This Ad Is Right for You," *New York Times* (February 27, 2016), https://www.nytimes.com /2016/02/28/sunday-review/ask-your-doctor-if-this-ad-is-right-for-you.html. As this article points out, New Zealand and the United States are the only countries that permit such marketing.

6. See Donald G. McNeil, Jr., "New Ebola Vaccine Gives 100% Protection," *New York Times* (December 22, 2016), https://www.nytimes.com/2016/12/22 /health/ebola-vaccine.html.

7. The number increased from 7.4 million to 15.9 million. Figures from American Society of Plastic Surgeons, "2015 Cosmetic Plastic Surgery Statistics: Cosmetic Procedure Trends," https://d2wirczt3b6wjm.cloudfront.net/News /Statistics/2015/cosmetic-procedure-trends-2015.pdf.

augmentation, face lift, liposuction, neck lift, thigh lift, and so forth.[8] One's body is not an individual whole but an amalgamation of features to be critiqued and improved—like a pizza with just the right amount of the right kinds of toppings.

The issue here goes deeper still. George Engel and, later, Jeffrey Bishop, have been leading critics of the ways in which they see modern medicine treating sick persons not as whole *persons* but as machines with malfunctioning parts. Engel argues that classical science, based on a Newtonian model of laws that govern motion, "readily fostered the notion of the body as a machine, of disease as the consequence of breakdown of the machine, and of the doctor's task as repair of the machine."[9] When Francis Bacon set aside questions of final causality, Bishop argues, the living body was left with "no first cause and no ultimate purpose."[10] For Bishop, this lack has a profound effect on the practice of medicine: "Since formal and final causation are nothing more than post hoc additions to the animal machine, life, as such, cannot have an intrinsic *telos* but only a terminus. Life begins and ends in nonliving matter. There is a paradox in all of this: the idea of life as locomotion of nonliving matter makes death nearly impossible because the failing motion of the body can be replaced by more effective machines. On the metaphysics of contemporary medicine, the body is a perpetual motion machine, potentially living forever, as long as its parts are replaced."[11] If in a consumer culture the process of commodification abstracts things from the contexts in which they have meaning in order to sell them,[12] here we have a case in

8. The report "2015 Cosmetic Plastic Surgery Statistics: Cosmetic Procedure Trends," identifies at least twenty-nine different cosmetic surgical procedures.

9. George Engel, "The Need for a New Medical Model: A Challenge for Biomedicine," *Psychodynamic Psychiatry* 40, no. 3 (2012): 377–96 at 382; reprint of an article with the same title in *Science*, New Series, 196, no. 4286 (April 8, 1977): 129–36.

10. Jeffrey Bishop, "On Medical Corpses and Resurrected Bodies," in *The Role of Death in Life: A Multidisciplinary Examination of the Relationship between Life and Death*, ed. John Behr and Conor Cunningham (Eugene, OR: Cascade Books, 2015), 169.

11. Jeffrey Bishop, *The Anticipatory Corpse* (Notre Dame, IN: University of Notre Dame Press, 2011), 97.

12. Think of Vincent Miller's example of the *Chant* album in Miller, *Consuming Religion: Christian Faith and Practice in a Consumer Culture* (New York: Continuum, 2005), 76.

which the ill or injured human body-person is engaged as a collection of parts that work more or less well, but *not* engaged as one with a source or destiny that provides life with meaning and orientation. When one is sick, one already faces the risk of separation from friends and family, isolation from community, and even alienation from God.[13] When one's care providers consciously or unconsciously adopt the worldview described by Bishop, there are consequences. M. Jennifer Glen explains:

> The sick body comes to be seen in abstraction from the totality of the person as a mechanism to be restored to good working order by the removal or adequate control of the pathological condition; or, failing arrest or cure, as an organism to be sustained in existence as long as its vital signs can be maintained, regardless of the human quality of life thereby preserved. In this context, the sick person may come to see himself through the eyes of others as a machine to be mended or maintained rather than as an integral human person. Thus is his alienation from the communion of humanity complete.[14]

As David Morris points out, this kind of mechanistic thinking is not restricted to providers of medical care. "In the United States," Morris writes, "an almost inescapable cultural teaching about bodies and illness suggests that the acceptable way for consumers to deal with such imperfections is by making a purchase that wipes them out, like underarm odor. It is not just medicine but the correct medical purchase that rescues the body from peril."[15]

Yet even the wisest series of "correct medical purchases" can end only in death. If the metaphysics of contemporary medicine posits a body that is theoretically immortal, in practice of course,

---

13. For discussion of this "multiple estrangement," see David Power, "The Sacrament of Anointing: Open Questions," *Concilium* 1991/92, ed. Mary Collins and David Power (London: SCM Press, 1991), 103; Daniel Sulmasy, *The Rebirth of the Clinic: An Introduction to Spirituality in Health Care* (Washington, DC: Georgetown University Press, 2006), 125–26. The phrase "multiple estrangement" appears in the Power text.

14. M. Jennifer Glen, "Sickness and Symbol: The Promise of the Future," *Worship* 54, no. 5 (1980): 397–411 at 401.

15. Morris, *Illness and Culture*, 159.

bodies wear out and die.[16] In a culture accustomed to abstraction and decontextualization, death, too, takes place without a sturdy framework of meaning. Indeed, not a few observers have argued that American culture denies death. Edward Thompson offers this assessment: "From euphemisms like 'life insurance' instead of 'death award,' to obituaries buried on back pages and not mentioning the cause of death, to hospices and palliative care settings hiding the dying from sight, to the craft of funeral directors masking the body with cosmetics to seem more lifelike and then artfully directing the wake and burial as if it was live theatre, to small, flat, concealed headstones replacing older slate and marble orchard cemeteries; death has been nearly banished from the ordinary and everyday aspects of people's lives."[17] Thompson's comments indicate the malleability of consumer culture. This culture offers goods and services that mesh well with a denial of death but if death were public and celebrated, advertisers and manufacturers could certainly address a need for, say, larger headstones.

Consumerism's malleability is a function of the fact that consumerism intends to serve a life with no intrinsic *telos*.[18] Bruce Rittenhouse draws on Nicholas Boyle to make an important point about consumerism and postmodernism and their shared aversion to overarching structures of meaning: "Boyle argues that postmodernism and consumerism are inseparable. One way in which their compatibility is seen is in many postmodern think-

16. The inevitability of death and the attendant awareness of finitude is a recurring theme in Sulmasy, *The Rebirth of the Clinic*.

17. Edward H. Thompson Jr., "Commentary: No Time for Dying," in *Practicing Catholic: Ritual, Body, and Contestation in Catholic Faith*, ed. Bruce Morrill, Joanna Zeigler, and Susan Rodgers (New York: Palgrave Macmillan, 2006), 53. See also Charles W. Gusmer, *And You Visited Me: Sacramental Ministry to the Sick and Dying* (Collegeville, MN: Pueblo, 1984), 173; Zygmunt Bauman, *Mortality, Immortality & Other Life Strategies* (Stanford, CA: Stanford University Press, 1992), 136; Susan K. Wood, "The Paschal Mystery: The Intersection of Ecclesiology and Sacramental Theology in Care of the Sick," in *Recovering the Riches of Anointing*, ed. Genevieve Glen (Collegeville, MN: Liturgical Press, 2002), 9; Jeffrey Bishop, *The Anticipatory Corpse*, 17.

18. Vincent Miller writes that advanced capitalism "seems capable of selling anything, including the values of its most committed opponents. It turned the 150th anniversary of the *Communist Manifesto* into a marketing opportunity." Miller, *Consuming Religion*, 18.

ers' wholesale rejection of meta-narratives, and the consequent fragmentation of meaning into discrete acts of subjective interpretation. . . . In consumerism, personal identity is spatially and temporally discontinuous. The institutions that formerly provided continuity to identity have faded in significance. Meaning exists in discrete acts of consumption and discrete acts of recognition by other persons."[19] In a world in which people fall ill and in which all eventually die, in a world in which consumerist abstraction has reached into the understanding and practice of medical care and in which personal identity is already fragmentary, the Catholic Church offers pastoral care to the sick, including the sacrament of anointing. I turn now to that sacrament first by presenting a brief history and then by discussing counter-narratives this sacrament offers to the ill and dying.

III. Anointing: Historical Overview

Writing in the 1980s, Charles Gusmer characterized the sacrament of the anointing of the sick as "the most misunderstood, most uncommunal, and most unliturgical of the seven sacraments of the Church."[20] He added that

> the sacrament of anointing continues to be *misunderstood* by those who for one reason or another continue to use the terms "extreme unction" or "last rites," or in an even more unconscious way by those who fatalistically regard the sacrament as a kind of religious pronouncement of death. Anointing has been the most *uncommunal* of sacraments: in the past, the family often felt compelled to leave the sick room, perhaps confusing the occasion of anointing with discretion required for sacramental confession. Anointing has been the most *unliturgical* of sacraments: we are still not far removed in time from priests darting into sickrooms for a quick dabbing with oil.[21]

19. Bruce Rittenhouse, *Shopping for Meaningful Lives: The Religious Motive of Consumerism* (Eugene, OR: Cascade Books, 2013), 44. Rittenhouse is drawing on Nicholas Boyle, *Who Are We Now? Christian Humanism and the Global Market from Hegel to Heaney* (Notre Dame, IN: University of Notre Dame Press, 1998), 79.

20. Gusmer, *And You Visited Me*, 181.

21. Ibid. (emphasis added).

I will return to Gusmer's claims about anointing being misunderstood, uncommunal, and unliturgical, but first I assess how this state of affairs came to be.

I do not intend to provide here a comprehensive treatment of the issue; a short treatment must suffice.[22] During the New Testament era and for centuries thereafter, Christians anointed sick persons and this practice was by no means restricted to or even primarily aimed at those who were dying. A fourth-century prayer for the blessing of the oil used in the rite indicates that recovery of health, if not always anticipated, was certainly hoped for:

> We invoke Thee, who hast all power and might, Saviour of all men, Father of our Lord Jesus Christ, and we pray Thee to send down from the heavens of Thy Only-begotten a curative power upon this oil, in order that to those who are anointed with these Thy creatures or who receive them, it may become a means of removing every disease and every sickness, of warding off every demon, of putting to flight every unclean spirit, of banishing all fever, all chill, and all weariness; a means of grace and goodness and the remission of sins; a medicament of life and salvation, unto health and soundness of soul and body and spirit, unto perfect well-being.[23]

A fifth-century papal letter provides evidence that both laity and clergy used blessed oil to anoint the sick; there is no mention of the severity of the illness required for anointing.[24]

Significant change begins to take root in the late eighth century and in a fashion that demonstrates this sacrament's connection to the sacrament of reconciliation. Reconciliation had been a once-

22. Standard historical treatments are available in Gusmer and in Joseph Martos, *Doors to the Sacred: A Historical Introduction to Sacraments in the Catholic Church*, rev. ed. (Liguori, MO: Liguori, 2014). See also Paul Palmer, ed., *Sources of Christian Theology*, vol. 2: *Sacraments and Forgiveness* (Westminster, MD: Newman, 1959); Bernhard Poschmann, *Penance and the Anointing of the Sick*, trans. Francis Courtney (New York: Herder & Herder, 1964).

23. From the Prayer Book of Serapion, circa 350 CE. Palmer, *Sources of Christian Theology* 2:280. Serapion is associated with the Egyptian city of Thmuis, near the Nile River.

24. See Pope Innocent I, Letter to Bishop Decentius of Gubbio [DS 216]. The letter is dated to 416 CE.

in-a-lifetime affair until the repeatable practice begun in Ireland in the fifth century started to make inroads on the continent in the sixth century. This repeatable form was not fully endorsed by the universal Western Church until Lateran IV in 1215,[25] however, and many of the faithful continued to postpone reconciliation until they were dying (so as to not blow their one chance at postbaptismal forgiveness of serious sin and to avoid the lifelong penitential practices that still applied in this era—including forgoing marital relations with one's spouse). Deathbed penance involved an anointing and, as Joseph Martos notes, "the fact that the passage on anointing in James 5 spoke of calling in the elders or presbyters and the forgiveness of sins led some churchmen in the later eighth century to suggest in their sermons that this was the practice to which the scriptural text was referring."[26] The administration of this penitential anointing was restricted to clergy. The faithful began to postpone their own requests for anointing in cases of sickness and, under Charlemagne, the practice of lay anointing was prohibited and began to fade out. The net result was that by the eleventh century, anointing of the sick lost its connection to hope for recovery, it became somewhat narrowly associated with forgiveness of sin on one's deathbed in hopes of escaping purgatory, and its administration was restricted to clergy. When Lyons II officially designated anointing of the sick as one of the seven sacraments of the Catholic Church in 1274, it was this practice the council had in mind—and hence the sacrament was referred to as extreme unction (last anointing).[27] Trent, seeking to beat back the challenge of Reformers who denied that extreme unction was a sacrament,[28] underscored Catholic teaching on this

25. DS 812. See the brief summary of the history of reconciliation in this book's chapter on reconciliation.

26. Joseph Martos, *Doors to the Sacred*, 384.

27. The Profession of Faith of Emperor Michael Paleologus, Second Council of Lyons, Session 4, contains the first official conciliar listing of seven sacraments [DS 860].

28. Memorably, Jean Calvin referred to extreme unction as a matter of "hypocritical stage-play" involving "half-dead carcasses." Calvin, *Institutes of the Christian Religion*, IV, 19, 18; IV, 18, 21; vol. 2, trans. Henry Beveridge (Grand Rapids, MI: Eerdmans, 1966), 636, 638.

point and solidified Catholic thought and practice with respect to this sacrament for the next four centuries.[29] Since the practice to which Trent referred in the 1500s had been taking shape since the 800s, we can say that when the Second Vatican Council took up the question of reform of the sacrament in the 1960s, that council was addressing patterns of thinking and acting that had been in place for more than a millennium.

Sacrosanctum Concilium, promulgated by the council in 1963, held that " 'extreme unction,' which may also and more fittingly be called 'Anointing of the Sick,' is not a sacrament intended only for those who are at the point of death" and "it is certain that as soon as any of the faithful *begins to be* in danger of death from sickness or old age, this is already a suitable time for them to receive this sacrament."[30] The revised rite clarifies that "a prudent or reasonably sure judgment, without scruple, is sufficient for deciding on the seriousness of an illness," and in a footnote the rite adds that "on the one hand, the sacrament may and should be given to anyone whose health is seriously impaired; on the other hand, it may not be given indiscriminately."[31] The rite offers options for celebration in a home or hospital, as well as in the context of Mass. It also provides for communal anointing. Some of the official prayers after anointing speak clearly of hope for physical recovery.[32] While certainly anointing can be appropriate

29. See the decrees and canons on extreme unction from Session 14 of Trent [DS 1694–1700; 1716–1719]. Norman Tanner, ed., *Decrees of the Ecumenical Councils,* vol. 2: *Trent to Vatican II* (Washington, DC: Georgetown University Press, 1990), 714–718.

30. *Sacrosanctum Concilium* 73 (emphasis added). By way of contrast, the 1917 *Code of Canon Law,* in 940/1 held that "extreme unction is not to be extended except to the faithful who, having obtained the use of reason, come into danger of death from infirmity or old age." There is greater emphasis on the proximity of death in the 1917 version. *The 1917 or Pio-Benedictine Code of Canon Law,* curated by Edward Peters (San Francisco: Ignatius, 2001), 328.

31. International Commission on English in the Liturgy, *Pastoral Care of the Sick: Rites of Anointing and Viaticum* (New York: Catholic Book Publishing, 1983) 8 and footnote. I will use this text throughout this book, citing the rite by paragraph number.

32. Pastoral Care of the Sick 125B asks God to "mercifully restore [the sick person] to full health" and 125E asks God that the sick person may be "reunited with

in terminal conditions, the rite nowhere uses the terms "extreme unction" or "last rites."

Turning to Charles Gusmer's description of anointing as misunderstood, uncommunal, and unliturgical, I will here comment on this characterization and then turn to what I see as the counter-consumerist narrative of the sacrament. Is the postconciliar rite misunderstood? Writing at about the same time as Gusmer, Jean Rabau contended that the rite was indeed "well understood and accepted by the Christian people."[33] Describing his efforts

---

us at your altar of praise." Nevertheless, Mary Collins holds that the rite does not often enough speak of recovery. For additional comment, see Collins, "The Roman Ritual: Pastoral Care and Anointing of the Sick," *Concilium* 1991/92, 3–17.

I have noted the Prayer Book of Serapion and its request that God empower the oil of the sick to banish all fever and chill, etc. The corresponding prayer in the seventh-century Gelasian Sacramentary asks that the oil dispel "all sufferings, all sickness, all illness of mind and body." From the time of Trent until the Second Vatican Council, the prayer asked that the oil "become a safeguard of mind and body for everyone who is anointed with this ointment of heavenly healing, to relieve every pain, every weakness, every ailment of mind and body." Nevertheless, at least from the time of Trent, the actual administration of the oil to the body of the sick person involved only petitions seeking forgiveness of sin, although some of the prayers after the anointing referred to a hoped-for recovery. The primary prayer of blessing of the oil after Vatican II asks God to "make this oil a remedy for all who are anointed with it; heal them in body, in soul, and in spirit, and deliver them from every affliction" and the sacramental formula asks that the Lord may "in his love and mercy help you with the grace of the Holy Spirit." The second part of the formula mentions sin but also a more expansive notion of vitality: "May the Lord who frees you from sin save you and raise you up."

The source for the passage from the Gelasian Sacramentary is Palmer, *Sources of Christian Theology*, 2:288; the sacramental formula in use after Trent and the prayers following the anointing are from *The Roman Ritual in Latin and English with Rubrics and Plainchant Notations*, vol. 1: *The Sacraments and Processions*, ed. and trans. Philip T. Weller (Boonville, NY: Preserving Christian Publications, 2016 [originally Bruce Publishing, 1950]), 339–45; for the blessing of the oil after Trent, the source is *The English-Latin Sacramentary for the United States of America* (New York: Catholic Book Publishing, 1966), 690; for the blessing of oil after Vatican II the source is Pastoral Care of the Sick 123; for the sacramental formula, the source is Pastoral Care of the Sick 124.

33. Jean Rabau, "The Anointing of the Sick: Renewal of the Sacrament," *Lumen Vitae* 41, no. 1 (1986): 49–61 at 49.

to catechize about the sacrament, however, Bruce Morrill wrote in 2006 that "my pastoral and classroom experience leads me to think that most Roman Catholics not only do not understand anointing within the entire rite of the Pastoral Care of the Sick, they in fact cling to the pre-Vatican II (medieval-tridentine) titles for this sacrament, Extreme Unction or Last Rites."[34] Beyond these conflicting anecdotes, there is data to consider from a 2001 survey of 3,365 chaplains conducted by CARA, the Center for Applied Research in the Apostolate. To the question of how often a patient requesting the sacrament of anointing understands the sacrament, respondents indicated that 66 percent of the time patients "usually" or "almost always" or "always" understood the sacrament. However, the number drops to 10 percent if the responses are restricted to "almost always" or "always."[35]

Is the rite uncommunal? Certainly, there are some severe illnesses or injuries that occur without warning, making it difficult for family and friends to be present—to say nothing of the challenge of arranging for the sacrament for more than one unexpectedly ill person at the same time. Yet there are parishes that celebrate the sacrament in the context of Mass three or four times a year or more. St. Ann's Monastery Basilica in Scranton, Pennsylvania, in fact, celebrates an annual Mass for the anointing of the sick at which hundreds are anointed.[36] In the CARA study, 53 percent of respondents reported that family and friends were "usually" or "almost always" or "always" included in the celebration of the sacrament; the number falls to 18 percent if responses are restricted to "almost always" or "always."[37]

34. Bruce Morrill, "Christ the Healer: An Investigation of Contemporary Liturgical, Pastoral, and Biblical Approaches," in Morrill, Ziegler, and Rogers, *Practicing Catholic*, 119.

35. CARA, "The Sacrament of the Anointing of the Sick: A Survey of Blessings and Needs" (April 2001), 9. This survey was made available to me by Philip Paradowski of the National Association of Catholic Chaplains, which commissioned the report. I am grateful to him for his assistance.

36. See Kathleen Bolus, "Hundreds Gather for Mass Anointing of the Sick at St. Ann's," *Times-Tribune* (July 24, 2015), n.p. Rich Shelp at the monastery confirmed this information in an email to me on September 23, 2016.

37. CARA, "The Sacrament of the Anointing of the Sick," 9.

Is the rite executed in an unliturgical manner? The CARA study offers this data.[38]

In your experience, how often do these occur when the Sacrament of Anointing is requested or administered?

	Percent Responding	Percent Responding
	"usually" or "always" or "almost always"	"always" or "almost always"
It is administered in a reverent and caring manner	86	45
It is administered in an intimate and comforting setting	67	23
It is administered in a perfunctory way	32	12

Although the majority numbers in the first two categories are decisive in the middle column, they drop significantly when the bar is set to "almost always" or "always"—by nearly half in the first case and more than half in the second case. Celebration of the sacrament is at least "usually" perfunctory in roughly one-third of cases; that number, too, shrinks by more than half when the bar is set to "almost always" or "always."

Further study is needed;[39] for example, how can 86 percent of respondents report that the sacrament is at least usually

38. Ibid.
39. Mary Gautier on the CARA staff advised me via email (September 14, 2016) that the National Association of Catholic Chaplains has not (yet) requested a second study.

administered in a reverent and caring way when 32 percent of respondents indicate that the sacrament is at least usually done in a perfunctory way? Yet even if the situation is not as bleak as Gusmer's diagnosis from the 1980s indicates,[40] clearly there is work to do by way of sacramental and liturgical formation around this sacrament. The following section seeks to provide such formation as a way of countering the consumerist and postmodern influences discussed earlier.

IV. Anointing of the Sick: Issues of Narrative and Identity

As has been noted by Bruce Rittenhouse above, consumerism is associated with a fragmented self. Lacking a permanent and abiding sense of identity, individuals in a consumer culture are left to negotiate and establish their identities again and again.[41] Rittenhouse contends that "the individual who lives a consumeristic form of life must continually consume new good-signs in order to update his or her deployment of signs to present the most advantageous system of signs possible" and that "it is not simply taste, character, or categorical identity that must be asserted

40. In the CARA survey, chaplains reported that 98 percent of the time anointing provides "somewhat" or "very much" comfort; 97 percent reported that it responded to spiritual needs "somewhat" or "very much"; 94 percent reported that it responded to emotional needs "somewhat" or "very much"; 89 percent reported that it was an experience of God's healing "somewhat" or "very much." When responses are restricted to "very much" only, the numbers fall to 84 percent for the question about comfort, 77 percent for the question about spiritual needs, 69 percent for the question about emotional needs, and 58 percent for the question about God's healing. All data from CARA, "The Sacrament of the Anointing of the Sick," 6. In a 2008 CARA survey of approximately 1,000 Catholics, 78 percent reported that anointing had been "somewhat" or "very meaningful" to them in light of their own anointing or the anointing of someone close to them. That number falls to 52 percent for "very meaningful" only. Data from CARA, "Sacraments Today: Belief and Practice among U.S. Catholics" (April 2008), 31.

41. See the comments on chronic reinvention of the self in my "Consumerism and the Liturgical Act of Worship," *Horizons* 38, no. 1 (2011): 54–74. David Morris ponders whether dissociative identity disorder (multiple personality disorder) may be the distinctive illness of the postmodern era. See Morris, *Illness and Culture*, 56–57.

through a consumeristic form of life, but *selfhood* itself."[42] Illness can compound this problem, as persons experience a "multiple estrangement"[43] from friends and family, church communities, co-workers, God, and even their own bodies.[44] The self of the sick person, already diminished by the very nature of consumer culture and now depleted by illness, is in a state of what one might call "spiritual powerlessness." Indeed, Charles Gusmer uses this very phrase to describe "the crisis that illness represents in the life of an ailing Christian as regards communication with self, others, and God" and for Gusmer, it is the degree of this powerlessness that is decisive when considering whether to anoint.[45] Anointing, then, is addressed to this state of powerlessness.

Anointing addresses this crisis by reinserting the sick person into the overarching Christian narrative of God's love. In direct opposition to consumerist modes of abstraction, the rite does not envision administration of the sacrament as an isolated instance of pastoral care.[46] Ministry to the sick includes companionable visits, covering household chores, providing meals, bringing Communion to the homebound, etc., and it is a responsibility that devolves upon the local Christian community as such—a point made by the rite in paragraphs 32, 33, 34, 35, 36, and 43. Numerous commentators have drawn attention to the idea that the sacrament of anointing is emptied of meaning if it is not part of a wider context of pastoral care; here I draw on James Empereur as a representative example: "Anointing cannot be seen as an isolated

---

42. Rittenhouse, *Shopping for Meaningful Lives*, 147 (emphasis added).

43. See Power, "The Sacrament of Anointing: Open Questions," 103.

44. "Illness," argues Rachelle Barina, "can lead to a perception that the 'I' who can think and thrive is separate from the body that fails the 'I.' This perception reflects and reinforces a body/soul dualism." Rachelle Barina, "Anticipating the Corpse or the Kingdom: Medicine and the Practice of Body/Soul (Dis)unity," *Heythrop Journal* 56, no. 5 (2015): 778–92 at 778.

45. Gusmer, *And You Visited Me*, 87.

46. Skye Jethani observes: "Alienation has conditioned consumers, including the religious variety, to believe context is irrelevant. Value is found only in something's immediate usefulness, in its ability to satisfy one's immediate desire." Citation from Skye Jethani, "The Unholy Trinity of Consumerism," *Cultural Encounters* 6, no. 1 (2010): 79–85 at 82.

ritual action but must mirror the acts of concern which precede and follow the anointing. As in the case of the other sacraments, the authenticity of anointing depends on the quality of religious experience being articulated."[47]

To put it another way, anointing of the sick is a profound statement of the church's belief that in illness "we should never have to stand alone."[48] Consumerism is twinned with the notion that one's worth and indeed one's *self*-worth is determined by the degree to which one is productive, remunerated, and able to engage in purchase after consumer purchase. Consequently, sicknesses that impinge upon one's productivity are viewed in American culture as private or even shameful.[49] In the pastoral care it extends to the sick, the Christian community instead endorses the view of St. Paul, namely, that when one member of the body suffers, all suffer (1 Cor 12:26).[50]

Those who are sick are not merely told "you do not stand alone." They are told "you stand *forth*." M. Therese Lysaught puts it this way: "The sick are challenged not to isolate themselves in embarrassment or fear. They are marked and anointed as a sign to the community of the meaning of death and discipleship in baptism, a sign that suffering is not 'useless' or 'meaningless' but in fact

---

47. James Empereur, *Prophetic Anointing: God's Call to the Sick, the Elderly, and the Dying* (Wilmington, DE: Michael Glazier, 1982), 205. Similar arguments may be found in Joan Mormul, "Sickness and the Paschal Mystery," *Liturgy* 25 (March–April 1980), 31–35 at 32–33; Gusmer, *And You Visited Me*, 155; Cor Traets, "The Sick and Suffering Person: A Liturgical/Sacramental Approach," in *God and Human Suffering*, ed. Jan Lambrecht and Raymond Collins, Louvain Theological and Pastoral Monographs 3 (Louvain: Peeters, 1990), 183–210 at 186; Donald Gelpi, *Committed Worship*, vol. 2: *The Sacraments of Ongoing Conversion* (Collegeville, MN: Liturgical Press, 1993), 190; Lizette Larson-Miller, *The Sacrament of Anointing of the Sick,* ed. John Laurance Lex Orandi Series (Collegeville, MN: Liturgical Press, 2005), xi; Morrill, *Divine Worship and Human Healing*, 158–59; S. Nazarene, "Anointing of the Sick Revisited from the Perspective of Social Justice," *Vidyajyoti Journal of Theological Reflection* 74, no. 5 (2010): 361–76 at 366.

48. *United States Catholic Catechism for Adults* (Washington, DC: United States Catholic Conference, 2006) 256.

49. See Morrill, "Christ the Healer," 122.

50. This verse is quoted in Pastoral Care of the Sick 32.

participates in the very work of God in Christ."[51] In baptism, one is plunged into the paschal mystery of Christ and summoned to live a life of discipleship, following the Master who freely embraced the cross and emptied himself for the sake of humanity. The fourth-century John Chrysostom had urged the newly baptized in his community to regard the robes in which they had been clad: "Now the robe you wear and the gleaming garments attract the eyes of all; if you should will to do so, by keeping your royal robes shining even more brightly than it now does, you will always be able to draw all who behold you to show the same zeal and praise for the Master."[52] Writing in our own day, Paul Meyendorff applies this baptismal theme to the sacrament of anointing: "Anointing of the sick, just like baptism, is not only for the forgiveness of sins, but for new birth, for enlightenment, for liberation from slavery, for adoption into sonship. The oil we are now using reminds us of the oil of gladness with which we were anointed prior to baptism, as well as the anointing with chrism we received immediately after we emerged from the font. We are thus reminded of the task that was set before us at our baptism: to 'shine with the radiance of the saints.'"[53] As we saw earlier in this book, this baptismal narrative is besieged by consumer culture, which seeks to undermine the notion of any all-embracing *telos*. The self and orientation of the sick person in a consumer culture is all the more threatened as noted above in the discussion of powerlessness.[54] Small wonder, then, that *Pastoral Care of the Sick* reminds readers that "the

51. M. Therese Lysaught, "Sharing Christ's Passion: A Critique of the Role of Suffering in the Discourse of Biomedical Ethics from the Perspective of the Theological Practice of Anointing of the Sick" (PhD diss., Duke University, 1992), 295.

52. John Chrysostom, *Fourth Instruction on Baptism* 18, in Paul Harkins, ed., *St. John Chrysostom: Baptismal Instructions* (Westminster, MD: Newman, 1963), 73. See the treatment of this theme in section VII, p. 18, of the chapter on baptism.

53. Paul Meyendorff, *The Anointing of the Sick* (Crestwood, NY: St. Vladimir's Seminary, 2009), 83.

54. Though it does not mention the baleful influence of consumer culture on those who are ill, Pastoral Care of the Sick 5 reminds the church that "those who are seriously ill need the special help of God's grace in this time of anxiety, lest they be broken in spirit and, under the pressure of temptation, perhaps weakened in their faith."

Church exhorts [those who are ill] to associate themselves *willingly* with the passion and death of Christ."[55] The 1994 *Catechism of the Catholic Church* goes even further: "By the grace of this sacrament the sick person *receives* the strength and the gift of uniting himself more closely to Christ's Passion: in a certain way he is consecrated to bear fruit by configuration to the Savior's redemptive Passion. Suffering, a consequence of original sin, acquires a new meaning; it becomes a participation in the saving work of Jesus."[56] We must address, then, what it means for the sick person to stand forth by uniting more closely with the paschal mystery of Christ.

A key word here is "willingly." Love is a decision/action freely undertaken or else it is not love. Robots do what they are programmed to do. God invites and even commands humans to love (see John 13:34), but there is no compulsion akin to what a calculator must do if I enter "7 x 8." The paradigm here is Jesus Christ himself, who, when speaking of his impending death, tells his disciples that "I lay down my life in order to take it up again. No one takes it from me, but I lay it down of my own accord" (John 10:17-18, NRSV). Eucharistic Prayer II is similarly clear that Jesus "entered willingly into his Passion." The suffering before him did not stop Jesus from loving his disciples "to the end" as Eucharistic Prayer IV puts it, drawing on John 13:1.[57] The Gospel of Luke has the crucified Jesus praying for divine forgiveness of his killers (Luke 23:34). Jesus was committed to a life narrative of love and service even when that narrative was besieged by sin and pride, by torture, suffering, and death.

When the Christian tradition speaks of union with Christ's passion, it is not endorsing suffering for the sake of suffering. Rather, it is reminding Christians that their vocation to love as part of God's overarching narrative of love does not take a vacation when Christians are sick. James Empereur correctly points out that "the sacrament of anointing includes those anointed as

---

55. Pastoral Care of the Sick 5 (emphasis added).

56. *Catechism of the Catholic Church* 1521 (emphasis added). See also *United States Catholic Catechism for Adults*, 254.

57. See Francis J. Moloney, " 'He Loved Them to the End': Eucharist in the Gospel of John," *Worship* 91, no. 1 (January 2017): 43–64.

on a par with any others in the church,"[58] adding elsewhere that "if
the liturgy emphasizes union with the suffering of Christ in such
a way as to make people content with suffering rather than be
challenged to free people from the weakness and hurt of sickness
and old age, then the liturgy is unjust."[59] Even if those who are
anointed are still physically weak or feeble, they are free to love
God and neighbor. This freedom may be impaired, but it is never
wholly compromised. The forms this love takes may be different
from a time when the sick person enjoyed better health but love,
in whatever form it takes, is a fulfillment of the Christian vocation.

When another person extends love to me, that person becomes
for me a sacrament of the encounter with God.[60] How much more
does this person become a sacrament if I am aware that this person
is engaging me in love even though he or she is suffering pain
or illness? Consider Yves Congar's comments on the challenge
of loving: "Precisely because there is selfishness inside us, it is
demanding and painful to face up to what we are supposed to
do for our neighbor. Sin inclines us to consider things selfishly or
too much according to our personal interest. This egotism gives
to our efforts to live for what is greater than ourselves—to our
sacrifice—an aspect of painful detachment. But such efforts to
live beyond ourselves can also succeed in bringing us our heart's
delight. This is what happens each time we truly love."[61] This base
egotism is compounded by the tendency to an egotistical closing
in on oneself that can accompany illness.[62] Indeed, a study published in 2000 found that thinking about death and mortality was

58. James Empereur and Christopher Kiesling, *The Liturgy that Does Justice*
(Collegeville, MN: Liturgical Press, 1990), 227 (emphasis added).

59. James Empereur, *Prophetic Anointing*, 190.

60. The parallel with the title of Edward Schillebeeckx, *Christ, the Sacrament of
the Encounter with God* (New York: Sheed & Ward, 1963) is deliberate.

61. Yves Congar, "The Structure of Christian Priesthood," in *At the Heart of
Christian Worship: Liturgical Essays of Yves Congar*, ed. and trans. Paul Philibert
(Collegeville, MN: Liturgical Press, 2010), 72. Originally published as "*Structure
du sacerdoce chrétien*," *La Maison-Dieu* 27 (1951): 51–85.

62. This caution about closing in one oneself was expressed by the Roman
Catholic bishops of Italy in their statement *Evangelizzazione e sacramenti della
penitenza e dell'unnzione degli infermi* (Torino: Elle Di Ci, 1974,1990) 140, quoted in

associated with increased materialistic tendencies.[63] The rite says that "the role of the sick in the Church is to be a reminder of the essential or higher things."[64] If that is true, then in at least some cases there may be a need for a sacramental-ecclesial intervention to counter the kind of weakness and powerlessness associated with suffering and compounded by the egotism and materialism that can manifest in serious illness.

Sacrosanctum Concilium 59 teaches that the sacraments of the church have a three-fold purpose: "to sanctify people, to build up the body of Christ, and . . . to worship God." My argument here is that the church anoints those who are seriously ill in part *so that* those who are ill may continue to build up the body of Christ by continuing to love. Unfortunately, this emphasis on continuing to love is not found in the English edition of *Pastoral Care of the Sick* but it is clear in the French edition, which speaks of the witness provided by the sick person continuing to love in the midst of suffering (*en continuant à aimer, au cœur de l'épreuve*).[65] Love builds up,[66] and the self-offering involved in love—the sacrifice of which Congar wrote—strengthens the bonds of communion. So much is

---

John Kasza, *Understanding Sacramental Healing: Anointing and Viaticum* (Chicago: Liturgy Training Publications, 2007), 89.

63. See Tim Kasser and Kennon M. Sheldon, "Of Wealth and Death: Materialism, Mortality Salience, and Consumption Behavior," *Psychological Science* 11, no. 4 (July 2000): 348–51. This study did not control for religious affiliation. Kasser also reports on and discusses the ways in which the acquisitiveness connected with consumerism is associated with health issues in Kasser, "The Good Life or the Goods Life? Positive Psychology and Personal Well-Being in the Culture of Consumption," in *Positive Psychology in Practice*, ed. P. Alex Linley and Stephen Joseph (Hoboken, NJ: John Wiley & Sons, 2004), 55–67.

64. Pastoral Care of the Sick 3.

65. *Sacrements pour les malades: pastorale et célébrations* 5 in Commission international de traduction pour les pays francophones, *Sacrements pour les malades: pastorale et célébrations* (Paris, 1977). Paragraph 55 of the French edition strikes a similar chord when it refers to the "loving attitude" of Jesus during his passion and death: "Dans le cas d'une maladie dont l'issue paraît fatale, le chrétien a également besoin de cette grâce pour vaincre l'angoisse de la mort à vivre l'espérance de la résurrection en s'associant à l'attitude aimante de Jésus Christ dans sa passion et sa mort (cf. Rom 8:17; Col 1:24; 2 Tim 2:11, 12)."

66. See 1 Cor 8:13.

this the case that in the end there is but the one self-offering of the one Son to the Father, to which all other sacrificial love is joined.

The narrative here involves Colossians 1:24, where the Pauline writer speaks of "rejoicing in my sufferings for your sake and in my flesh I am completing what is lacking in Christ's afflictions for the sake of his body, that is, the church"[67] (NRSV). An extended citation from Yves Congar will allow us to relate the all-sufficiency of Christ's sacrifice on the cross to the question of making up what is "lacking" in Christ's sacrifice:

> Christ is our Alpha and Omega, as we read in the Book of Revelation (1:8; 21:6; 22:13). But Christ is our Alpha all by himself, even though he is such for our sake (*hyper ēmōn*, for our benefit), whereas we are the Omega along with him and he cannot be that without us. . . .
>
> In order to pass *from* the state of plenitude that belongs uniquely to the Son *over* to the fullness of the body, the sacrifice and priesthood of Christ needs to be appropriated by the faithful. *Only One is priest*, but he allows many to be priests in him and through him; only one sacrifice has efficacious value, but it gives value to all of our sacrifices. It *contains* them, but they give it a new kind of fulfillment and abundance by actualizing its transcendent value. Without the participation of the members, the sacrifice of Christ would not be total. . . .
>
> The role of the sacraments is to reproduce in a particular mode of being [as sign] that is precisely symbolic-real, what Jesus did for us in the days of his flesh. This allows the root to bear its fruits—to make the Christ Alpha produce within us over time the reality of life in such a way as to form the Christ Omega.[68]

The sacraments, in other words, have a role to play in the coming-to-be of Christ Omega. Those who are anointed have a role to play

---

67. Col 1:24 is specifically mentioned in paragraphs 5 and 55 of *Sacrements pour les malades*. It is found as well in Pastoral Care of the Sick 3 and 5 (footnote), but with no reference to loving as Christ did.

68. Congar, "The Structure of Christian Priesthood," 82, 83, 85. One is reminded of Pope Leo the Great's maxim that "what was visible in our Savior has passed over into his mysteries [=sacraments]." See the quotation from his Sermon 74.2 in *Catechism of the Catholic Church* 1115.

in God's plan "for the fullness of time, to gather up all things in him [Christ], things in heaven and things on earth" (Eph 1:10, NRSV). By continuing to love in the midst of their suffering, those who are ill partake in the total sacrifice of the Christian community, the realization of which, following Congar, is the "attachment to God of '. . . the entire redeemed city.' "[69] Against the postmodern and consumerist claim that there is no stable self and that there is nothing but a fragmentary narrative, the anointing of the sick posits a narrative that is nothing less than eschatological.

Consumerism is associated with productivity and remuneration for that productivity, as was mentioned earlier. The sacrament of anointing challenges this understanding of productivity. The American bishops wrote that those who are ill "are *believed* to be and seen as *productive* members of the community, contributing to the welfare of all by associating themselves freely with Christ's passion and death."[70] There is a matter of justice here in allowing those who are ill or frail to grasp that the consumerist idea of productivity is not the only way to understand the contributions one makes to society or the church. What James Empereur and Christopher Kiesling say here about the elderly applies as well to the seriously ill:

> The old are in need of liberation. . . . Their success is no longer measured by their achievements. The meaning of their lives does not come from job, status, or special abilities. Liberation comes to the elderly when they find the meaning of their lives in being old, when they need not try to relive the past, and are not threatened by their former failures and weaknesses. Injustice is inflicted on the old when they are made to feel guilty about their uselessness to society. Justice here is the support and at-

69. Congar, "The Structure of Christian Priesthood," 79. Congar takes the line about the entire redeemed city from the treatment of sacrifice in Augustine, *City of God* 10.6.

70. National Conference of Catholic Bishops, *Study Text 2: Pastoral Care of the Sick and Dying*, rev. ed. (Washington, DC: United States Catholic Bishops, 1984), 21. I have emphasized the word "productive." See the discussion of this study text in M. Therese Lysaught, "Suffering, Ethics, and the Body of Christ: Anointing as a Strategic Alternative Practice," *Christian Bioethics* 2, no. 2 (1996): 172–201.

mosphere which makes it possible to believe in the worth of one's own life.[71]

Part of the worth of the ill and frail is that, in the words of Lizette Larson-Miller, they are "prophets of the reign of God in our midst."[72] Indeed, one of the prayers after anointing asks that the one anointed "may give us all an example of patience and joyfully witness to the power of your love."[73] Going back to the seventh-century Gelasian Sacramentary through the prayer book in use at the time of Vatican II, the blessing of the oil of the sick mentioned the oil used to bless "priests, kings, prophets, and martyrs."[74] The blessing of oil currently in use in the Catholic Church makes no reference to priests, kings, prophets or martyrs. That is a loss, in my view, but the prophetic function of persons who are ill or frail abides.

V. Conclusion

In this chapter, I have detailed some of the challenges presented by consumer culture to those who are ill or frail. Already predisposed to understanding themselves in a fragmentary way, those who are ill are faced with additional forms of alienation and fragmentation sometimes even from their very bodies. I then turned to the history of the sacrament of anointing the sick, noting how its initial association with a vibrant sense of well-being was reduced to a more or less exclusive link with forgiveness of sin in preparation for a good death. I discussed the reforms implemented following Vatican II. Survey results from the Center for Applied Research in the Apostolate underscored the need for additional sacramental

71. Empereur and Kiesling, *The Liturgy that Does Justice*, 221.

72. Larson-Miller, *The Sacrament of Anointing of the Sick*, xv.

73. Pastoral Care of the Sick 125D. Larson-Miller observes, however, that this is "one of the few places where the prayers acknowledge what the sick do for us, rather than solely what the Church does for the sick." Larson-Miller, *The Sacrament of Anointing of the Sick*, 27.

74. For the Gelasian Sacramentary, see Palmer, *Sources of Christian Theology*, 2:288; for the prayer in use up to Vatican II, see *The English-Latin Sacramentary for the United States of America* 690.

formation, a sketch of which I provided in the third part. Based on the work of Yves Congar addressed in the third part of the chapter, we can understand now why Pope Francis claims that "all love is meant to share in the complete self-gift of the Son of God for our sake."[75] In a special way, those who are ill are called to be living signs of this truth, prophets helping the ecclesial community deepen its living out of the paschal mystery.

By way of bringing this chapter to a close, I would hope for at least two future steps. First, the church needs a follow-up to the CARA study of 2001. CARA completed a study on sacramental belief and practice among American Catholics in 2008,[76] but that survey addressed all seven sacraments and did not parallel the depth of the 2001 study on anointing. A CARA study of American parishes in 2011 did not address the anointing of the sick.[77]

Second, there is the matter of formation in the sacramental thought and practice of the church. Rachelle Barina writes that "formation in the practices and intellectual habits that embody sacramental theology should animate Christian practices of care for the sick."[78] This chapter offers one such effort. The fact that the number of medical schools offering at least one course on the relationship between medical care and religious beliefs jumped from five to sixty in between 1992 and 2000 is a positive development.[79] So, too, is the creation of institutions such as the Program on Medicine and Religion at the University of Chicago and the program in Theology, Medicine, and Culture at Duke Divinity School. Much work remains, of course, but every effort to love makes a difference.

---

75. Pope Francis, Encyclical Letter on Faith (*Lumen Fidei*, June 29, 2013) 32, http://w2.vatican.va/content/francesco/en/encyclicals/documents/papa-francesco_20130629_enciclica-lumen-fidei.html.

76. CARA, "Sacraments Today."

77. CARA, "The Changing Face of U.S. Catholic Parishes" (2011).

78. Barina, "Anticipating the Corpse or the Kingdom," 779.

79. Larson-Miller, *The Sacrament of Anointing of the Sick*, 96 citing information in *Faith, Spirituality, and Medicine: Toward the Making of the Healing Practitioner*, ed. Dana King (New York: Haworth, 2000), xiii.

Chapter Six

MARRIAGE
AND CONSUMER CULTURE

I. Introduction

Among official enumerations of the seven sacraments of the Roman Catholic Church, one often finds marriage occupying the last spot.[1] Marriage was also the last of the church rites to be formally designated as a sacrament, making the list in the profession of faith of Emperor Michael Paleologus at Lyons II in 1274, where, however, it was listed in the sixth place.[2] Part of the reason why marriage did not achieve such recognition earlier is connected, of course, to the ambivalence of the Christian tradition toward sex. To offer just a few examples, St. Jerome, Doctor of the Church, wrote that "in view of the purity of the body of Christ,

---

1. Marriage was listed in the seventh spot in 1547 by the Council of Trent (session 7, can. 1; DS 860); in 1566 by the *Catechism of the Council of Trent* (DS 1601); in 1870 by Vatican I in the Profession of Faith by Pius IX; in 1963 by Vatican II in *Sacrosanctum Concilium*, which addresses reform of the sacraments in paragraphs 64–78, treating marriage in paragraphs 77–78; in 1965 by Vatican II in *Lumen Gentium* 10; and in the current *Catechism of the Catholic Church*. Bernard Cooke, however, places what he calls the "sacrament of human friendship" in the first place and his discussion of the seven sacraments begins with marriage. See Bernard Cooke, *Sacraments and Sacramentality* (Mystic, CT: Twenty-Third Publications, 2004), 78–92.

2. Extreme unction was listed in the seventh place. See DS 860. A general treatment of the history of the sacrament of marriage is available in Joseph Martos, *Doors to the Sacred*, rev. ed. (Liguori, MO: Liguori, 2014), 405–62.

all sexual intercourse is unclean."[3] Saint Augustine, another Doctor of the Church, echoed St. Paul's advice about marrying rather than burning with lust;[4] and there is no question that Augustine prized the chastity of celibacy over the chastity of marriage.[5] Yet as we turn to the question of consumerism and the sacrament of marriage, a second objection to its sacramental status arises, this time from financial quarters. Edward Schillebeeckx observes that as the issue of the sacramental status of marriage was being debated between roughly 1150 and 1250, "canonists, anxious to prevent simony, were hardly able to accept that the marriage contract, which was accompanied by so many financial transactions between the two families in connection with the arrangement of the dowry, was capable of conferring grace."[6] Indeed, the 1453 Sarum Manual in England had the priest inquiring into the matter of the dowry![7]

Perhaps more than any other sacrament, marriage has been entangled with commerce and finance. On the other hand, writing in 1997, Susanne Friese contended that "little has been written about

3. Jerome, *Against Jovinianus*, I.20, in Philip Schaff and Henry Wace, eds., *Nicene and Post-Nicene Fathers of the Church*, Series II, vol. 6: *Jerome: Letters and Select Works* (Peabody, MA: Hendrickson, 2004), 361. While not as harsh as Jerome, the earlier Origen held that "when conjugal acts are being done, the presence of the Holy Spirit will not be granted." Homilies on Numbers 6.3.7 in Origen, *Homilies on Numbers*, trans. Thomas Scheck, ed. Christopher Hall (Downers Grove, IL: IVP Academic, 2009), 23.

4. See Augustine, *The Excellence of Marriage*, 10.10–11, in David G. Hunter, ed., *The Works of Saint Augustine: A Translation for the 21st Century I/9: Marriage and Virginity: The Excellence of Marriage, Holy Virginity, The Excellence of Widowhood, Adulterous Marriages, Continence*, trans. Ray Kearney (Hyde Park, NY: New City, 1999), 41–42.

5. See Augustine, *The Excellence of Marriage*, 23.28, in Augustine, *Marriage and Virginity*, 54; Augustine, Sermon 354.9 in John Rotelle, ed., *The Works of Augustine: A Translation for the 21st Century: Sermons III/10 (341–400) on Various Subjects*, trans. Edmund Hill (Hyde Park, NY: New City, 1995), 161–62.

6. Edward Schillebeeckx, *Marriage: Human Reality and Saving Mystery*, trans. N.D. Smith (New York: Sheed & Ward, 1965), 332. Schillebeeckx refers here to G. Le Bras, "Mariage," in *Dictionnaire de Théologique Catholique*, vol. 9 (Paris: Librairie Letouzey et Ané, 1927), col. 2208.

7. See *Documents of the Marriage Liturgy*, ed. Mark Searle and Kenneth W. Stevenson (Collegeville, MN: Liturgical Press, 1992), 165.

the ritual and traditions of the wedding as these relate to consumer behavior or marketing."[8] The situation has changed since then with the appearance of works such as Cele C. Otnes and Elizabeth H. Pleck, *Cinderella Dreams*, and Rebecca Mead, *One Perfect Day*.[9] Yet a search for the conjoined key words "marriage" and "consumerism" in the ATLA Religion Database yielded zero hits.[10]

I intend here to fill some of that gap by addressing first how consumer culture does or does not prepare would-be couples to undertake marriage. I will turn to a particular aspect of this "preparation"—namely, the ways in which consumer culture encourages couples to make of their wedding a display of the self. I will argue next that the church offers a different understanding of an ecclesially and socially rooted self, grounded in the full sacramental life of the church and with an eye towards a mission in the world. I will conclude with some suggestions for tackling challenges presented by consumer culture.

II. Consumer Culture and Preparation for Marriage

In his 2016 apostolic exhortation on love in the family, Francis warned against "a cultural decline that fails to promote love or self-giving" and a "culture of the ephemeral." He continued:

> Here I think, for example, of the speed with which people move from one affective relationship to another. They believe, along the lines of social networks, that love can be connected or disconnected at the whim of the consumer, and the relationship quickly "blocked." I think too of the fears associated with permanent

8. Susanne Friese, "A Consumer Good in the Ritual Process: The Case of the Wedding Dress," *Journal of Ritual Studies* 11, no. 2 (1997): 47–58 at 47.

9. Cele C. Otnes and Elizabeth H. Pleck, *Cinderella Dreams: The Allure of the Lavish Wedding* (Berkeley, CA: University of California, 2003); Rebecca Mead, *One Perfect Day: The Selling of the American Wedding* (New York: Penguin, 2007). Though it is not written with respect to weddings per se, there is also Kurt Armstrong, *Why Love Will Always Be a Poor Investment: Marriage and Consumer Culture* (Eugene, OR: Wipf & Stock, 2012). Note as well that *Cinderella Dreams* and *One Perfect Day* are helpful but *secular* assessments of consumerism and marriage.

10. Search conducted April 24, 2017. There were likewise no hits for "wedding" and "consumerism."

commitment, the obsession with free time, and those relationships that weigh costs and benefits for the sake of remedying
loneliness, providing protection, or offering some service. We
treat affective relationships the way we treat material objects
and the environment: everything is disposable; everyone uses
and throws away, takes and breaks, exploits and squeezes to the
last drop. Then, goodbye.[11]

Expanding on this theme in an address he gave in Rome a few
months after the exhortation was promulgated, Francis raised
the question of the nullity of (some) Catholic marriages: "This is
why a part of our sacramental marriages are null, because they
[the spouses] say, 'Yes, for a lifetime,' but they do not know what
they are saying because they have another culture. They say it,
and they mean well, but they do not have the awareness."[12]

Surely consumer culture socializes persons to "have it your
way," in the words of a well-known ad campaign run by a major
fast-food franchise,[13] and consumer tolerance for discomfort is

11. Pope Francis, Post-Synodal Apostolic Exhortation on Love in the Family
(*Amoris Laetitia*, March 19, 2016) 39. Francis's comment here about using and
throwing away is a clear link to the denunciation of the "throwaway culture"
in his encyclical *Laudato Si'* (May 24, 2015). See especially paragraphs 16, 22, and
43 of that document. In a general audience on March 4, 2015, Francis lamented
the effects of the throwaway culture on the elderly: "It's brutal to see how the
elderly are thrown away, it is a brutal thing, it is a sin! No one dares to say it
openly, but it's done! There is something vile in this *adherence to the throw-away
culture.*" See https://w2.vatican.va/content/francesco/en/audiences/2015
/documents/papa-francesco_20150304_udienza-generale.html. Mutatis mutan-
dis, this principle applies to "affective relationships."

12. Pope Francis, "Many Sacramental Marriages Are Null," *Origins* 46, no. 12
(July 28, 2016): 184–98 at 188. The address was given on June 16, 2016. On the
same page, Francis laments the influence of a "culture of the provisional." Richard
Gaillardetz had made a similar exculpatory point in 2007: "Many of the difficulties
that couples face in remaining faithful to their marriage commitment are not due
to any moral failing but are rather the consequence of living in a culture that is
inhospitable to keeping commitments of any kind." Gaillardetz, *A Daring Promise:
A Spirituality of Christian Marriage* (Liguori, MO: Liguori/Triumph, 2007), xi.

13. Burger King's "Have It Your Way" campaign ran from 1974–2014. See
"Burger King changes slogan to 'Be Your Way' after four decades of 'Have It
Your Way'" *New York Daily News* (May 19, 2014), http://www.nydailynews
.com/life-style/eats/burger-king-slogan-article-1.1798278.

no virtue on Madison Avenue. Sociologist Juliet Schor writes that "[in 1929] the general director of General Motors' Research Labs, Charles Kettering, stated the matter baldly: business needs to create a 'dissatisfied consumer'; its mission is 'the organized creation of dissatisfaction.' Kettering led the way by introducing annual model changes for GM cars—planned obsolescence designed to make the consumer discontented with what he or she already had."[14] Ever ready to cater to dissatisfied consumers, entrepreneurs in 2002 launched AshleyMadison.com, a dating website promising discreet connections to those seeking extramarital affairs, with the slogan "Life is short. Have an Affair."

These more or less overt attempts to generate or appeal to a sense of dissatisfaction are certainly worthy of note but they are only part of the story; they do not take place in an otherwise neutral cultural environment. Among others, Frederic de Coninck has pointed out that trends in the workforce have for some time undermined notions of commitment on the part of one's employer, generating uncertainty among employees. This development, he argues, "is supported by an ideology that wants each person to become a combatant in an uncertain and fluctuating universe, relying only on himself/herself."[15] Having to "prove oneself constantly" in the spheres of work, friends, and intimates creates "a burden that crushes one."[16] In other words, what is at issue here is not merely social cultivation of discontent but anxiety about when or if the other (one's employer, one's friends, one's intimate partner) might jump ship first. Continuity is hard to come by, and, as Kathleen Fischer and Thomas Hart suggest, this instability has consequences even for the willingness to undertake marriage in the first place, arguing that "to live in the West today is to be accustomed to moving geographically, to holding a succession of jobs,

---

14. Juliet Schor, *The Overworked American* (New York: Basic, 1991), 120. Schor's source here is Charles F. Kettering, "Keep the Consumer Dissatisfied," *Nation's Business* (January 1929); the line about organized creation of dissatisfaction is from Roland Marchand, *Advertising the American Dream: Making Way for Modernity* (Berkeley, CA: University of California Press, 1985), 156.

15. Frederic de Coninck, "Le défi de la fidélité dans une société dominée par le temps court," *Foi et vie* 109, no. 5 (2010): 26–34 at 29. My translation.

16. Ibid., 29. My translation.

to relating to a changing circle of friends, to being bombarded with a confusing variety of philosophies and values. Having learned to expect and live flexibly with change, many people experience a strong reluctance to enter into a lifetime commitment to another individual in marriage."[17] Certainly the number of Catholic weddings is falling. Citing statistics from the *Official Catholic Directory*, one recent study found that "since 1985 the US Catholic population that is connected to a parish has grown by 30 percent, but Catholic marriages are *down* by 57 percent."[18]

One alternative, of course, is the choice to merely cohabit. Writing in 1981, Jo McGowan had observed that merely cohabiting implied "that the central relationship of one's life is nobody's business but one's own. To live together is a decision reached privately and put into motion alone."[19] Cohabiting is a phenomenon connected to consumer culture not only insofar as it lacks permanence but also insofar as one's choice of partner is a private choice, not unlike one's decision to buy a yellow toaster rather than a blue toaster or to have pizza for dinner instead of burritos. The US bishops were correct in 2009 when they asserted in *Marriage: Love and Life in the Divine Plan* that "at the heart of cohabitation lies a reluctance or refusal to make a public, permanent commitment."[20] Yet that sixty-page document makes only

17. Kathleen Fischer and Thomas Hart, "The Contemporary Setting for Marriage: Sociobehavioral Insights," in *Alternative Futures for Worship*, vol. 5: *Christian Marriage*, ed. Bernard Cooke (Collegeville, MN: Liturgical Press, 1987), 18–19.

18. Charles E. Zech et al., *Catholic Parishes of the 21st Century* (New York: Oxford University Press, 2017), 142.

19. Jo McGowan, "Marriage Versus Just Living Together," *Commonweal* 108, no. 5 (March 13, 1981): 142–45 at 143.

20. United States Conference of Catholic Bishops, *Marriage: Love and Life in the Divine Plan* (November 17, 2009), 27. In 2000, the Pontifical Council for the Family had argued that some "persons who live together justify this choice because of economic reasons or to avoid legal difficulties. The real motives are often much deeper. In using this type of pretext, there is often an underlying mentality that gives little value to sexuality. This is influenced more or less by pragmatism and hedonism, as well as by a conception of love detached from any responsibility." Citation from Pontifical Council for the Family, *Family, Marriage, and 'De Facto' Unions* (July 26, 2000) 5. Linking consumerism and hedonism is easy enough but I am not sure that it is helpful to refer to economic factors as in all cases a "pretext."

two references to consumerism and neither reference concerns cohabitation or indeed any respect in which consumer culture forms persons for marriage.[21]

Despite the silence of the US bishops in their 2009 document, it is clear that consumer culture and the rugged economic individualism that accompanies it are associated with baneful influences on the formation of persons for marriage. So, then, according to consumer culture, what is a marriage about? To that question we turn.

III. A Display of Self

The website Brides.com offers advice to brides interested in religious wedding ceremonies. According to one source, the first question guests will ask concerns the length of the ceremony.[22] On the same website, Erin Celletti advises that parish officials might have objections to strapless gowns.[23] Celletti also states

---

See Fenaba Addo, "Debt, Cohabitation, and Marriage in Young Adulthood," *Demography* 51 (2014): 1677–1701; Jamaal Abdul-Alim, "Student Debt is Causing New Graduates to Delay Making Major Life Moves," *Diverse Issues in Higher Education* 33, no. 10 (June 16, 2016): 8. Addo finds that "credit card debt is positively associated with cohabitation for men and women" (1677), and Abdul-Amin reports on a recent survey that found 49 percent of respondents "would delay engagement or marriage because of their own debt" and 33 percent of respondents "would be reluctant to marry someone who was also repaying loans." I will return to the question of consumerism and hedonism in the chapter on holy orders.

21. *Marriage: Love and Life in the Divine Plan* refers to a consumer mentality regarding procuring children via in vitro fertilization (20) and to "consumer-oriented versions of sex" (46) that set impossibly high standards for delights in bed. The 2000 Vatican document *Family, Marriage, and 'De Facto' Unions* does not mention consumer culture at all nor does *Preparation for Marriage*, a 1996 document also issued by the Pontifical Council for the Family.

22. See Jaimie Mackey, "What Do We Need to Tell Guests Before Our Religious Wedding Ceremony?," *Brides*, June 18, 2016, http://www.brides.com/story/religious-wedding-ceremony-what-to-tell-guests.

23. Erin Celletti, "6 Essential Details about Getting Married in a Catholic Church," *Brides*, February 14, 2017, http://www.brides.com/story/essential-details-getting-married-catholic-church. Though standards of decorum may vary from parish to parish, there are in fact no rubrics in either the 1969 *Rite of Marriage* or the revised 2016 *Order of Celebrating Matrimony* concerning what the bride and groom may or must wear.

that "many times the Catholic Church will request that the maid or matron of honor and best man be of the Catholic faith," indicating that either Celletti or the parishes she investigated are unaware of the Vatican policy that members of "other Churches or ecclesial Communities may be witnesses at the celebration of marriage in a Catholic church."[24]

As much as the warning about strapless gowns misses the mark about the meaning and significance of a Catholic wedding, Celletti's comment is quite instructive for our current purposes. The wedding is about how the couple (but especially the bride) puts on a display of self. Alison Winch and Anna Webster provide a glimpse of the bewildering array of options presented to couples on a wedding website based in the United Kingdom:

> A . . . salient feature of [Confetti.co.uk] is the abundance of consumer options and its attendant niches, including: wedding dresses and fashions, venues, cakes, florists, hen and stag dos, honeymoons, weddings abroad, invitations and stationery, brides, maids and mothers, reception, table top, favours, personalized products, wedding gifts, confetti, make up and beauty, photographers and cars. Within each category there are hundreds of further options to choose from. Search under stationery and there are 20 professionally printed items, 187 blank cards and envelopes, 88 trims and bows, 81 ribbons and wraps, 120 table planning options, 27 craft paper items, 5 pens and glue and 20 invitation kits and tags.[25]

Among the many items listed by Winch and Webster, the wedding gown of course occupies a primary place. So much is this the case that, according to Rebecca Mead, "Kleinfeld, the storied

---

24. Celletti, "6 Essential Details"; the Vatican policy is taken from the Pontifical Council for Promoting Christian Unity, *Directory for the Application of Principles and Norms on Ecumenism* (March 25, 1993) 128, 136, http://www.vatican.va/roman_curia/pontifical_councils/chrstuni/documents/rc_pc_chrstuni_doc_25031993_principles-and-norms-on-ecumenism_en.html.

25. Alison Winch and Anna Webster, "Here Comes the Brand: Wedding Media and the Management of Transformation," *Continuum: Journal of Media and Cultural Studies* 26, no. 1 (February 2012): 51–59 at 53.

New York wedding-dress emporium, greets women who make an appointment with a letter announcing, 'We believe the day you choose your wedding gown should be as joyful and memorable as the day you wear it.' "[26] Cele Otnes and Elizabeth Pleck write of the "talismanic power of the wedding gown."[27] In her study of the significance of wedding gowns, Susanne Friese observed that "the participants wanted to express themselves and their individuality in the choice of their dress . . . finding something that would invoke their own sense of identity."[28] Participants in the study offered comments such as "I can see myself in it. I didn't feel weird in the dress," "It looked like it said Lydia all over it," and "The marriages I attended recently, or people I talked to, I think almost all of them chose their dresses, I mean, me included, 'cos that's what we wanted—to show ourselves."[29] Fascination with wedding gowns has led to the long-running television program *Say Yes to the Dress* and even a spin-off series, *Say Yes to the Dress: Bridesmaids*, that lasted four seasons. The desire to fit into one's dress, along with the general desire to look one's best on the day of one's wedding has spawned a bridal boot camp industry, with crash courses in physical fitness, nutrition, and weight loss.[30]

Yet the list compiled by Winch and Webster contains many other items and choices as well. To assist couples (especially brides) with the task of navigating these seas, in 2003 the Madison Avenue

26. Mead, *One Perfect Day*, 77.

27. Otnes and Pleck, *Cinderella Dreams*, 101. Otnes and Pleck point out that "[bridal] salons in Canada, and even the bridal sections of department stores in that country, request that potential clients and their entourages remove their shoes and leave them at the door before entering the salon" (97). The parallel with Moses at the burning bush (Exod 3:5) is striking and disconcerting.

28. Susanne Friese, "The Wedding Dress: From Use Value to Sacred Object," in *Through the Wardrobe: Women's Relationships with Their Clothes*, ed. Ali Guy, Eileen Green, and Maura Banim (Oxford: Berg, 2001), 63.

29. Ibid.

30. Brides.com identifies one such program clocking in at $4040 for a week of training at Lake Austin Resort in Austin, TX. Staff Author, "The Best Bridal Boot Camps," *Brides*, October 3, 2012, http://www.brides.com/gallery/best-bridal -boot-camps-wedding-fitness.

Business Improvement District and Condé Nast (publisher of many bridal magazines) arranged the "Wedding March," which provided each attendee with an opportunity to "get her MBA in getting married."[31] Those who view such training as useful reflect a situation in which the to-do list supplied for would-be brides by *Brides* expanded from twenty-one tasks in 1959 to forty-seven tasks just eleven years later.[32] One way to appreciate at least some of the chores of preparing a wedding is to look briefly at the celebrity wedding of Trista Rehn and Ryan Sutter, broadcast by the ABC television network in December 2003. Renée Sgroi offers this synopsis, noting the services of a wedding planner:

> First, Trista visits with wedding planner Mindy Weiss. Weiss, Trista tells viewers, has planned weddings for celebrities including Adam Sandler and Gwen Stefani. Next, Trista, Ryan, and Weiss visit florist Mark's Garden, where they see tables decorated with elaborate floral arrangements, and discuss their plans for the wedding. They then make their way to Lenox, where Trista and Ryan meet with a designer to have their own personalized china designed. At Lair and Black, Trista and Ryan are shown examples of specialized engagement and wedding invitations created for them. . . . After Lair and Black, Trista and Ryan are seen at Perfect Endings, where they sample various decadent cakes. Following the cake tasting, the couple meets with a designer at Tacori, the jewelry makers, where they will plan their own wedding bands. In the next sequence, Trista and Ryan, along with Weiss, examine the Villa at Rancho Lodge, where the wedding and reception will occur. . . . Next, Trista and her mother visit designer studio Badgely Mischka. The two are treated to a fashion show of bridal gowns, as they discuss the possibilities for Trista's own dress. At Amsale, Trista and

31. Mead, *One Perfect Day*, 15. The MBA reference was made by Peter K. Hunsinger, then the president of Condé Nast Bridal Group. That Hunsinger judged such a reference to be apt indicates that marriage and money are indeed entangled!

32. See Otnes and Pleck, *Cinderella Dreams*, 61. The authors point out that the timetable recommended by *Brides* also expanded from two months before the wedding in 1959 to six months before the wedding in 1970. The authors do not mention whether the list has been updated since 1970.

her bridesmaids choose the bridesmaid dresses, while the men try on tuxedos at Kenneth Cole. . . . The episode ends with one final shopping sequence, where Trista and Ryan invest in dance lessons from the "Dance Doctor," in preparation for their wedding.[33]

Sgroi argues that "the ways in which these products are personalized to their specifications, suggests that the choices they make for the wedding are significant because these choices speak to the couple's identities and individualism," adding that "whether or not viewers wish—or have the economic means—to emulate *Trista and Ryan's Wedding* perhaps matters less than the central point made through the attention to minute details: that individuality, taste, personality, and identity are expressed as a function of consumer choice."[34] Wedding planner Colin Cowie puts it this way: "Your wedding is not just another big party; it is your opportunity to make a statement of style to your family and friends and your new family and friends . . . [so] everything you do should be an expression of self. . . . My advice to the bride is, be guided by your own sense of style. So long as you are not offending anyone and your personality is shining through, then embrace that idea to the fullest."[35]

It is little wonder, then, that Otnes and Pleck argue that "the greatest fear of the bride and groom on their wedding day is not that their marriage will end in divorce . . . but that they will stage an event unworthy of prolonged (and positive) discussion among family members and friends."[36] Attention is directed to planning the *wedding* perhaps at the expense of planning for marriage. One

---

33. Renée Sgroi, "Consuming the Reality TV Wedding," *Ethnologies* 28, no. 2 (2006): 113–31 at 120.

34. Ibid., 123. The estimated cost of this wedding was $5,160,973 (in 2018 dollars). That such celebrity weddings have at least some impact on wedding trends is supported by Otnes and Pleck, who noted that in response to demand after the royal wedding of Prince Charles and Lady Diana Spencer in 1981, a new trade group was formed (the Association of Bridal Consultants). See Otnes and Pleck, *Cinderella Dreams*, 50.

35. Quoted in Mead, *One Perfect Day*, 119.

36. Otnes and Pleck, *Cinderella Dreams*, 268.

trade publication even warned retailers about brides who are more intent on preparing for their marriage than they are on preparing for their wedding.[37] On the other hand, a bride in the study conducted by Susanne Friese confessed that "I had the wedding organized, piece of cake, really no problem . . . but I am married now, OOPS, I haven't planned on that part."[38] Colin Cowie, the wedding planner, flatly denied interest in the post-wedding day fates of the couples he has worked with. " 'I don't really care,' he said. 'I just get 'em down the aisle.' "[39]

IV. Marriages in Ecclesial Context

Colin Cowie's remark is instructive about a key phenomenon associated with consumerism, namely, the commodified abstraction of goods and services from the conditions under which they were produced or in which they originally had meaning. For Cowie, weddings are quite literally divorced from the marriages to which they give rise. Cowie goes so far as to say that "there are no rules today in weddings,"[40] and thus all that matters is the push to display one's own style and to produce a unique wedding experience.[41] Yet there is pushback with regard to the pressure to be unique. An unscientific study conducted by *US Catholic* in 2006 found that for 72 percent of respondents "the focus on a perfect, unique wedding ceremony and reception detracts from the true meaning of the sacrament and works at cross-purposes to what the church teaches about marriage."[42] Here, then, I turn to the notion of an ecclesially and socially rooted self, grounded in the full sacramental life of the church, and to the notion of marriage as entailing a mission in the world.

37. See Mead, *One Perfect Day*, 56.
38. Friese, "A Consumer Good in the Ritual Process," 55.
39. Quoted in Mead, *One Perfect Day*, 122.
40. Quoted in ibid., 119.
41. See also the discussion of uniqueness in Francien Broekhuizen and Adrienne Evans, "Pain, Pleasure, and Bridal Beauty: Mapping Postfeminist Bridal Perfection," *Journal of Gender Studies* 25, no. 3 (2016): 335–48.
42. Peg Conway, "A Modest Wedding Proposal," *U.S. Catholic* 71, no. 11 (November 2006): 24–28 at 27.

Speaking at a general audience in May 2015, Pope Francis remarked that "marriage is first and foremost the discovery of a call from God."[43] Christian marriage, then, is the faith-filled response to this call. In the words of Michael Lawler, "it is not the naked intention to marry, even to marry in some religious rite, that makes valid Christian sacrament. It is the Christian faith-informed intention to marry in a ritual that publicly proclaims to the spouses, to the Church, and to the world not only 'I love you,' but also 'I love you in Christ and in his Church.' That active and faith-informed proclamation creates not only a marriage but specifically a Christian marriage."[44] To "love you in Christ and in his Church" is a matter not only of the unfolding of each spouse's baptismal call to holiness,[45] but of situating one's marriage in the arc of salvation history itself. Hence it is important to note that *Sacrosanctum Concilium* 78 calls for readings from Scripture during the celebration of a wedding, regardless of whether the celebration takes place in the context of a Mass.[46] Those who gather for the wedding recall their place in the history of God's people. Indeed, the preconciliar form of the nuptial blessing made specific reference to the bride taking her place in a line of biblical figures: "Let her ever follow

43. Pope Francis, General Audience, May 27, 2015, https://w2.vatican.va/content/francesco/en/audiences/2015/documents/papa-francesco_20150527_udienza-generale.html.

44. Michael Lawler, *Marriage in the Catholic Church: Disputed Questions* (Collegeville, MN: Liturgical Press, 2002), 53.

45. William P. Roberts writes: "The sacramental life of Christian marriage ought to be chosen as a particular way in which the couple see they can best grow in Christian holiness and participate in Christ's mission. In marriage they renew their baptismal commitment and give it new direction." William P. Roberts, "Toward a Post-Vatican II Spirituality of Marriage," in *Marriage*, Readings in Moral Theology 15, ed. Charles E. Curran and Julie Hanlon Rubio (New York: Paulist, 2009), 129. See also *Lumen Gentium* 11, 41; *Gaudium et Spes* 49; Jorge Medina Estévez, *Marriage*, Sacrament Series (Washington, DC: USCCB, 2015), 12.

46. Paul Turner observes that at least between the time of Trent and the time of the Second Vatican Council, "Catholic weddings included no readings from Scripture." All weddings took place outside of Mass, even though a Mass may have followed. For Turner's comments, see Paul Turner, *Inseparable Love: A Commentary on* The Order of Celebrating Matrimony *in the Catholic Church* (Collegeville, MN: Liturgical Press, 2016), xvii.

the model of holy women—dear to her husband like Rachel, wise like Rebecca, long-lived and faithful like Sarah."[47] The blessing currently in use alludes to the "example of those holy women whose praises are sung in Scripture";[48] it is both less specific and more inclusive.

A key change to the nuptial blessing came about in the English-speaking world with the promulgation of the third edition of the Roman Missal in 2011. For the first time, this blessing contained a clear epiclesis: "Look now with favor on these your servants, joined together in Marriage, who ask to be strengthened by your blessing. Send down on them the grace of the Holy Spirit and pour your love into their hearts, that they may remain faithful in the Marriage covenant."[49] This revision brings the celebration of matrimony into line with other sacramental rituals of the church that feature the structure anamnesis/epiclesis. Prior to the revision, Mark Searle and Kenneth Stevenson had offered this analysis:

> The role of remembering or anamnesis is to situate this marriage in a larger context of God's creative and redemptive work, to identify these two people with the couples who flit across the history of that work as recorded in the Scriptures, and to turn them into icons of the redeeming Christ and redeemed humanity. . . . Out of anamnesis flows intercession, as the memory of God's economy prompts the request for help on behalf of those who are to be participant in it.

---

47. Excerpt from the nuptial blessing in *The Roman Ritual in Latin and English with Rubrics and Plainchant Notation* vol. 1: *The Sacraments and Processions,* ed. Philip T. Weller (Boonville, NY: Preserving Christian Publications, 2016), 469. Wives of the patriarchs are found in nuptial blessings as early as the one contained in the Veronese/Leonine Sacramentary from the sixth century. See *Documents of the Marriage Liturgy,* 40–44.

48. 2016 Order of Celebrating Matrimony 74. All citations of the 2016 order will be from *The Order of Celebrating Matrimony* (Collegeville, MN: Liturgical Press, 2016).

49. *The Roman Missal, Third Typical Edition* 1181. See also Order of Celebrating Matrimony 74 and 105, which have this same phrasing. The nuptial blessings in paragraphs 207 and 209 also invoke the Holy Spirit, but with different wording. For the significance of the epiclesis, see also Turner, *Inseparable Love,* 135–36.

This pattern is common enough, but in the solemn blessings of the Roman Rite—the blessing of the font, the prayer of ordination, the Eucharistic prayer—the first and chief blessing that is invoked is the descent of the Holy Spirit upon the action of the Church, to ensure that the sacramental sign be capable of effecting what it signifies. The nuptial blessing is the equivalent prayer of the marriage rite and becomes the central element in the nuptial liturgies of the West. Yet, for all its similarities to the other solemn prayers, it passes directly from *anamnesis* to intercession without an *epiclesis* invoking the Spirit.[50]

Correcting this omission, the new blessing gives to the rite of marriage an anamnesis/epiclesis structure that recalls God's saving deeds and asks that God continue to be a saving God in the present context, in this case by empowering the newly married couple to be a sacramental sign to all by remaining faithful to each other with the very power and vitality of the Holy Spirit. The wedding ceremony and the marriage it seals is situated in the wide scope of God's saving plan, which, as the *Catechism of the Catholic Church* reminds its readers, "begins with the creation of man and woman in the image and likeness of God and concludes with a vision of the wedding-feast of the Lamb."[51]

As is the case with all the sacraments, the sacrament of marriage presupposes and requires faith.[52] Affiliation with the Christian faith and participation in Christian living begins in baptism, is sealed in confirmation, and reaches its fullness in the Eucharist. If marriage is abstracted from its relationship to these other sacraments, especially baptism and Eucharist, then the meaning of marriage is subject to distortion. For this reason, Karl Lehmann has written that "through baptism, a person is incorporated into the Church of Jesus Christ. . . . It is above all an ontological and existential incorporation into the Body of Christ. In consequence, two baptized persons who contract marriage are not entitled to decide on their

---

50. *Documents of the Marriage Liturgy*, 263–64.

51. *Catechism of the Catholic Church* 1603.

52. See the Order of Celebrating Matrimony 16. See also *Sacrosanctum Concilium* 59.

own what their union is to mean and what it is to be."[53] The sacrament of marriage is not a free-floating signifier; I will be returning to this point, but for the moment I wish merely to take note of a summary offered by Pope John Paul II: "Christian marriage, like the other sacraments, 'whose purpose is to sanctify people, to build up the body of Christ, and finally, to give worship to God,' is in itself a liturgical action glorifying God in Jesus Christ and in the Church. By celebrating it, Christian spouses profess their gratitude to God for the sublime gift bestowed on them of being able to live in their married and family lives the very love of God for people and that of the Lord Jesus for the Church, His bride."[54]

Besides being grounded in their baptisms, the spouses are also to find the meaning of their marriage grounded in Eucharist. The *Catechism of the Catholic Church* points out that "in the Latin Rite the celebration of marriage between two Catholic faithful normally takes place during Holy Mass, because of the connection of all the sacraments with the Paschal mystery of Christ . . . . It is therefore fitting that the spouses should seal their consent to give themselves to each other through the offering of their own lives by uniting it to the offering of Christ for his Church made present in the Eucharistic sacrifice."[55] Participation in the Eucharist is a fitting capstone for a wedding but with the US bishops it must be stressed that "marriage *continually* sends the believing Catholic back again to the Eucharist."[56] The bishops observe that the mutual love of the spouses is a recurrent inducement to gratitude and

53. Karl Lehmann, "The Sacramentality of Christian Marriage: The Bond between Baptism, Faith, and Marriage," in *Contemporary Perspectives on Christian Marriage: Propositions and Papers from the International Theological Commission*, ed. Richard Malone and John Connery (Chicago: Loyola University Press, 1984), 106. See also the Order of Celebrating Matrimony 7; Cormac Burke, *The Theology of Marriage: Personalism, Doctrine, and Canon Law* (Washington, DC: Catholic University of America Press, 2015), 6.

54. John Paul II, apostolic exhortation *Familiaris Consortio* (November 22, 1981) 56. The phrase in quotes is taken from *Sacrosanctum Concilium* 59.

55. *Catechism of the Catholic Church* 1521. See also the Order of Celebrating Matrimony 35.

56. *Marriage: Love and Life in the Divine Plan*, 55 (emphasis added).

the Eucharist *is* "thanksgiving."[57] The Pontifical Council for the Family contends that "the Eucharist develops the affective love proper to marriage in daily giving to one's spouse and children."[58] *Lumen Gentium* points out that eucharistic celebration expresses and reinforces the holiness of all of life. Speaking of the laity, the document notes that "all their works, if accomplished in the Spirit, become spiritual sacrifices acceptable to God through Jesus Christ: their prayers and apostolic undertakings, family and married life, daily work, relaxation of mind and body, even the hardships of life if patiently borne (see 1 Pet 2:5). In the celebration of the Eucharist, these are offered to the Father along with the body of the Lord. And so, worshipping everywhere by their holy actions, the laity consecrate the world itself to God."[59] Eucharist also provides a link to the claim that Christian existence—including married Christian existence—entails having a mission in the world. In *Amoris Laetitia*, Francis teaches that "the celebration of the Eucharist thus becomes a constant summons for everyone 'to examine himself or herself,' to open the doors of the family to greater fellowship with the underprivileged, and in this way to receive the sacrament of that eucharistic love which makes us one body."[60]

An important illustration of this sense of mission attached explicitly to marriage is found in one option for the solemn blessing that concludes the celebration of the sacrament regardless of whether the context is a Mass. The blessing in question contains these lines: "May you be witnesses in the world to God's charity, so that the afflicted and needy who have known your kindness may one day receive you thankfully into the eternal dwelling of God."[61] What is at issue here is that the love of the couple, though

---

57. Ibid., 55.

58. *Preparation for the Sacrament of Marriage*, 41

59. *Lumen Gentium* 34. It is worth noting that *Familiaris Consortio* 56 also makes explicit reference to *Lumen Gentium* 34 in a passage not quoted in this book.

60. Francis, *Amoris Laetitia* 186. The phrase in quotes is drawn from 1 Cor 11:28, Paul's critique of eucharistic worship in Corinth.

61. 2016 Order of Celebrating Matrimony 77. The corresponding text in the 1969 rite was perhaps stronger: "May you always bear witness to the love of God in this world so that the afflicted and the needy *will find in you* generous friends, and welcome you into the joys of heaven." Citation from (1969) Rite

certainly exclusive in one sense, is not meant to curve in on itself. Karl Rahner puts its well: "Marriage is not the act in which two individuals come together to form a 'we,' a relationship in which they set themselves apart from the 'all' and close themselves against this. Rather it is the act in which a 'we' is constituted which opens itself lovingly precisely to *all*."[62] Francis has emphasized this point more than once: "A family that is closed in on itself is like a contradiction, a mortification of the promise that gave birth to it and enables it to live. Never forget: the identity of a family is always a promise that expands, and it expands to the whole family and also to all of humanity."[63] Earlier, we encountered Michael Lawler's claims about brides and grooms when they say "I love you in Christ and in his Church." For Francis, to thus marry in the Lord "entails a missionary dimension, which means having at heart the willingness to be a medium for God's blessing and for the Lord's grace to all."[64] In *Familiaris Consortio*, John Paul II had this

---

of Marriage 125 (emphasis added). See also the 1969 Rite of Marriage 37 for a reference to the couple's being "willing to help and comfort all who come" to them in need. Paragraph 37 was approved for particular use in the United States. The US bishops draw on paragraph 125 of the 1969 rite in their 2009 document on marriage: "Their family, with its heightened awareness of human dignity, reaches out in hospitality to the poor and to anyone in need, in keeping with the words of the final blessing from the ritual of weddings." *Marriage: Love and Life in the Divine Plan*, 52.

62. Karl Rahner, "Marriage as a Sacrament," in *Theological Investigations*, vol. 10: *Writings of 1965–67* (London: Darton, Longman & Todd, 1973), 207. Rahner pursues this topic for the next few pages. For other comments on the temptation to curve in and withdraw, see Walter Kasper, *Theology of Christian Marriage*, trans. David Smith (New York: Crossroad, 1980), 10–11; *Preparation for the Sacrament of Marriage*, 38; United States Conference of Catholic Bishops, *A Family Perspective in Church and Society: Tenth Anniversary Edition* (Washington, DC: United States Catholic Conference, 1998) 18.

63. Francis, General Audience, October 21, 2015, https://w2.vatican.va /content/francesco/en/audiences/2015/documents/papa-francesco_20151021 _udienza-generale.html. See also *Amoris Laetitia* 181, 187.

64. Francis, General Audience, May 6, 2015, https://w2.vatican.va/content /francesco/en/audiences/2015/documents/papa-francesco_20150506_udienza -generale.html. In *Amoris Laetitia*, released two months before this audience, Francis had written that "a married couple who experience the power of love know that this love is called to bind the wounds of the outcast, to foster a cul-

to say about marriage and mission: "The Christian family's faith and evangelizing mission also possesses [a] catholic missionary inspiration. The sacrament of marriage takes up and reproposes the task of defending and spreading the faith, a task that has its roots in baptism and confirmation, and makes Christian married couples and parents witnesses of Christ 'to the end of the earth,' missionaries, in the true and proper sense, of love and life."[65] This sense of mission finds important expression in the revised *Rituel romain de la célébration du mariage,* the Rite of Marriage for use in French-speaking Canada. That *rituel* offers two forms for the "questions before the consent" in paragraphs 71 and 72. (The 2016 English Order of Celebrating Matrimony 60 offers only one option.) In each French-language form, there is a concluding optional question that the presider may ask the couple: "Are you prepared to accept together your mission as Christians in the world and in the Church?" The couple responds: "Yes."[66] There is no equivalent question in the English-language edition of the rite, nor in the 1969 French-language rite.

---

ture of encounter and to fight for justice" (183). See also the comments on the "ecstatic" quality of married love in Benedict XVI, Encyclical Letter on Christian Love (*Deus Caritas Est,* December 25, 2005) 6; and on the other-directedness of married love in Donald L. Gelpi, *Committed Worship: A Sacramental Theology for Converting Christians,* vol. 2: *The Sacraments of Ongoing Conversion* (Collegeville, MN: Liturgical Press, 1993), 41.

65. John Paul II, *Familiaris Consortio* 54. This passage draws on *Lumen Gentium* 11 for its reference to baptism and confirmation and on Acts 1:8 for its reference to the ends of the earth. The 2016 Order of Celebrating Matrimony 18 strongly recommends but not does not absolutely require that the spouses be confirmed prior to their wedding. For reasons of space the present chapter will not address the issue of confirmation. George Bebawi claims that Cyril of Alexandria also related marriage to the task of spreading the good news of the resurrection in *Exegesis eis to kata Ioannan Euangelion,* trans. and ed. Edward Pusey (Oxford: Clarendon Press, 1872), 3:36. My research could not confirm this claim. See George Bebawi, "The Crown of Life: An Orthodox Perspective," *Ecumenical Review* 34, no. 3 (1982): 263–70 at 267.

66. Rituel romain de la celebration du mariage 71 in *Rituel romain de la célébration du mariage* (Ottawa: Conférence des évêques du Canada, 2011). My translation. There is no equivalent question in *Rituel pour la célébration du mariage à l'usage des dioceses de France* (Paris: Brepols, 1969).

Notably, the Coptic wedding rite also expresses a sense of mission. During the rite, the couple are anointed with oil. The oil is blessed with this prayer:

> Master and Lord,
> God and ruler of all that is,
> Father of our Lord,
> God and Savior, Jesus Christ.
> You anointed priests, kings and prophets
> with fresh olive oil.
> We pray and beseech you, Lord,
> lover of humankind,
> you who are good,
> to pour out your blessing upon this oil
> Let it be an oil of sanctification for your servants.
> Amen.
> A weapon of truth.
> Amen.
> And of justice.
> Amen.[67]

The Copts, and Churches of the East generally, celebrate a rite of crowning the bride and groom as part of the wedding rite. These crowns recall the crown of martyrdom (i.e., of giving witness to one's faith[68]) as well as the notion of being king and queen of creation after the pattern of Adam and Eve.[69] A mission indeed.

V. Conclusion

Consumer culture abstracts a wedding from its original context of meaning. Consumer culture seeks to confer meaning on a wedding in and through the use and consumption of consumer goods.

---

67. "The Coptic Rite" in *Documents of the Marriage Liturgy*, 92.

68. See *An Orthodox Prayer Book*, trans. John von Holzhausen and Michael Gelsinger (Brookline, MA: Holy Cross Orthodox Press, 1977), 86, 94.

69. See "Marriage Rites as Documents of Faith," in *Documents of the Marriage Liturgy*, 262–63. See also Alexander Schmemann, *For the Life of the World* (Crestwood, NY: St. Vladimir's Seminary, 1963), 89–91.

Responding to these challenges will involve at least catechesis and an emphasis on simplicity.

Back in 1981, John Paul II had called for a three-stage preparation for marriage patterned in broad strokes after the three-stage process employed in the Rite of Christian Initiation of Adults. Identifying these stages as times of remote, proximate, and immediate preparation, he wrote:

> Remote preparation begins in early childhood, in that wise family training which leads children to discover themselves as being endowed with a rich and complex psychology and with a particular personality with its own strengths and weaknesses. It is the period when esteem for all authentic human values is instilled, both in interpersonal and in social relationships, with all that this signifies for the formation of character, for the control and right use of one's inclinations, for the manner of regarding and meeting people of the opposite sex, and so on. Also necessary, especially for Christians, is solid spiritual and catechetical formation that will show that marriage is a true vocation and mission, without excluding the possibility of the total gift of self to God in the vocation to the priestly or religious life.
>
> Upon this basis there will subsequently and gradually be built up the proximate preparation, which—from the suitable age and with adequate catechesis, as in a catechumenal process—involves a more specific preparation for the sacraments, as it were, a rediscovery of them. This renewed catechesis of young people and others preparing for Christian marriage is absolutely necessary in order that the sacrament may be celebrated and lived with the right moral and spiritual dispositions. The religious formation of young people should be integrated, at the right moment and in accordance with the various concrete requirements, with a preparation for life as a couple. This preparation will present marriage as an interpersonal relationship of a man and a woman that has to be continually developed, and it will encourage those concerned to study the nature of conjugal sexuality and responsible parenthood, with the essential medical and biological knowledge connected with it. It will also acquaint those concerned with correct methods for the education of children, and will assist them in gaining the basic requisites for

well-ordered family life, such as stable work, sufficient financial resources, sensible administration, notions of housekeeping.

Finally, one must not overlook preparation for the family apostolate, for fraternal solidarity and collaboration with other families, for active membership in groups, associations, movements and undertakings set up for the human and Christian benefit of the family.

The immediate preparation for the celebration of the sacrament of Matrimony should take place in the months and weeks immediately preceding the wedding, so as to give a new meaning, content and form to the so-called premarital enquiry required by Canon Law. This preparation is not only necessary in every case, but is also more urgently needed for engaged couples that still manifest shortcomings or difficulties in Christian doctrine and practice.[70]

Francis has also encouraged this "catechumenate" approach to marriage preparation.[71] However, while the US bishops in their 2005 *National Directory for Catechesis* teach that "the family is the most effective school for catechesis on Christian marriage and family life,"[72] that publication does not mention the three stages identified in 1981. Their 2009 document *Marriage: Love and Life in the Divine Plan*, does so however.[73]

What is clear, at any rate, is that the "rediscovery" of the sacraments called for by John Paul II has not yet arrived. No solution to the consumerist challenges to marriage will work if it does not include re-envisioning sacramental thought and practice as a whole. Karl Lehmann, whose remarks about baptismal incorporation into the Body of Christ were noted earlier, also wrote that his "remarks are not convincing unless one takes into account

70. John Paul II, *Familiaris Consortio* 66.

71. See Francis, *Amoris Laetitia* 206; Francis, Address to the Officials of the Tribunal of the Roman Rota for the Inauguration of the Judicial Year (Clementine Hall, January 21, 2017), http://w2.vatican.va/content/francesco/en/speeches/2017/january/documents/papa-francesco_20170121_anno-giudiziario-rota-romana.html.

72. United States Conference of Catholic Bishops, *National Directory for Catechesis* (Washington, DC: USCCB, 2005), 143.

73. *Marriage: Love and Life in the Divine Plan*, 44.

the original structure of baptism. Unfortunately, this structure is sometimes misconstrued by a ritualization of the sacrament, as well as by a doctrinalization of the word, and an externalizing perception which makes of baptism nothing more than a juridical sign of incorporation into the Church."[74] Concerning the connection between marriage and Eucharist, it is likely that most Catholics think in terms of the ban on receiving Communion that is applied to Catholics who divorce and remarry without an annulment,[75] but one wonders whether those deprived of Communion think about that one sacrament and not about how marriage and Eucharist refer back to each other.

At the same time, there are at least some couples who pursue commodified design-your-own weddings who yearn for a more fulsome context within which to ground their celebration. For example, as part of her research, Rebecca Mead interviewed freelance wedding officiant Joyce Gioia. For Gioia, according to Mead, a "wedding was an expression of the couple's inner spirituality, rather than of their submission to the spiritual authority of a larger institution. It was also an expression of their taste when it came to religious ritual—their selection among the array of elements Gioia could offer."[76] Yet Gioia could also tell Mead: "People say after my wedding ceremonies, 'I want to attend your services, where

74. Lehmann, "The Sacramentality of Christian Marriage," 106. See the chapter on baptism in the present volume for additional discussion of this sacrament.

75. In 2015, the United States Conference of Catholic Bishops published a seven-volume series on the sacraments. The volume on marriage runs about thirty-nine pages. The author, Cardinal Jorge Medina Estévez, discusses the ban on Communion for divorced and remarried Catholics in the third paragraph of this short book (6). He makes one passing reference to families attending Mass in one sentence (38–39). One wonders about the relative priorities of the author. Pope Francis's comments in chapter 8 of *Amoris Laetitia* concerning reception of Communion in the case of Catholics who divorce and remarry have drawn a great deal of attention. Treatment of that subject exceeds the scope of the present effort.

76. Mead, *One Perfect Day*, 136–37. It is worth noting that among the array of elements on offer from Gioia is an "Apache" wedding prayer whose authenticity dates to the 1950 Western film *Broken Arrow*. According to Mead, this prayer was penned by the movie's writers and has no connection at all to Apache belief or practice. See Mead, *One Perfect Day*, 131, 136.

is your church?' . . . I want to say, 'I don't have one. It is against my religion.' "[77] Though Mead's study did not control for religious affiliation, there is perhaps a lesson here about the importance of a larger institutional tradition for those seeking to marry.

One might consider here the example of the use of crowns, already noted above. George Bebawi observes that "the baptismal service in the Coptic and Syrian churches attaches considerable importance to crowns. . . . It is essential to understand that the similarity between the Eastern baptismal and marriage rites indicates an essential relationship between the two."[78] I am not necessarily suggesting that the Latin Rite of the Roman Catholic Church start using crowns in baptisms and weddings; I *am* suggesting that the Catholic Church find ways to make the connection between these sacraments clear.

As I turn to the question of simplicity, I do so again with a sense of the connection between baptism and marriage. Writing in North Africa in the early third century, Tertullian wrote the following on baptism:

> It is all very simple, without exterior show. No extraordinary setting is necessary and no expense. A person descends into the water and is sprinkled while a few words are said. That person comes up out of the water not much cleaner, if at all. It seems all the more incredible, then, that the result is eternal life.
>
> Believe me, it is quite different in the ceremonies, public or secret, in honour of false gods, for what raises their credibility and authority is the show, the preparation and the expense. What miserable incredulity is shown by denying God's simplicity and power.[79]

God's power and God's grace do not rely upon or require human grandeur. What this might mean for weddings Tertullian himself discussed in a treatise to his wife:

---

77. Ibid., 128.

78. George Bebawi, "The Crown of Life," 264, 267.

79. Tertullian, *On Baptism* 2 in *Wellsprings of Faith*, vol. 11: *A New Beginning: Tertullian, Cyril and Augustine on Baptism*, trans. Mary Dominique, Mary Bernard, D. Mary Groves, and Anthony Meredith (Trowbridge: Redwood Books, 1998), 4–5.

[God] it is who clothes the lilies of the field in such beauty; who feeds the birds of the air, though they labor not; who bids us not to be concerned about the morrow, what we shall eat or what we shall put on. He assures us that He knows what is necessary for each of His servants. And this, certainly, is not a mass of jeweled pendants, nor a surfeit of clothing, nor mules brought in from Gaul, nor porters from Germany. Such things do lend lustre to a wedding, but what is necessary for us is, rather, a sufficiency which is consistent with sobriety and modesty.[80]

Perhaps a century and a half later, Paulinus of Nola penned a lengthy ode on the occasion of a wedding. Among the most noteworthy passages for our purposes are the following:

Let our joy be sober and our prayers discreet.
Let the name of Christ echo everywhere
from the lips of his devoted people.
Let there be no dancing crowds in decorated streets,
nor strewing of the ground with leaves,
nor of the threshold with foliage.
Let there be no riotous parades
through a city where Christ dwells.[81]

Let there be no trays overflowing with useless gifts,
for character, not wealth, is the sign of true worth.
The holy wife of a bishop's son,
the spouse of a boy already consecrated,
must receive as dowry the light of life.
For her no garments tricked with gold or purple,
the splendor of God's grace will be her robe of gold.
Necklaces of motley jewels are not for her:
for she herself shall be a shining jewel
for the Lord her God.[82]

Someone who seeks a reputation by the way they dress
is only cheapened and devalued thereby.

---

80. Tertullian, *To His Wife* 1.4, in *Tertullian: Treatises on Marriage and Remarriage To His Wife, An Exhortation to Chastity, Monogamy*, Ancient Christian Writers 13, ed. and trans. William P. LeSaint (Westminster, MD: Newman, 1951), 16.
81. Paulinus of Nola, *Poem 25* in *Documents of the Marriage Liturgy*, 32.
82. Paulinus of Nola, *Poem 25* in ibid., 33.

> Such misconceived pursuits sorely blind the mind
> and the body decked in gaudiness coarsens the soul.
> Shamelessness fails to realise the foulness
> of garments which cheapen the wearer.[83]

One can also find cautions about extravagance in more recent church statements.[84] On the one hand, such cautions are an indication that the opposite is happening in practice. On the other hand, 86 percent of respondents in the 2006 survey conducted by *US Catholic* referenced earlier indicated that they "would welcome simpler, more sacramental wedding ceremonies and receptions" and more than half (55 percent) indicated that they had "been to a wedding that was so opulent I was uncomfortable."[85]

In addition to keeping outside wedding planners away from the wedding rite itself—a policy firmly recommended by the Episcopal Diocese of New York[86]—churches might also consider the question of liturgical vestment for the bride and groom. Peg Conway wrote in 2006: "Eschewing secular finery, the bride and groom would don a symbolic garment like an alb, the white robe worn by liturgical ministers, deacons, and priests. The wearing of such

---

83. Paulinus of Nola, *Poem 25* in ibid. For similar comments from antiquity, see John Chrysostom, *Homily 48*, 29–30 in *Homilies on Genesis*, The Fathers of the Church: A New Translation 87, trans. Robert C. Hill (Washington, DC: Catholic University of America Press, 1992), 40–41; can. 53 of the Synod of Laodicea in Philip Schaff and Henry Wace, eds., *Nicene and Post-Nicene Fathers of the Church*, Series II, vol. 14: *The Seven Ecumenical Councils* (Peabody, MA: Hendrickson, 2004), 156.

84. See John Paul II, *Familiaris Consortio* 67; Francis, *Amoris Laetitia* 212; and quite emphatically in *Preparation for the Sacrament of Marriage*, which addresses the issue in paragraphs 61, 62, and 67. The US bishops direct concern to this issue in "Ten Tips for Keeping Your Catholic Wedding Focused on Faith," *For Your Marriage*, http://www.foryourmarriage.org/catholic-marriage/planning -a-catholic-wedding/ceremony-options/. See also the remarks about wedding costs by the Episcopal Diocese of New York in "The Liturgical Commission on Marriage," https://www.dioceseny.org/administration/for-clergy/liturgical -and-sacramental/liturgical-commission/marriage/.

85. Conway, "A Modest Wedding Proposal," 26, 27.

86. "We suggest that they be forbidden to attend rehearsals and under no circumstances may questions about the liturgy be referred to them. The clergy of our church are the only wedding advisors we recognize." Episcopal Diocese of New York, "The Liturgical Commission on Marriage."

a vestment, which evokes Baptism, would locate marriage within the context of church life and stand in sharp contrast to cultural practices."[87] The use of albs would not only make the connection between baptism and marriage clear, but also point ahead to the white pall at funerals. Here, I turn to the *Order of Christian Funerals*: "If it is the custom in the local community, a pall may be placed over the coffin when it is received at the church. A reminder of the baptismal garment of the deceased, the pall is a sign of the Christian dignity of the person. The use of the pall also signifies that all are equal in the eyes of God. . . . Only Christian symbols may rest on or be placed near the coffin during the funeral liturgy. Any other symbols, for example, national flags, or flags or insignias of associations, have no place in the funeral liturgy."[88] The alb is also a liturgical garment and since the Catholic Church holds that the spouses minister the sacrament to each other,[89] the alb is fitting on these grounds as well. As noted above, the funeral pall has an equalizing element to it; so, too, would the use of albs in a wedding. Like its predecessor, the marriage rite of 2016 holds that "no favoritism be shown to private persons or classes of persons."[90]

87. Conway, "A Modest Wedding Proposal," 25.

88. Order of Christian Funerals 38.

89. See *Catechism of the Catholic Church* 1623. Kenneth W. Stevenson has pointed out that emphasis on the liturgical role of the couple can have unintended consequences: "Whatever may have been intended by making the couple the sole ministers of the sacrament, it is certainly true that many people today, including theologians, see in the isolation of consent something not only stark but also lacking in the ecclesial dimension. . . . So the *Praenotanda*'s insistence on the nuptial blessing is an important way of stressing the liturgical and ecclesial character of the sacrament, presided over by an ordained representative of the rest of the Church." Kenneth W. Stevenson, *To Join Together: The Rite of Marriage* (New York: Pueblo, 1987), 167. Stevenson is referring to paragraph 6 of the 1969 Rite of Marriage. The same insistence on the nuptial blessing is found in the 2016 Order of Celebrating Matrimony 35. It should be noted, however, that the 1983 *Code of Canon Law* makes provision in canon 1112 for bishops to permit lay persons to officiate at weddings in situations where there is a lack of priests and deacons. It should be noted as well that in the Orthodox Church and in the Byzantine and Syriac Churches in communion with Rome, it is the priest (and not the spouses) who is the minister.

90. 2016 Order of Celebrating Matrimony 31. See also the 1969 Rite of Marriage 9. Both passages refer to *Sacrosanctum Concilium* 32.

The question of venue is also a matter of equality. The *Code of Canon Law* specifies that "a marriage between Catholics or between a Catholic party and a non-Catholic baptized party is to be celebrated in a parish church. It can be celebrated in another church or oratory with the permission of the local ordinary or pastor."[91] It is the *Ceremonial of Bishops*, however, that clarifies why the venue should be a parish church: "To prevent his participation from bearing the mark of favoritism, or from being a mere sign of outward show, it should be the bishop's normal practice not to assist at marriages in a private chapel or home but in the cathedral or parish church. In this way the ecclesial character of the celebration of the sacrament will more surely stand out and the local community will have the opportunity to participate in the celebration."[92] The rite of marriage, even down to the venue, is not a free-floating signifier. It is not merely a family affair that happens to take place in a church building.[93] It is not a private occasion for display of self. It is, rather, an instantiation of the paschal mystery of Christ in the lives of the couple, who die to themselves and rise anew as effective signs of God's love.

In a variant of the axiom *lex orandi, lex credendi*, Rebecca Mead has written that "the American wedding—in all its excesses and all its sentimentality—tells us what principles we are all married to."[94] A wide and enriched catechesis about the sacraments and a renewed emphasis on liturgical simplicity in the wedding rite can begin the process of divorce from consumer excess and sentimentality.

91. *Code of Canon Law* 1118/1, http://www.vatican.va/archive/ENG1104/__P40 .HTM. The next line, 1118/2, notes that "the local ordinary can permit a marriage to be celebrated in another suitable place."

92. Ceremonial of Bishops 598 in *Ceremonial of Bishops* (Collegeville, MN: Liturgical Press, 1989).

93. See the concerns expressed about this sentiment in Paul Covino, "Christian Marriage: Sacramentality and Ritual Forms," in *Bodies of Worship: Explorations in Theory and Practice*, ed. Bruce Morrill (Collegeville, MN: Liturgical Press, 1999), 109.

94. Mead, *One Perfect Day*, 224.

Chapter Seven

HOLY ORDERS
AND CONSUMER CULTURE

I. Introduction

In his 1992 Post-Synodal Apostolic Exhortation on the Formation of Priests (*Pastores Dabo Vobis*), Pope John Paul II warned
about the impact of consumerism on religious vocations. He
wrote of children and young people as "prisoners of the fleeting
moment [who] seek to 'consume' the strongest and most gratify-
ing individual experiences at the level of immediate emotions
and sensations, inevitably finding themselves indifferent and
'paralyzed' as it were when they come face to face with the summons to embark upon a life project which includes a spiritual
and religious dimension and a commitment to solidarity."[1] He
added: "The lure of the so-called 'consumer society' is so strong
among young people that they become totally dominated and
imprisoned by an individualistic, materialistic, and hedonistic
interpretation of human existence. Material 'well-being,' which
is so intensely sought after, becomes the one ideal to be striven
for in life, a well-being which is to be attained in any way and at
any price. There is a refusal of anything that speaks of sacrifice
and a rejection of any effort to look for and to practice spiritual

---

1. John Paul II, Post-Synodal Apostolic Exhortation on the Formation of Priests
(*Pastores Dabo Vobis*, March 25, 1992) 7, http://w2.vatican.va/content/john
-paul-ii/en/apost_exhortations/documents/hf_jp-ii_exh_25031992_pastores
-dabo-vobis.html.

and religious values."[2] Bruce Rittenhouse contends that for John Paul, "the motivation for consumerism is hedonism."[3] Indeed, John Paul refers to hedonism three times in *Pastores Dabo Vobis*.[4] Certainly, one should not underestimate the degree to which North Atlantic culture in particular prizes pleasure over forbearance and sacrifice.[5] However consumerism is about more than (immediate) gratification. Given the decline of once stable social networks, identity construction and maintenance is more and more associated with what one purchases. Networks such as family, neighborhood, place of employment, and religious affiliation no longer allow one to construct and maintain one's self with the predictability and reliability of the past. Zygmunt Bauman argues that shopping offers an important mode of identity construction:

> With a mind-boggling profusion of brand new, eye-catching and alluring identities never further from reach than the nearest shopping mall, the chances of any particular identity being placidly accepted as the ultimate one, calling for no further overhaul or replacement, are equal to the proverbial survival chances of a snowball in hell. Indeed, why settle for what one has already finished building, warts and all, if new self-assembly kits promise excitements never before experienced and—who knows—throw open gates leading to delights never before enjoyed? "If not fully satisfied, return goods to the shop": is it not the first principle of the consuming life strategy?[6]

2. *Pastores Dabo Vobis* 8.

3. Bruce Rittenhouse, *Shopping for Meaningful Lives: The Religious Motive of Consumerism* (Eugene, OR: Cascade Books, 2013), 51.

4. See *Pastores Dabo Vobis* 7, 8, 48. See also the condemnations of "superdevelopment" in John Paul II, Encyclical Letter for the Twentieth Anniversary of *Populorum Progressio* (*Sollicitudo Rei Socialis*, December 30, 1987) 28, 31, 35, as well as the denunciations of consumerism in John Paul II, Encyclical Letter on the Hundredth Anniversary of *Rerum Novarum* (*Centesimus Annus*, May 1, 1991) 36, 37, 41, 55.

5. See p. 74, n. 34. See also my "A Holy and Living Sacrifice," *Liturgical Ministry* 18 (Spring 2009): 59–67.

6. Zygmunt Bauman, *Consuming Life* (Malden, MA: Polity, 2007), 112. On the next page, Bauman adds: "Andrzej Stasiuk, an outstanding Polish novelist and particularly perceptive analyst of the contemporary human condition, suggests

My purpose here is to attend where necessary to the issue of consumerism as hedonism insofar as this phenomenon has an impact on the theology and practice of ordination and ordained ministry in the Roman Catholic Church, but also to attend to the question of consumerism and identity construction.[7] First, I will provide some statistics on the Catholic priesthood. Second, I will discuss Catholic law and custom concerning the acquisition of wealth by ordained persons. Third, I will examine the trend of regarding ordained persons as holier and more exalted than others in the church. Fourth, I will turn attention to the status of orders after the Second Vatican Council. Finally, I will explore notions of mutuality and relation insofar as these ideas may resituate the identity of ordained persons in the present day.

II. Statistics

According to data compiled by the Center for Research in the Apostolate (CARA) in a major study undertaken in 2012, the high water mark for the number of priests in the United States was approximately 60,000 in the year 1969.[8] As of 2017, that number had

---

that 'the possibility of becoming someone else' is a present day substitute for the now largely discarded and uncared-for salvation or redemption. One would add: a substitute far superior to the original, since it is instantaneous rather than being vexingly slow in coming, and multiple as well as revocable instead of being the 'one and only' and ultimate." More than three decades before Bauman's book, a Vatican document had reached a similar conclusion: "Ideas today are in a process of radical revision. Society does not stress the stability of vocation, but rather the opposite." Citation from Sacred Congregation for Catholic Education, "Formation in Celibacy" 15. The text is available in *Origins* 4, no. 5 (June 27, 1974): 65–76 at 70.

7. It is interesting to note that the *Directory on the Ministry and Life of Priests* issued by the Sacred Congregation for the Clergy on March 31, 1994, makes no mention at all of consumerism. Hence, it does not address the impact of consumerism on vocations or on the life and identity of priests. There are passing references to materialism in paragraphs 45 and 66. See http://www .vatican.va/roman_curia/congregations/cclergy/documents/rc_con_cclergy _doc_31011994_directory_en.html.

8. Data taken from Charles Zech et al., *Catholic Parishes of the 21st Century* (New York: Oxford University Press, 2017), 20–21. These figures include diocesan priests and priests who are members of religious orders.

fallen to approximately 37,181.[9] The number of priests has fallen but the number of Catholics overall has increased from approximately 30 million in 1950 to approximately 70 million by 2000.[10] At the time of the last comprehensive study of Catholic parishes in the United States (the Notre Dame Study in the 1980s), there were approximately 900 Catholics per ordained priest. In 2012, by comparison, the ratio had increased to approximately 1,728 Catholics per ordained priest.[11] Given the falloff in the number of priests, it is not surprising to find a decrease in the number of Catholic parishes in the United States. CARA indicates that in the year 2000, there were in excess of 19,000 parishes, but by 2010 that number stood at 17,800.[12] With the decrease in the number of parishes and the increase in the Catholic population, the size of a typical parish has shifted. According to the Notre Dame Study, in 1987 an average parish had about 2,300 members on the parish rolls. By 2012, that number had jumped to 3,300.[13] Data concerning the median age of people in the workforce indicate that in 2009

9. Data taken from "Frequently Requested Church Statistics," Center for Applied Research in the Apostolate (CARA), http://cara.georgetown.edu /frequently-requested-church-statistics/.

10. Data taken from Zech et al., *Catholic Parishes of the 21st Century*, 7, which claims that "at the dawn of the 21st century US Catholics numbered well over 70 million." CARA provides a figure of 68.5 million as of 2017 at "Frequently Requested Church Statistics." The discrepancy may be a matter of who self-identifies as Catholic and who is actually registered at a Catholic parish.

11. Data taken from Zech et al., *Catholic Parishes of the 21st Century*, 22. The authors specify that the 900:1 ratio was derived from numbers in 1982. Globally, the authors report that in 2013 the ratio of lay Catholics to priests was approximately 3000:1 (20).

12. Data taken from Zech et al., *Catholic Parishes of the 21st Century*, 15. The authors add that there were about 17,800 parishes in the United States in 1965. From 1965 to 2000, then, the number jumped from 17,800 to more than 19,000 and then fell back to the lower number in the space of about ten years. The authors note that since 2004 the number of parishes in the United States has exceeded the number of priests in diocesan ministry (41). The authors also observe that among the most severely affected dioceses is that of Green Bay, Wisconsin. As of 2015, that diocese had sixty-four active diocesan priests but 157 parishes. More than half of the parishes in the diocese did not have a resident pastor (43).

13. Data taken from Zech et al., *Catholic Parishes of the 21st Century*, 17. The authors observe that these numbers constitute a 39 percent increase in the number of parishioners in an average parish.

"the median age of the general labor force increased just slightly (5 percent) from 39.8 to 41.8 [since 1970]. . . . Active diocesan priests, by contrast, have a median age in 2009 of fifty-nine, an increase of 31 percent from the 1970 figure."[14] Finally, the authors of the CARA study note: "[At present there are] about 450 to 550 new priests ordained each year for ministry in the United States. However, the sobering reality is that this is only about a third the number needed to compensate for the large numbers of elderly priests who are dying, retiring, or otherwise leaving pastoral ministry. And this does not take into account the other reality: that the Catholic population in the United States is continuing to increase at about 1 percent per year."[15]

Of themselves, these numbers indicate only *that* ratios are changing. The numbers do not indicate *why* the ratios are changing. Just as it is difficult to establish why Catholics are not seeking sacramental reconciliation with the frequency that characterized Catholic practice in the mid-twentieth century, so too is it difficult to establish why fewer Catholic men are seeking ordination.[16] A 2008 CARA study indicated that 83% of male Catholics "never considered" life as a priest or religious brother.[17] Moreover, 68% of respondents answered "no" when they were asked if they would encourage their own (hypothetical) child to pursue a vocation as a priest, deacon, religious brother, nun, or sister.[18]

The falling numbers, of course, have an impact on the identity of clerics, especially priests. The percentage of priests indicating that having "too much work" is a "great problem" for them has

14. Mary L. Gautier, Paul M. Perl, and Stephen J. Fichter, *Same Call, Different Men: The Evolution of the Priesthood since Vatican II* (Collegeville, MN: Liturgical Press, 2012), 2. The median age for priests in 1970 was forty-five, still above the median age for all workers.

15. Zech et al., *Catholic Parishes of the 21st Century*, 23.

16. Rates of participation in the Catholic sacraments have fallen across the board. See CARA, *Sacraments Today: Belief and Practice among U.S. Catholics* (April 2008), online at https://cara.georgetown.edu/sacraments.html.

17. Data taken from CARA, *Sacraments Today*, 69.

18. Data taken from CARA, *Sacraments Today*, 80. This question was directed to Catholics who were parents and Catholics who were not parents, with no significant difference between the two groups (66 percent of parents answered "no," and 68 percent of those who were not parents answered "no").

more than doubled between 1970 and 2012 (from 8 percent to 17 percent).[19] Demands on the time of priests can lead to a kind of functionalism, against which the Vatican warned in its 1994 *Directory on the Ministry and Life of Priests*:

> Pastoral charity faces the danger, today especially, of being emptied of its meaning through so-called "functionalism." It is not rare, in fact, to perceive, even in some priests, the influence of an erroneous mentality which reduces the ministerial priesthood to strictly functional aspects. To merely play the role of the priest, carrying out a few services and ensuring completion of various tasks would make up the entire priestly existence. Such a reductive conception of the identity of the ministry of the priest risks pushing their lives towards an emptiness, an emptiness which often comes to be filled by lifestyles not consonant with their very ministry.[20]

Indeed, priests have voiced concerns about becoming "sacramental machines"[21] and "purely functionary."[22] Hector Welgampola,

19. Gautier, Perl, and Fichter, *Same Call, Different Men*, 66.

20. *Directory on the Ministry and Life of Priests* 44. The same document warns about "exterior activism" in para. 40 and "overwork" in para. 83. See also the comments in Joseph Ratzinger, "Life and Ministry of Priests," in Congregation for the Clergy, *Priesthood: A Greater Love: International Symposium on the Thirtieth Anniversary of the Promulgation of the Conciliar Decree* Presbyterorum Ordinis (Philadelphia: Archdiocese of Philadelphia, 1997) 126–27. The conference papers in this volume feature essays by Cardinal Anthony Bevilacqua of Philadelphia, implicated in the cover-up of clerical sexual abuse there and from Marcial Maciel Degollado, founder of the Legionaries of Christ, who sexually abused boys and young men and who also fathered children with at least two women. For Bevilacqua, see the Grand Jury Report (September 17, 2003) compiled by Philadelphia District Attorney Lynne Abraham. For Degollado, see Reuters, "Legionaries of Christ Denounce Founder Marcial Maciel Degollado," *New York Times* (February 6, 2014), at https://www.nytimes.com/2014/02/07/world/legionaries -of-christ-denounce-founder-marcial-maciel-degollado.html. Their presence at the conference is an indication of a severely warped sense of clerical privilege.

21. Anonymous priest quoted in Dean Hoge and Jacqueline Wenger, *Evolving Visions of the Priesthood: Changes from Vatican II to the Turn of the New Century* (Collegeville, MN: Liturgical Press, 2003), 19.

22. Anonymous priest quoted in Hoge and Wenger, *Evolving Visions of the Priesthood*, 36.

an Asian observer commenting on perceptions of Catholic priests there, wrote that "priests are often viewed distantly, as little more than Sacrament-dispensing zombies."[23] An American priest laments that his "ministry is becoming more and more sacramental. Priests just do sacraments. I don't do counseling anymore."[24]

I will return later to the issue of how consumerism affects priests in relation to other priests and to the assemblies they pastor. For the present, it suffices to say that I think that John Paul's assessment, with which this chapter began, is not without merit but I also think it does not tell the whole story. The problem of consumerism is more insidious than mere hedonism. Nevertheless, it is to the question of orders and wealth that I now turn.

III. Holy Orders and Wealth

Though it is anachronistic to equate the *episkopoi*, *presbyteroi*, and *diakonoi* of the New Testament with the bishops, priests, and deacons of today it is certain that the New Testament warned Christian communities about *episkopoi* who were "greedy of filthy lucre" in the memorable phrasing of Titus 1:7 in the King James Version. First Timothy 3 employs the same phrasing in verse 3 to warn about *episkopoi*, and verse 8 applies the caution to *diakonoi*.[25] The early church order known as the *Didache*, evidently dependent in some measure on these traditions, repeats the warnings about *episkopoi* and *diakonoi* who are attracted to money.[26] According to

---

23. Hector Welgampola, "Living Church in Asia," *UCA* News Column (August 27, 2007), quoted in David Ranson, *The Contemporary Challenge of Priestly Life: A Meditation on the Paschal Paradox* (New York: Paulist, 2009), 40.

24. Anonymous priest quoted in Gautier, Perl, and Fichter, *Same Call, Different Men*, 75. In a 2001 survey, 43 percent of priests said that they would be "very or somewhat dissatisfied" if their ministry were restricted to sacramental and liturgical duties. However, the same survey found that 44 percent of respondents would be "very or somewhat satisfied" with such restrictions. More study is needed. See Hoge and Wenger, *Evolving Visions of the Priesthood*, 39.

25. The NRSV translates Titus 1:7 as "greedy for gain," 1 Tim 3:3 as "lover of money," and 1 Tim 3:8 as "greedy for money."

26. See *Didache* 15.1, in *The Apostolic Fathers*, vol. 1: *I Clement, II Clement, Ignatius, Polycarp, Didache, Barnabas*, trans. Kirsopp Lake (Cambridge, MA: Harvard University Press, 1959), 331.

Acts 6, the office of *diakonos* had its origins in the Christian community's care for widows but that some who later had this function abused their positions is suggested by the mid-second century *Shepherd* of Hermas, which castigates those *diakonoi* "who ministered amiss, and devoured the living of widows and orphans, and made gain for themselves from the ministry which they had received to administer."[27] Polycarp, writing to the church in Philadelphia around the year 130, counseled *presbyteroi* as well to refrain from love of money and to have a care for widows, orphans, and the poor.[28] Origen (d. 253) denounced bishops and other church figures who sought wealth and land: "You will say the like in the case of him who seeks the office of a bishop for the sake of glory with men, or of flattery from men, or for the sake of the gain received from those who, coming over to the word, give in the name of piety; for a bishop of this kind at any rate does not 'desire a good work,' nor can he be without reproach, nor temperate, nor sober-minded, as he is intoxicated with glory and intemperately satiated with it. And the same also you will say about the elders and deacons."[29] In the mid-third century, one finds in the fourth

27. *Shepherd* of *Hermas*, Similitude 9.26.2. I am using the text in *The Apostolic Fathers*, vol. 2: *The Shepherd of Hermas, The Martyrdom of Polycarp, The Epistle to Diognetus*, trans. Kirsopp Lake (Cambridge, MA: Harvard University Press, 1959), 281. Commenting on this passage, Paul Bradshaw writes: "It is not entirely clear whether the *diakonoi* who are mentioned in Similitude 9.26.2 as having 'ministered badly' and embezzled funds intended for the relief of widows and orphans are 'deacons' as such or whether the term is being used in a more general sense as *diakonia* is in Similitude 9.27.2; but because *diakonoi* are listed along with apostles, teachers, and bishops in Vision 3.5.1, it seems more likely that that specific officials are intended." Paul Bradshaw, *Rites of Ordination: Their History and Theology* (Collegeville, MN: Liturgical Press, 2013), 27.

28. See Polycarp, *Letter to the Philippians*, 6.1, in *The Apostolic Fathers* 1:291. Though it is not my purpose here to trace the evolution of the ministerial and administrative responsibilities of bishops, priests, and deacons, it is worth noting Paul Bradshaw's observation on this passage that "there is no explicit mention of [presbyteroi] presiding at worship or of exercising the ministry of the word." Bradshaw, *Rites of Ordination*, 31.

29. Origen, *Commentary on Matthew* 11.15, in Allan Menzies, ed., *Ante-Nicene Fathers The Writings of the Fathers Down to A.D. 325*, vol. 9: *The Gospel of Peter, The Diatessaron of Tatian, The Apocalypse of Peter, The Vision of Paul, The Apocalypses of the Virgin and Sedrach, The Testament of Abraham, The Acts of Xanthippe and Polyxena, The*

paragraph of the *Didascalia Apostolorum* more references to 1 Timothy 3, concerning the conduct of bishops:

> And let [the bishop] be *watchful and chaste and staid* and orderly; and let him not be turbulent, *and let him not be one that exceeds in wine; and let him not be a backbiter; but let him be quiet, and not be quarrelsome; and let him not be money-loving* [1 Tim 3.2-3]. . . . And let his hand be open to give; and let him love the orphans with the widows, and be a lover of the poor and of strangers. . . . And let the bishop be also without respect of persons, and let him not defer to the rich nor favour them unduly; and let him not disregard or neglect the poor, nor be lifted up against them. And let him be scant and poor in his food and drink, that he may be able to be watchful in admonishing and correcting those who are undisciplined. And let him not be crafty and extravagant, nor luxurious, nor pleasure-loving, nor fond of dainty meats. . . . Let not the bishop therefore be *a lover of filthy lucre* [1 Tim 3.8], and especially from the heathen . . . . And let him not be lustful, nor money-loving: for all these things are of the agency of demons.[30]

This document cautions deacons about "filthy lucre,"[31] and later warns about "filthy lucre" and care for widows and orphans:

> Do you the bishops and the deacons be constant therefore in the ministry of the altar of Christ—we mean the widows and the orphans. . . . Make it your care and endeavor therefore to minister to widows out of the ministry of a clean conscience, that what

---

Narrative of Zosimus, The Apology of Aristides, The Epistles of Clement (complete text), Origen's Commentary on John Books 1–10, and Commentary on Matthew Books 1, 2, and 10–14 (Peabody, MA: Hendrickson, 2004), 444. The reference to "a good work" is from 1 Tim 3:1. Origen engages in similar criticism elsewhere (e.g., *Homily 16 on Genesis*, 5 in *Origen: Homilies on Genesis and Exodus*, trans. Ronald E. Heine [Washington, DC: Catholic University of America Press, 1982], 221). For commentary on these passages, see Han van Campenhausen, *Ecclesiastical Authority in the Church of the First Three Centuries* (Stanford, CA: Stanford University Press, 1969), 252.

30. *Didascalia Apostolorum* 4. I am using the text in R. Hugh Connolly, *Didascalia Apostolorum: The Syriac Version Translated and Accompanied by the Verona Latin Fragments* (Oxford: Clarendon, 1929), 32, 34, 35. All citations of this text will come from the Connolly book. The Scripture references are from Connolly, who apparently applies 1 Tim 3:8 to bishops, though the scriptural context clearly refers to deacons.

31. *Didascalia Apostolorum* 16.

they ask and request may be granted them at once upon their praying for it. But if there be bishops who are careless and give no heed to these matters, through respect of persons, or for the sake of filthy lucre . . . they shall render no ordinary account.[32]

Canon 18 of the Council of Elvira (ca. 300 CE) held that "bishops, presbyters, and deacons may not leave their own places for the sake of commerce, nor are they to be traveling about the provinces, frequenting the markets for their own profit,"[33] and canon 3 of the Council of Chalcedon (451 CE) warned against members of the clergy "involving themselves in worldly business, neglecting the service of God, frequenting the houses of worldly persons and taking over the handling of property out of avarice."[34]

Fast-forwarding more than a millennium to around the turn of the sixteenth century, Rome was haunted by bankruptcy, but still Pope Julius II and his successor Leo X spent money quite lavishly.[35] The profligacy in Rome drew the attention of many critics, including, notably, Martin Luther, who complained bitterly about the financial drain on Germany imposed by various ecclesiastical tactics to identify and exploit revenue streams.[36] The details of

32. *Didascalia Apostolorum* 18. However, according to *Didascalia Apostolorum* 9, the "account" which the bishop must render is never to any human person: "And thou shalt require no account of the bishop, nor observe him, how he dispenses and discharges his stewardship, or when he gives, or to whom, or where, or whether well or ill, or whether he gives fairly; for he has One who will require, even the Lord God, who delivered this stewardship into his hands and held him worthy of the priesthood of so great an office."

33. Council of Elvira, can. 18. I am using the text in *The Faith of the Early Fathers*, ed. William Jurgens (Collegeville, MN: Liturgical Press, 1970), 1:254.

34. Council of Chalcedon, can. 3. I am using the text in Norman Tanner, ed., *Decrees of the Ecumenical Councils*, vol. 1: *Nicaea I to Lateran V* (Washington, DC: Georgetown University Press, 1990), 88.

35. See Owen Chadwick, *The Pelican History of the Church*, vol. 3: *The Reformation* (New York: Penguin, 1986), 40.

36. See Martin Luther, *To the Christian Nobility of the German Nation*. Relevant passages are in Martin Luther, *Three Treatises from the American Edition of Luther's Works* (Philadelphia: Fortress, 1985), 28. Later in this treatise, Luther writes: "The Roman See should do away with all the *official*, and cut down the creeping, crawling swarm of vermin at Rome, so that the pope's household can be supported out of the pope's own pocket. The pope should not allow his court to surpass the courts of all kings in pomp and extravagance, because this kind of thing not

the theological debate over these tactics (e.g., indulgences) need not concern us here. What is important for our purposes is the attempt by the Council of Trent to reestablish a correct relationship between holy orders and wealth. Trent reminded clerics of the "divine command to know their sheep, to offer sacrifice for them, to nourish them by preaching God's word, by administering the sacraments and by the example of good works of every kind, to have fatherly care of the poor and of all others who are wretched."[37] Along the same lines, the council prohibited clerics from taking lengthy absences from their assignments and declared:

> If, however, anyone (and may it never happen) is absent in contravention of this decree, the holy synod decrees that, in addition to the other penalties imposed against non-residents under Paul III and hereby renewed, and the guilt of mortal sin thereby incurred, such a one will not receive revenues in proportion to the length of absence; nor can he in conscience retain these funds even if no claim is made on them, but he is obliged to dispose of them (or in his default it is to be done by a higher ecclesiastic) on the fabric of the churches or the poor of the locality.[38]

The *Catechism of the Council of Trent*, promulgated by Pope Pius V three years after the close of the council, had this warning about those who aspire to ordained ministry:

> In these days the faithful often sin gravely in this respect. Some there are who embrace [the clerical state] to secure the necessaries of life, and who, consequently, seek in the priesthood, just as other men do in the lowest walks of life, nothing more or less than gain. Though both the natural and divine law lay down, as the Apostle remarks, that he who serves the altar should live

---

only never has been of any use to the cause of the Christian faith, but has kept the courtesans from study and prayer until they are hardly able to speak about the faith at all." *To the Christian Nobility of the German Nation*, 51–52.

37. Council of Trent, Session 23, Decree on Reformation, can. 1. I am using the text in Norman Tanner, ed., *Decrees of the Ecumenical Councils*, vol. 2: *Trent to Vatican II* (Washington, DC: Georgetown University Press, 1990), 744.

38. Council of Trent, Session 23, Decree on Reformation, chap. 1. I am using the text in Tanner, *Decrees of the Ecumenical Councils*, 2:745.

by the altar; yet to approach the altar for the sake of gain and money is one of the very gravest of sacrileges.

Some are attracted to the priesthood by ambition and love of honors; while there are others who desire to be ordained simply in order that they may abound in riches, as is proved by the fact that unless some wealthy benefice were conferred on them, they would not dream of receiving Holy Orders.[39]

The fact that the 1917 *Code of Canon Law* repeats earlier prohibitions on clerical engagement in business ventures suggests on the one hand constancy in teaching but perhaps also persistent problems with observance of the teaching.[40] Writing about the duties of the Catholic priest about two decades later, Pope Pius XI taught:

He must holily spurn all vile greed of earthly gains, since he is in search of souls, not of money, of the glory of God, not his own. He is no mercenary working for a temporal recompense, nor yet an employee who, whilst attending conscientiously to duties of his office, at the same time is looking to his career and personal promotion. . . . Woe to the priest who, forgetful of these divine promises should become 'greedy of filthy lucre'. . . . On the other hand, by sincere disinterestedness the priest can hope to win the hearts of all. For detachment from earthly goods, if

---

39. *Catechism of the Council of Trent for Parish Priests*, eds. John McHugh and Charles Callan (Rockford, IL: TAN Books, 1982), 319. The *Catechism* was issued in 1566. The Scripture reference here is to 1 Cor 9:13. The phenomenon of seeking economic security or gain was not new in the sixteenth century, of course. In the fourth century, John Chrysostom had lamented that in his day "many of these ordinations happen not by divine grace but by human ambition." Citation from John Chrysostom, *On the Priesthood* 4, 1 as quoted in Paul Bradshaw, *Ordination Rites of the Ancient Churches of East and West* (Collegeville, MN: Liturgical Press, 1990), 26. R. Scott Appleby points out that during the Great Depression, seminary life offered daily meals, advanced education, and subsequent job security in an era when such things were hard to come by. See R. Scott Appleby, "Part I: The Transformation of the Roman Catholic Parish Priesthood," in *Transforming Parish Ministry: The Changing Roles of the Catholic Clergy*, ed. Jay P. Dolan (New York: Crossroad, 1990), 3–107 at 22, quoted in Hoge and Wenger, *Evolving Visions of the Priesthood*, 10.

40. See the 1917 *Code of Canon Law*, can. 142. Text available in *The 1917 or Pio-Benedictine Code of Canon Law*, curated by Edward Peters (San Francisco: Ignatius Press, 2001), 71.

inspired by lively faith, is always accompanied by tender compassion towards the unfortunate of every kind.[41]

The same pontiff wrote approvingly of priests who embraced austerity: "a priest who is really poor and disinterested in the Gospel sense may work among his flock marvels recalling a Saint Vincent de Paul, a Cure of Ars, a Cottolengo, a Don Bosco and so many others."[42] On the eve of Vatican II, Pope John XXIII repeated these words of praise.[43]

For its part, Vatican II charged bishops to be "zealous in promoting the holiness of their clergy, religious and laity according to the vocation of each individual, remembering that they themselves are obliged to give an example of sanctity in charity, humility and simplicity of life."[44] Along the same lines, bishops "should be especially solicitous for the poor and weaker folk whom the Lord has commissioned them to evangelize."[45] For their part, priests should serve all in their care but remember that "the poor and the

---

41. Pope Pius XI, Encyclical Letter on the Catholic Priesthood (*Ad Catholici Sacerdotii*, December 20, 1935) 48–50, http://w2.vatican.va/content/pius-xi /en/encyclicals/documents/hf_p-xi_enc_19351220_ad-catholici-sacerdotii.html.

42. Pope Piux XI, Encyclical Letter on Atheistic Communism (*Divini Redemptoris*, March 19, 1937) 63, https://w2.vatican.va/content/pius-xi/en/encyclicals /documents/hf_p-xi_enc_19370319_divini-redemptoris.html.

43. Pope John XXIII, Encyclical Letter on St. John Vianney (*Sacerdotii Nostri Primordia*, August 1, 1959) 16, http://w2.vatican.va/content/john-xxiii/en /encyclicals/documents/hf_j-xxiii_enc_19590801_sacerdotii.html. The Vatican's English language translation of John's encyclical follows the Latin of *Divini Redemptoris* more closely than does the Vatican translation of *Divini Redemptoris*. The Latin text (https://w2.vatican.va/content/pius-xi/la/encyclicals/documents /hf_p-xi_enc_19370319_divini-redemptoris.html) states: "Quotidianis enim experimentis cognitum est tenuioris vitae sacerdotes, qui ex evangelica doctrina suis reipsa utilitatibus nullo modo inserviant, mirifica *semper* conferre in christianam plebem beneficia : uti exemplis S. Vincentii a Paulo, S. Ioannis B. Vianney, S. Iosephi B. Cottolengo, S. Ioannis Bosco, innumerabilium aliorum confirmatur" (emphasis added); "semper" means "always." The Vatican's English translation of this passage in *Sacerdotii Nostri Primordia* is: "priests who live modestly and follow the teaching of the Gospel by paying little attention to their own interests, *always* confer wonderful benefits on the Christian people." Emphasis added.

44. *Christus Dominus* 15.

45. *Christus Dominus* 13.

weaker ones have been committed to their care in a special way."[46] Moreover, "priests and bishops alike are to avoid everything that might in any way antagonize the poor."[47]

The first universally obligatory rite of consecration of a bishop, the 1595 Pontifical promulgated by Pope Clement VIII, contained a question for the bishop-elect concerning his willingness to "be kind and compassionate in the name of Lord to the poor and to strangers and to all who are in need."[48] Sharon McMillan points out that this question concerning care for the poor is the only one of the original eight questions from the 1595 edition to be retained in the revised Examination of the Candidate in the 1968 Rite of Ordination of a Bishop.[49] The sample homily provided in the rite of 1968 (which has no precedent in the rite of 1595) tells the bishop-elect to "love the poor and infirm, strangers and the homeless."[50] Neither the 1968 prayer for the consecration of a

---

46. *Presbyterorum Ordinis* 6.

47. *Presbyterorum Ordinis* 17. See also *Lumen Gentium* 41 on bishops, priests, and deacons as examples for others to follow.

48. *Pontificale Romanum* 1595, 84, quoted in Sharon L. McMillan, *Episcopal Ordination and Ecclesial Consensus* (Collegeville, MN: Liturgical Press, 2005), 262. This question appears in the Roman Pontifical of 1962; see *Pontificale Romanum Editio Iuxta Typica* (Rome: Marietti, 1962) 42. Paragraph 19 of the 1968 Rite of Ordination of a Bishop asks: "Are you resolved to show kindness and compassion in the name of the Lord to the poor and to strangers and to all who are in need?" The more recent translation of this question asks essentially the same thing: "Do you resolve, for the sake of the Lord's name, to be welcoming and merciful to the poor, to strangers, and to all who are in need?" See Ordination of a Bishop 40, in Congregation for Divine Worship and the Discipline of the Sacraments, *The Roman Pontifical* (Vatican City: Vox Clara Committee, 2012), which will be the source for all references to the 2012 translation of this rite, unless otherwise noted.

49. See McMillan, *Episcopal Ordination and Ecclesial Consensus*, 262. Other questions, such as the question of obedience to the pope, appear elsewhere in the 1968 rite—but not in the Examination of the Candidate. As noted above, the question about care for the poor is retained in Ordination of a Bishop 40 in the English pontifical of 2012. Here it is among the questions listed under "Promise of the Elect."

50. 1968 Ordination of a Bishop 18. The 2012 translation of the sample homily says essentially the same thing: "With the charity of a father and brother, love all whom God places in your care, especially the Priests and Deacons who are your co-workers in the ministry of Christ, but also the poor and the weak, immigrants, and strangers." 2012 Ordination of a Bishop 39.

bishop nor its successor makes reference to the poor but the 1994 *Catechism of the Catholic Church* teaches that the grace of episcopal ordination "is first of all a grace of strength . . . the grace to guide and defend his Church with strength and prudence as a father and pastor, with gratuitous love for all and a preferential love for the poor, the sick, and the needy."[51] Concerning the 1968 Rite of Ordination of a Priest and its successor, neither the sample homily nor the prayer of consecration makes reference to the poor,[52] but the 1968 prayer for the consecration of a deacon does: "May he excel in every virtue: in love that is sincere, in concern for the sick and the poor, in unassuming authority, in self-discipline, and in holiness of life."[53]

Canon 282/1 of the 1983 *Code of Canon Law* directs clerics "to foster simplicity of life and . . . to refrain from all things that have a semblance of vanity."[54] Repeating prohibitions going back to at least the Council of Elvira, canon 286 holds that "clerics

---

51. *Catechism of the Catholic Church* 1586. The prayer of consecration of a bishop in force at the time of the Second Vatican Council also makes no reference to the poor.

52. There is no mention of the poor in the Rite of Ordination of a Priest in the Roman Pontifical of 1962, either. The vow of poverty applies to those entering religious communities/orders, but it does not apply to typical diocesan clergy. I am restricting analysis here to diocesan clergy who are, in the words of Vatican II, "invited to embrace voluntary poverty" (*Presbyterorum Ordinis* 17).

53. 1968 Ordination of a Deacon 21. The ordination of a deacon according to the Roman Pontifical of 1962 made no reference to the poor in the prayer of consecration. The 2012 translation of this prayer says essentially the same thing as the 1968 version: "May there abound in him every Gospel virtue: unfeigned love, concern for the sick and poor, unassuming authority, the purity of innocence, and the observance of spiritual discipline." Citation from 2012 Ordination of Deacons 235. Additionally, the sample homily of 1968 cautions those to be ordained to the diaconate to regard "all defilement and avarice as serving false gods" (1968 Ordination of a Deacon 14). The echo of scriptural warnings about greed and idolatry (see Eph 5:5 and Col 3:5) is no doubt intentional. The sample homily in the 2012 translation of this rite says essentially the same thing: "Since no one can serve two masters, look upon all defilement and avarice as serving false gods" (2012 Ordination of Deacons 227).

54. I am using the text of the 1983 *Code of Canon Law* at http://www.vatican .va/archive/ENG1104/__PY.HTM. Paragraph 2 of this canon states that clerics "are to wish to use for the good of the Church and works of charity those goods which have come to them on the occasion of the exercise of ecclesiastical office

are prohibited from conducting business or trade personally or through others, for their own advantage or that of others, except with the permission of legitimate ecclesiastical authority."[55] In the 1992 document with which this chapter began, John Paul II hailed the importance of priestly poverty by characterizing it as "urgently needed in affluent and consumeristic societies: 'A truly poor priest is indeed a specific sign of separation from, disavowal of and non-submission to the tyranny of a contemporary world which puts all its trust in money and in material security.'"[56] In 1999, writing of the bishops in the United States, John Paul II addressed the conversion required by the gospel that "demands especially of us Bishops a genuine identification with the personal style of Jesus Christ, who leads us to simplicity, poverty, responsibility for others and the renunciation of our own advantage."[57]

In the fifth edition of the *Program for Priestly Formation* approved by the bishops of the United States in 2006, one finds reference to shaping future priests to live "a life of gratitude for the material blessings of God's creation coupled with a simple and generous lifestyle that cares for and is in solidarity with the poor, works for universal justice, makes itself ready and available for all those in need, administers the goods of the community with

---

and which are left over after provision has been made for their decent support and for the fulfillment of all the duties of their own state."

55. See also the discussion of young men seeking economic security via priesthood in Petrus B. Timang, "Priestly Ministry and Voluntary Poverty in Light of Vatican Council II" (Thesis, Pontifical University of St. Thomas Aquinas, 1986), xvi. Timang refers here to C. Groenen, "Muda-Mudi Indonesia dalam Komunitas Injili," *Rohani* 28, no. 10 (1981): 291–97, 302. For an American context, see George Wilson, *Clericalism: The Death of Priesthood* (Collegeville, MN: Liturgical Press, 2008), 28; and the account of R. Scott Appleby on p. 176, n. 39.

56. *Pastores Dabo Vobis* 30. John Paul is here quoting proposition 10 of the working document of the synod.

57. John Paul II, Post-Synodal Apostolic Exhortation on the Way to Conversion, Communion and Solidarity in America (*Ecclesia in America*, January 22, 1999) 28, http://w2.vatican.va/content/john-paul-ii/en/apost_exhortations/documents/hf_jp-ii_exh_22011999_ecclesia-in-america.html. The words here are quoted from proposition 76 of the synod's working document. In paragraph 39 of this exhortation, John Paul asserts that priests must grow above all "in solidarity with the poor."

utmost honesty, and offers a courageous prophetic witness in the world."[58] The same document later makes specific reference to consumerism:

> The formation program should articulate the distinctive qualities of simplicity of life appropriate for one preparing for priestly leadership. Simplicity of life is particularly important in our own age when human needs and desires are so consciously manipulated and exploited. A consumer society often reduces people to things, which are used and then discarded, plunging society more deeply into a world of objects, which ironically seem to possess us. In a consumer society, a right attitude toward the world and earthly goods is easily lost. That is why a seminarian has to be helped to cultivate personal self-discipline and asceticism. It is an important pastoral obligation of all priests who accompany people through the journey of life to acquire a sound and balanced perspective about earthly goods and possessions so that they can impart right attitudes to others.[59]

Yet the long-standing emphasis on clerical simplicity has been marred not only by events of the past (e.g., those denounced by Hermas and Origen and the lavishness preceding the Protestant Reformation of 1517) but also by recent headlines. In the United States alone, there have been cases such as the priests Michael Jude Fay in 2006,[60] Jonathan Wehrle in 2017,[61] and Henryk Pawelec

---

58. United States Conference of Catholic Bishops, *Program of Priestly Formation* (Washington, DC: USCCB, 2006) 26. See also the ninth bullet point of para. 76 of the program.

59. *Program of Priestly Formation* 98. The present author contacted a local seminary and an institute for priestly formation. Representatives of each institution said that their institution had no particular resources for assisting future priests to minister in a culture marked by consumerism.

60. See Susan Shultz and Joshua Fisher, "Father Fay, 58, Dies of Cancer in Prison," *Darien Times* (August 15, 2009), http://www.darientimes.com/22673 /father-fay-58-dies-of-cancer-in-prison/.

61. See Dan Morris-Young, "Alleged Embezzlement by Lansing Priest Approaches $5 Million," *National Catholic Reporter* (July 11, 2017), https://www.ncr online.org/blogs/ncr-today/alleged-embezzlement-lansing-priest-approaches -5-million.

in 2018.[62] Fay was convicted of embezzling more than $1 million, Wehrle is accused of embezzling more than $5 million, and Pawelec has repaid the $236,000 he stole. Fay died in prison 2009, and as of this writing Wehrle's case is making its way through the legal system. Among American bishops, there are the examples of William Murphy (2002), Edward Braxton (2005), John Myers (2014), Wilton Gregory (2014), Dennis Sullivan (2014), Patrick McGrath (2018), and Michael Bransfield (2019). Civil authorities have not filed any formal charges against these bishops, but Catholics have raised serious questions about the cost of renovating episcopal residences in the cases of Murphy ($920,000)[63] and Braxton ($150,000),[64] purchasing episcopal residences in the cases of Gregory ($2.2 million)[65] and Sullivan ($500,000),[66] and of spending on

62. See Martin Vassolo, "Priest Pays Back $236,000 He Stole from Pompano Beach Church, Archdiocese of Miami Says," *Miami Herald* (August 19, 2018), https://www.miamiherald.com/news/local/community/broward/article 216989025.html.

63. See John Rather, "After Cardinal Law, Questions for Murphy," *New York Times* (December 22, 2002), http://www.nytimes.com/2002/12/22/nyregion /after-cardinal-law-questions-for-murphy.html. Newspaper columnist Jimmy Breslin was unsparing in his criticism of the Rockville Centre (NY) bishop he called "Mansion Murphy." See Jimmy Breslin, "LI Bishop's Mansion: Biggest Waste of Money, Bar Nun," *Newsday* (October 8, 2002), http://www.bishop -accountability.org/news/2002-10-08-Breslin-CommentaryLI.htm.

64. According to news reports, the Diocese of Belleville (IL) did not confirm the cost of renovations. The $150,000 figure was provided by one of those protesting the renovation. Reports indicate that the diocese covered $25,000 for basic repairs and that the remainder of the cost was defrayed by gifts given to Braxton. See Lisa P. White, "Renovation of Bishop's House Draws Fire from Laity Group: Protesters Question Priorities of Diocese," *Belleville News-Democrat* (April 14, 2005), 1A.

65. Purchase price reported in Jim Walsh, "Camden Bishop among Those under Fire for Costly Homes," *Courier-Post* (April 13, 2014), https://www .courierpostonline.com/story/news/local/south-jersey/2014/04/12/camden -bishop-among-fire-costly-homes/7651903/. At the time, Wilton Gregory was archbishop of Atlanta, GA; in 2019 he became archbishop of Washington, DC. Following protests over the purchase, Gregory moved out of the home. See Emma Fitzsimmons, "Atlanta Archbishop Says He'll Sell Mansion," *New York Times* (April 6, 2014), https://www.nytimes.com/2014/04/06/us/atlanta-archbishop -says-hell-sell-mansion.html.

66. Purchase price reported in Walsh, "Camden Bishop."

retirement facilities in the cases of Myers ($500,000)[67] and McGrath ($2.3 million).[68] Bransfield, the former bishop of Wheeling, West Virginia, was found by a church investigation to have spent $4.6 million on renovations of his residence, $182,000 on deliveries of flowers to his chancery, and $350,000 in gifts to other members of the clergy.[69] Perhaps the best-known case is that of Franz-Peter Tebartz-van Elst, the former bishop of Limburg, Germany. Tebartz-van Elst spent approximately $42 million on renovations to his episcopal residence. According to news outlets, this figure included "$474,000 for carpentry and cupboards, $610,000 for art, $135,000 for windows for a private chapel, $34,000 for a conference table, [and] $20,000 for a bathtub."[70] This news broke in October 2013; in that same month Francis suspended Tebartz-van Elst,[71]

67. Figure reported in Walsh, "Camden Bishop." Myers is the former bishop of Newark.

68. Purchase price reported in John Woolfolk, "San Jose Diocese Buys Bishop $2.3 Million Retirement Home," *The Mercury News* (August 26, 2018), https:// www.mercurynews.com/2018/08/26/san-jose-diocese-buys-bishop-2-3-million -retirement-home/. Following backlash over the purchase, McGrath reversed course. See Jason Green, "Retiring S.J. Bishop Confesses Error in Judgment, Won't Move into $2.3 Million Home," *The Mercury News* (August 27, 2018), https:// www.mercurynews.com/2018/08/27/retiring-san-jose-bishop-wont-move -into-2-3-million-home/.

69. The report lists additional cases of extravagant spending on the part of Bransfield. See Michele Boorstein, Shawn Boburg, and, Robert O'Harrow Jr., "W.Va. Bishop Gave Powerful Cardinals and Other Priests $350,000 in Cash Gifts before His Ouster, Church Records Show," *Washington Post* (June 5, 2019), https://www.washingtonpost.com/investigations/a-wva-bishop-spent-millions -on-himself-and-sent-cash-gifts-to-cardinals-and-to-young-priests-he-was -accused-of-mistreating-confidential-vatican-report-says/2019/06/05/98af7a e6-7686-11e9-b3f5-5673edf2d127_story.html. Notably, the author of the church report, Archbishop William Lori of Baltimore, initially deleted his own name from the list of those to whom Bransfield had given gifts. See "Archbishop Lori: Mistake Not to List Priests Who Received Gifts from Bransfield," *The Intelligencer* (June 12, 2019), http://www.theintelligencer.net/news/top-headlines/2019/06 /archbishop-lori-mistake-not-to-list-priests-who-received-gifts-from-bransfield/.

70. Alison Smale, "German Outrage Swells over a Bishop's Spending," *New York Times* (October 12, 2013), http://www.nytimes.com/2013/10/13/world/europe /german-outrage-swells-over-a-bishops-spending.html.

71. See Alison Smale, "Vatican Suspends German Bishop Accused of Lavish Spending on Himself," *New York Times* (October 23, 2013), https://www.nytimes

and in March 2014 the pope accepted the bishop's resignation from the see of Limburg.[72]

It is true, of course, that on the whole the ordained have less opportunity to engage in wanton displays of consumerist hedonism. I have related recent incidents that are newsworthy but also somewhat exceptional. Yet, there are at least two points to make about orders and wealth. The first concerns bishops, whose authority in their respective dioceses is nearly supreme. George Wilson relates the account of a diocesan business manager who protested a bishop's directive to transfer $1 million from the diocesan general fund to the bishop's discretionary fund. The manager contended that this money was the "people's money." The bishop replied, "Well, from now on it's my money."[73] One wonders about the ways in which this bishop's view of his authority over diocesan monies informed also his view of pastoral matters. Are there ways in which episcopal control over money—even when exercised responsibly—colors episcopal judgment in other matters?

A second point concerns the financial standing of priests and bishops. Even as most priests and bishops are not lavish in their spending, for some, at least, their lives are reasonably comfortable in a way and on a level that is foreign to some economic strata. Here is Michael Papesh's view:

> Few of the people in the pews have four weeks of vacation each year, with a week of retreat and a week of continuing education above that, as priests do. . . . Nearly no one today has anything like the absolute job security priests take so for granted. Few people other than priests and bishops in our culture retire, as the priests of St. Paul and Minneapolis do, to a lovely retirement residence on prime wooded property along the Mississippi River, with three meals a day, housekeeping and laundry service—all for the low, low price of $955 per month. Most of the faithful, if

---

.com/2013/10/24/world/europe/vatican-suspends-german-bishop-known-for-spending.html.

72. See Melissa Eddy, "Pope Accepts Bishop's Resignation," *New York Times* (March 27, 2014): A6.

73. Anonymous incident reported in Wilson, *Clericalism*, 31–32.

they fully understood a priest's circumstances, would be green with envy.[74]

Perhaps shielded in some ways from consumerism because of their typically modest salaries, in other ways priests may also be shielded from the economic concerns that can preoccupy those to whom and among whom they minister.

IV. Orders and Holiness[75]

The Torah impressed upon Israelites that God's people were summoned to holiness: "you shall be holy," says the Lord, "for I am holy" (Lev 11:44, NRSV).[76] Yet even though the Israelites were to be a "priestly kingdom and a holy nation" (Exod 19:6, NRSV), the priestly class was set apart to say and do things that other Israelites were not authorized to say and do (notably the offering of sacrifice). The Old Testament frequently condemns spiritual leaders who fail to provide adequate models to the people of what it means to observe the Law.[77]

Hosea 4:7-9 is of particular note for the present consideration. Here I cite the NRSV:

> The more they increased,
>> the more they sinned against me;
>> they changed their glory into shame.
> They feed on the sin of my people;
>> they are greedy for their iniquity.
> And it shall be like people, like priest;
>> I will punish them for their ways,
>> and repay them for their deeds.

74. Michael Papesh, *Clerical Culture: Contradiction and Transformation* (Collegeville, MN: Liturgical Press, 2004), 114.

75. For a brief overview of the history of the clerical state as superior in holiness to the lay state, see Friedrich Wulf, "Introductory Remarks on Chapters V and VI," in *Commentary on the Documents of Vatican II*, ed. Herbert Vorgrimler (London: Burns & Oates, 1966), 1:253–60.

76. See also Lev 11:45; 19:2.

77. See, for example, Isa 28:7; Jer 2:8, 26; 5:31; 8:10; 32:32; Ezek 22:26; 44:15.

The idea of "like people, like priest" is taken up in *Didascalia Apostolorum* 4: "And whatever of good there be that is found in men, let the same be in the bishop. For when the pastor shall be remote from all evil, he will be able to constrain his disciples also and encourage them by his good manners to be imitators of his good works; as the Lord has said in the Twelve Prophets: *The people shall be even as the priest.* For it behooves you to be an example to the people, for you also have Christ for an example."[78] The notion that ordained persons should be models for other Christians finds clear expression as well in the prayer over the one to become a bishop in the fourth-century *Canons of Hippolytus*: "Make him shepherd your people blamelessly, so that he may be worthy of tending your great and holy flock; make his life higher than [that] of all his people, without dispute; make him envied by reason of his virtue by everyone."[79] The same petition occurs in the prayer over one to become a priest in canon 4,[80] while over a candidate for the diaconate these words were prayed: "Make his life without sin before all men and an example for many, so that he may save a multitude in the holy Church without shame."[81] The "blameless" quality of bishops and priests is grounded in admonitions found in the New Testament letters, where being blameless is sometimes associated with all members of a local church (e.g., Phil 1:13; 1 Cor 1:8; Col 1:22) and sometimes with specific office-holders (1 Tim 3:10 for a *diakonos*; Titus 1:6 for a *presbyteros*; and Titus 1:7 for an *episkopos*). Several early church orders include a petition for the blamelessness of those being ordained.[82]

78. *Didascalia Apostolorum* 4.

79. *Canons of Hippolytus* 3, quoted in Bradshaw, *Ordination Rites*, 110.

80. *Canons of Hippolytus* 4, quoted in Bradshaw, *Ordination Rites*, 111.

81. *Canons of Hippolytus* 5, quoted in Bradshaw, *Ordination Rites*, 111.

82. For bishops, see *Apostolic Tradition* 3, in Bradshaw, *Ordination Rites*, 107; *Apostolic Constitutions* 8.5, in Bradshaw, *Ordination Rites*, 114; *Testamentum Domini* 1.21 in Bradshaw, *Ordination Rites*, 118. For priests, see *Apostolic Constitutions* 8.16 in Bradshaw, *Ordination Rites*, 115. For deacons, see *Apostolic Tradition* 8 in Bradshaw, *Ordination Rites*, 109; *Apostolic Constitutions* 8.18 in Bradshaw, *Ordination Rites*, 115; *Testamentum Domini* 1.38 in Bradshaw, *Ordination Rites*, 120. The *Apostolic Tradition* dates from some time in the third or early fourth century. The *Apostolic Constitutions* date from the late fourth century and the *Testamentum Domini* is from the fifth century.

The New Testament letters at times apply "blamelessness" to all Christians and indeed the New Testament never refers to any person as "priest" except for Jesus and in reference to Jewish temple priests. Rather, passages such as 1 Pet 2:9 and Rev 1:6; 5:10 apply the term "priests" to all Christians. Nevertheless, by the early third century Tertullian was writing about the difference between ordained and laity,[83] and by the late fourth century one finds John Chrysostom drawing sharp distinctions between the status and holiness of the ordained and the holiness of those who are not. His treatise *On the Priesthood* provides striking examples of his thought:

> When one is required to preside over the Church, and to be entrusted with the care of so many souls . . . we must bring forward those who to a large extent surpass all others, and soar as much above them in excellence of spirit as Saul overtopped the whole Hebrew nation in bodily stature: or rather far more . . . let the distinction between the pastor and his charge be as great as that between rational man and irrational creatures, not to say even greater, inasmuch as the risk is concerned with things of far greater importance.[84]

> For indeed what is it but all manner of heavenly authority which He has given them when He says, "Whose sins ye remit they are remitted, and whose sins ye retain they are retained?" What authority could be greater than this? "The Father hath committed all judgment to the Son?" But I see it all put into the hands of these men by the Son. For they have been conducted to this dignity as if they were already translated to Heaven, and had transcended human nature, and were released from the passions to which we are liable.[85]

---

83. See Tertullian, *Exhortation to Chastity* 7, in *Tertullian: Treatises on Marriage and Remarriage To His Wife, An Exhortation to Chastity, Monogamy*, Ancient Christian Writers 13, ed. and trans. William P. LeSaint (Westminster, MD: Newman, 1951), 53.

84. John Chrysostom, *On the Priesthood* 2.2, in Philip Schaff, ed., *Nicene and Post-Nicene Fathers of the Christian Church*, Series I, vol. 9 (Grand Rapids, MI: Eerdmans, 1989, reprint), 40. Elsewhere in this same treatise, of course, Chrysostom had lamented that in his day "many of these ordinations happen not by divine grace but by human ambition." John Chrysostom, *On the Priesthood* 4.1, quoted in Bradshaw, *Ordination Rites*, 26.

85. Chrysostom, *On the Priesthood* 3.5 in *Nicene and Post-Nicene Fathers of the Christian Church* I, 9:47.

> Wherefore they might not only be more justly feared by us than rulers and kings, but also be more honored than parents; since these begat us of blood and the will of the flesh, but the others are the authors of our birth from God.[86]

> For as though he were entrusted with the whole world and were himself the father of all men, he draws near to God . . . and he ought as much to excel in every respect all those on whose behalf he prays, as rulers should excel their subjects.[87]

> Priests are the salt of the earth.[88]

Remarks such as these lead Kenan Osborne to make this observation: "Even though at times Chrysostom speaks of the human side of the priest, it is clear that he places the priest at a very high level. Such a theology of the priest could not help but divide the clergy and lay even more. The dignity of the priest was greater than angels, and it was the closeness to the Eucharist which both demanded and bestowed holiness and purity. Since Chrysostom's work was an immediate 'best seller,' its influence on the theology and spirituality of the priesthood remained dominant for centuries."[89]

Given this kind of thinking and given the late fourth-century emphasis on the correctness of Nicaea's teaching on how Father and Son are *homoousios*, it is not surprising that awe before the Eucharist increased (after all, it was the Son of God—who was truly *God*—who came to presence in the consecrated elements) and frequency of communion decreased. Chrysostom himself challenged his assembly: "In vain do we stand before the altar;

---

86. Chrysostom, *On the Priesthood* 3.6 in ibid., 9:47.

87. Chrysostom, *On the Priesthood* 6.4 in ibid., 9:76.

88. Ibid.

89. Kenan Osborne, *Priesthood: A History of Ordained Ministry in the Roman Catholic Church* (New York: Paulist Press, 1988), 150. Osborne's text directed me to Chrysostom's treatise on priesthood. For a comparison between priests and angels, see John Chrysostom, *On the Priesthood* 3.5 in *Nicene and Post-Nicene Fathers of the Christian Church* I, 9:47. See also Gregory of Nyssa, *Sermon on the Day of Lights/On the Baptism of Christ*, in *The Faith of the Early Fathers*, ed. William Jurgens (Collegeville, MN: Liturgical Press, 1970), 2:58–59 for the claim that ordination sets a man apart from and over "the multitude." Gregory was a contemporary of Chrysostom.

there is no one to partake."[90] Paul Bradshaw and Maxwell Johnson offer an important assessment of this trend:

> Contrary to Chrysostom's advice, many people apparently stayed until the time for communion and then left the church. Indeed, the ecclesiastical authorities were eventually forced to accept this practice, and in the end they began to make provision in the rites at the time of the communion for a formal blessing and dismissal of non-communicants in order to encourage a more orderly departure. . . . This development also had a significant effect on people's understanding of the Eucharist. It made it possible for them to think of the rite as complete and effective without the need for them to receive communion and thus helped to further the idea that liturgy was something that the clergy did on their behalf, which ultimately did not even require their presence. The more professionalized clergy of this period increasingly dominated public worship, and the people were content to let them do it, the pure acting for the impure, the experts for the ignorant.[91]

In this emerging understanding of holy orders, two related phenomena take shape. One is that clerics begin to develop an identity involving not only having authority and responsibility in the church but also a measure of superiority with respect to holiness. A second is that ecclesial assemblies begin to regard the clergy as the actors and agents of liturgical spectacle. This trend will be exacerbated by later consumerist forms of spectatorship (e.g., in front of televisions or movie screens). Laity are the consumers and clergy are the experts staging a performance. We will return to this point.

In part as a response to Martin Luther's emphasis on the universal priesthood of all believers, the Council of Trent and the catechism that followed stressed the distinctiveness of the ordained. As we have already seen, Trent reminded clerics of their duty to

90. John Chrysostom, *Homilies on Ephesians* 3, in Philip Schaff, ed., *Nicene and Post-Nicene Fathers of the Christian Church*, Series I, vol. 13: *Saint Chrysostom: Homilies on Galatians, Ephesians, Philippians, Colossians, Thessalonians, Timothy, Titus, and Philemon* (Grand Rapids, MI: Eerdmans, 1988, reprint), 64.

91. Paul Bradshaw and Maxwell Johnson, *The Eucharistic Liturgies: Their Evolution and Interpretation* (Collegeville, MN: Liturgical Press, 2012), 66.

provide an example to those in their care.[92] The Tridentine catechism underscored the difference between lay and ordained in
dramatic terms:

> Bishops and priests being, as they are, God's interpreters and
> ambassadors, empowered in His name to teach mankind the
> divine law and the rules of conduct, and holding, as they do,
> His place on earth, it is evident that no nobler function than
> theirs can be imagined. Justly, therefore, are they called not only
> Angels, but even gods, because of the fact that they exercise in
> our midst the power and prerogatives of the immortal God.
>
> In all ages, priests have been held in the highest honour; yet
> the priests of the New Testament far exceed all others. For the
> power of consecrating and offering the body and blood of our
> Lord and of forgiving sins, which has been conferred on them,
> not only has nothing equal or like to it on earth, but even sur-
> passes human reason and understanding.[93]

It is little wonder that this catechism later adds that "it will readily
be seen that what the Apostle Peter says of all the faithful: You are a
chosen generation, a kingly priesthood, a holy nation, applies especially and with much greater reason to the ministers of the Church."[94]

It is important to note that the Catechism of the Council of Trent
was the exclusive universal catechism of the Catholic Church until
the second universal catechism was promulgated in the 1990s.
For generations, the self-understanding of clerics and the identity
these clerics had in the eyes of other Catholics were shaped by
this teaching. In a 1904 letter, for example, Pope Pius X not only
repeated the maxim from Hosea 4:9, but again stressed the difference between lay and ordained: "To bring about the reign of Jesus

92. Council of Trent, Session 23, Decree on Reformation, chap. 1. I am using the
text in Tanner, *Decrees of the Ecumenical Councils*, 2:744. See also canons 3 and 4 in
Trent's canons on the sacrament of orders (DS 1773 and 1774), which declare that
ordination is not merely a means by which one is chosen to preach and administer
sacraments and that once one is ordained, one's priesthood cannot be undone.

93. *Catechism of the Council of Trent for Parish Priests* 318.

94. *Catechism of the Council of Trent for Parish Priests* 325. The Scripture passage
at issue is 1 Pet 2:9.

Christ in the world, nothing is more essential than a saintly clergy who, by their example, their preaching and their learning will be the guides of the faithful; an old proverb says that the people will always be like their priests: Sicut sacerdos, sic populus."[95] In his 1908 apostolic exhortation *Haerent Animo*, the same pope repeated a theme found as early as John Chrysostom: "There should be as much difference between the priest and any other upright man as there is between heaven and earth . . . [even though] a priest cannot avoid daily contact with a corrupt society."[96] This expectation concerning clerical conduct was enshrined in canon 124 of the 1917 *Code of Canon Law*, which declared that "clerics must lead an interior and exterior life holier than that of laity and should excel in rendering them an example of virtue and good deeds."[97] In the writings of Pius XI and Pius XII, one finds reference to the "ineffable greatness of the human priest" (Pius XI),[98] and the idea that the lives of clerics "should be even more hidden with Christ in God than the lives of Christian lay-folk" (Pius XII).[99] Referring to the 1917 *Code*, Pius XII wrote that "the Church has promulgated appropriate and wise laws, whose purpose is to safeguard sacerdotal sanctity from the cares and pleasures of the laity."[100]

95. Pius X, Letter concerning clerical discipline addressed to Cardinal Respighi (May 5, 1904). This portion of the letter appears in Pius X, Apostolic Exhortation on Priestly Sanctity (*Haerent Animo*, August 4, 1908), endnote 5, https://www.ewtn.com/library/PAPALDOC/P10HAER.HTM. Pius X is not the author of this endnote, but he is the author of the letter itself, which appears in this endnote.

96. Pius X, *Haerent Animo* 1, 2.

97. I am using the text in *The 1917 or Pio-Benedictine Code of Canon Law*, 65. Pius XI uses similar phrasing in his *Ad Catholici Sacerdotii* 38.

98. Pius XI, *Ad Catholici Sacerdotii* 16. Paragraph 31 of this document refers to the dignity of the priesthood as "most sublime."

99. Pius XII, Apostolic Exhortation on the Development of Holiness in Priestly Life (*Menti Nostrae*, September 23, 1950) 9, http://www.ewtn.com/library/papaldoc/p12clerg.htm.

100. Pius XII, Encyclical Letter on Consecrated Virginity (*Sacra Virginitas*, March 25, 1954) 56, http://w2.vatican.va/content/pius-xii/en/encyclicals/documents/hf_p-xii_enc_25031954_sacra-virginitas.html. Pius is referring to cans. 124–42.

Vatican II continues the tradition of regarding bishops and priests as examples for other Christians.[101] The council continues as well the teaching on the "excellence" of priesthood.[102] Yet in its Decree on the Ministry and Life of Priests, the council scaled back the rhetoric of distinction and separation:

> The priests of the New Testament are, it is true, by their vocation and ordination, set apart in some way within the people of God, but this is not in order that they should be separated from that people or from any person, but that they should be completely consecrated to the task for which God chooses them (see Acts 13:2). They could not be the servants of Christ unless they were witnesses and dispensers of a life other than that of this earth. On the other hand they would be powerless to serve people if they remained aloof from their life and circumstances.[103]

Still, with echoes of canon 124 of the 1917 *Code of Canon Law*, this same decree taught that "priests are especially bound to attain perfection."[104]

We have seen, then, from an initial understanding of universal priesthood in the very early church, the notion of the clerical state took on a sense of differentiation and distinction that included a sense of superiority with respect to the virtues and holiness of the non-ordained. Many of the laity indeed shared this view.[105] In its Dogmatic Constitution on the Church, however, Vatican II declared that it is "quite clear that all Christians in whatever state or walk in life are called to the fullness of christian life and to the

---

101. For bishops, see *Lumen Gentium* 26 and *Christus Dominus* 15. For priests, see *Presbyterorum Ordinis* 4.

102. See *Presbyterorum Ordinis* 1 and 11.

103. *Presbyterorum Ordinis* 3. Commenting on this paragraph of *Presbyterorum Ordinis* at a Vatican conference in 1995, Cardinal Joseph Ratzinger stated that "we can find . . . newness in comparison with Trent in so far as . . . vital unity is emphasized and the common life of the whole Church." Joseph Ratzinger, "Life and Ministry of Priests," in Congregation for the Clergy, *Priesthood: A Greater Love* 117. See also the comments in Luke H. T. Liu, "Priest: Pastor and Leader of the Community," in the same volume (96).

104. *Presbyterorum Ordinis* 12.

105. See Hoge and Wenger, *Evolving Visions of the Priesthood*, 10.

perfection of charity."[106] Yet the conciliar Decree on the Ministry and Life of Priests—and as we shall see in the next section, post-conciliar Vatican documents—insists as well on the excellence of priesthood. For George Wilson, these claims are difficult to reconcile: "Those who are called to orders are not thereby holier than their lay brothers and sisters. It is not then belittling of their dignity to say that nothing more is expected of them by way of Christian virtue or life than of the laity, *because the call to the fullness of perfection was already given in their baptism.*"[107]

The reader may ask why I have devoted space to a discussion of the distinctive holiness of the ordained in a chapter addressing holy orders and consumerism. The answer is that the understanding of consumerism that informs this book concerns primarily questions of identity—how to arrive at one's identity, how to maintain one's identity, how to change or revise one's identity. Whatever other strengths or weaknesses one may associate with a two-tiered structure of Christian identity according to which the ordained are holier than the laity, this structure did indeed provide a clear identity to the ordained. What happens, though, when this structure starts to break down as happened after the council? That question is for the next section.

V. Orders after Vatican Council II

Two years after the close of the council, Pope Paul VI taught that "to his children in Christ, the priest is a sign and a pledge of that sublime and new reality which is the kingdom of God; he dispenses it and he possesses it to a more perfect degree."[108] Paul added in the same document that the asceticism "proper to [the priesthood is] more demanding than that which is required of the

---

106. *Lumen Gentium* 40.

107. Wilson, *Clericalism*, 46.

108. Paul VI, Encyclical Letter on the Celibacy of the Priest (*Sacerdotalis Caelibatus*, June 24, 1967) 31, http://w2.vatican.va/content/paul-vi/en/encyclicals/documents/hf_p-vi_enc_24061967_sacerdotalis.html.

other faithful."[109] The 1971 Synod of Bishops issued a document declaring in part that priestly ministry is "not only is to be considered as a fully valid human activity but indeed as more excellent than other activities."[110] Three years later, the Sacred Congregation for Catholic Education promulgated a document on clerical celibacy, which taught that "if it is true that every Christian is consecrated to God in Christ and to the service of his brothers, it is no less true that consecration to God in the priesthood demands an even more generous and complete dedication."[111] The same document later compared biological parenthood with the spiritual fatherhood of a priest: "There is something sublime in the qualities roused in a man's heart by natural fatherhood: an altruistic spirit, the assumption of heavy responsibilities, a capacity for love and a dedication enough to make any sacrifice, daily bearing of life's burdens and difficulties, prudent care for the future, etc. However, all this is equally true of spiritual paternity. Moreover, spiritual fatherhood, not being confined to the natural order, is even more responsible and heroic."[112]

---

109. *Sacerdotalis Caelibatus* 70. It is interesting to note that in a 1974 document, the Sacred Congregation for Catholic Education quoted this passage, changing a key word: "Young students must be convinced of the necessity of a very special asceticism in their lives, one that is far more demanding than what is required of the *ordinary* faithful and which is special to those aspiring to the priesthood." Sacred Congregation for Catholic Education, "Formation in Celibacy" 2 (emphasis added).

110. 1971 Synod of Bishops, *The Ministerial Priesthood and Justice in the World* (Washington, DC: National Conference of Catholic Bishops, 1982), 16.

111. Sacred Congregation for Catholic Education, "Formation in Celibacy" 8.

112. Sacred Congregation for Catholic Education, "Formation in Celibacy" 32. Commenting some twenty years later on priestly celibacy and the absence of natural family life, Archbishop Miloslav Vlk of Prague insisted on the superiority of priestly family life:

Celibacy is not a renunciation of family. If God, who is love, has created marriage as an expression and image of his Trinitarian life, why would he deprive the priest of such a "good" thing? The truth is that God, far from depriving priests of this good, invites them to live in a more beautiful family, more akin to conditions in paradise, the family which was formed among the apostles, who could say: "Lord, to whom shall we go? You alone have the words of life."

In a 1979 letter to priests, John Paul II asserted that even though all Christians have a responsibility for the salvation of others, "nevertheless you Priests are expected to have care and commitment which are far greater and different from those of any lay person."[113] Later in this letter, however, John Paul struck a tone different from that of Pope Paul regarding the discipline of celibacy and the challenges of married life: "the commitment to married fidelity, which derives from the sacrament of Matrimony, creates similar obligations in its own sphere."[114] Indeed, in 1992's *Pastores Dabo Vobis*, John Paul wrote that "the ministerial priesthood does not of itself signify a greater degree of holiness with regard to the common priesthood of the faithful."[115] Echoes of canon 124 of the 1917 *Code* persist in this 1992 document, however: "What the apostle Paul says of all Christians, that they must attain 'to mature manhood, to the measure of the stature of the fullness of Christ' (Eph 4:13), can be applied specifically to priests, who are called to the perfection of charity and therefore to holiness, even more so because their pastoral ministry itself demands that they be living models for all the faithful."[116] In an important (but brief) passage, however, John Paul later mentions that priests can draw "spiritual nourishment" from the efforts of laity to live out lives of discipleship.[117]

The priest, too, needs a family. And [the priest] feels the deprivation of a natural family, clearly so, unless he comes to realize [family] concretely among priests, with Jesus, the priest in their midst. In this type of family, he does not experience personal loneliness, nor does he feel the need for other affective ties. Miloslav Vlk, "The Call of Priests to Perfection," in Congregation for the Clergy, *Priesthood: A Greater Love* 227–28.

113. John Paul II, Letter to All the Priests on the Occasion of Holy Thursday (April 9, 1979) 5, https://w2.vatican.va/content/john-paul-ii/en/letters/1979/documents/hf_jp-ii_let_19790409_sacerdoti-giovedi-santo.html.

114. Ibid. 9.

115. *Pastores Dabo Vobis* 17.

116. Ibid. 72.

117. Ibid. 78. The 1971 Synod of Bishops had said something similar: "In the exercise of his ministry the priest is enlightened and strengthened by the action of the Church and the example of the faithful." 1971 Synod of Bishops, *The Ministerial Priesthood and Justice in the World*, 18.

Turning to rites of ordination, the prayer of consecration of a bishop in force at the time of Vatican II invoked God as the source of all dignity,[118] but the corresponding prayer in the rite of 1968 hearkens back to *Apostolic Tradition* 3, which makes no reference to dignity, honor or advancement in rank.[119] However, the sample homily in the 1968 rite refers to the "position in the Church to which our brother is about to be raised" and the current sample homily restores the language of rank: "consider carefully the nature of the rank in the Church to which our brother is about to be raised."[120]

The prayer for the ordination of a priest at the time of the council invoked God as "the source of every honor and dispenser of all dignities,"[121] and it asks that God confer upon the candidate the "dignity of the Priesthood."[122] The corresponding prayer in the rite of 1968 identifies God as "the source of every honor and dignity,"[123] and it asks God to confer upon the ordinands "the dignity of the priesthood."[124] The current prayer invokes God as "author of human dignity" and it is God "who apportion[s] all graces."[125] The prayer later asks God to grant "to this your servant the dignity of the Priesthood."[126] Though the notion of "honor" is

---

118. See *Pontificale Romanum Editio Iuxta Typica* 45.

119. See *Apostolic Tradition* 3 in Bradshaw, *Ordination Rites of the Ancient Churches of East and West*, 107. For the rite of 1968, see Ordination of a Bishop 26. For the 2012 version of this prayer, which again makes no reference to dignity, honor or advancement, see 2012 Ordination of a Bishop 47.

120. 1968 Ordination of a Bishop 18; 2012 Ordination of a Bishop 39.

121. *The Rite of Ordination According to the Roman Pontifical*, trans. J. S. M. Lynch, 4th ed. (New York: Catholic Library Association, 1918), 59. The relevant Latin text from the Roman Pontifical of 1962 is identical to the Latin text Lynch has translated.

122. *The Rite of Ordination According to the Roman Pontifical*, 60. The relevant Latin text from the Roman Pontifical of 1962 is identical to the Latin text Lynch has translated.

123. 1968 Ordination of a Priest 22.

124. Ibid.

125. Ordination of Priests 159 in United States Conference of Catholic Bishops, *Rites of Ordination of a Bishop, of Priests, and of Deacons, Second Typical Edition* (Washington, DC: USCCB, 2003).

126. Ibid.

absent and the current prayer also speaks of (one) human dignity, the capitalization of "Priesthood" sets the dignity of the ordinands apart from others.[127]

The prayer for the ordination of a deacon at the time of Vatican II refers to God as the giver of all honors and orders.[128] The corresponding prayer in the rite of 1968 says of God that "you are the source of all honor, you assign to each his rank, you give to each his ministry,"[129] whereas the current prayer refers to God as the "giver of every grace, who apportion[s] every order and assign[s] every office."[130] There is no longer a reference to honor, leading Jan Michael Joncas to assert that " 'orders' and 'offices' are no longer imaged as a form of social advancement but as manifestation of divine benevolence."[131] Nevertheless, the current sample homily invites those gathered for a diaconal ordination to "consider carefully the nature of the rank in the Church to which he is about to be raised."[132]

We have seen that George Wilson points out the tension between the conciliar pronouncement on the call to universal holiness and various statements identifying the ordained as especially bound to seek perfection. One result of this tension is confusion. Dean Hoge and Jacqueline Wenger explain: "The years after Vatican II were a time of uncertainty for priests. On balance, they had as much to lose as to gain from the council's actions. Its emphasis on the 'priesthood of the laity' and on the church as 'the people of God' demanded that the role and identity of priests be reconsidered. . . . Many priests now felt confused, since their earlier role

---

127. For additional commentary on the absence of "honor," see Jan Michael Joncas, "The Public Language of Ministry Revisited: *De Ordinatione Episcopi, Presbyterorum et Diaconorum* 1990," *Worship* 68, no. 5 (1994): 386–403 at 398.

128. See *The Rite of Ordination According to the Roman Pontifical*, 47. The relevant Latin text from the Roman Pontifical of 1962 is identical to the Latin text Lynch has translated.

129. 1968 Ordination of a Deacon 21.

130. 2012 Ordination of Deacons 235.

131. Jan Michael Joncas, "The Public Language of Ministry Revisited," 397.

132. 2012 Ordination of Deacons 227. The sample homily of 1968 invited the assembly to "consider carefully the ministry to which he is to be promoted." Citation from 1968 Ordination of a Deacon 14.

and their secure status were lost; large numbers resigned between 1968 and 1974."[133] It is reasonable to suppose that questions about priestly identity contributed in at least some way to the resignations of priests and perhaps also to the lower numbers of men seeking holy orders. In turn, these lower numbers exacerbate the tendency for priests to be pressed into service as "functionaries" or "machines."

The 2001 survey of priests to which we have already referred found that only 5 percent of priests were "very happy" with "the image of the Catholic priesthood in America today."[134] While it is also true that this same survey found that only 3 percent of priests found "the lack of a clear idea of what a priest is" to be "a great problem for me personally,"[135] nearly two-thirds of priests (64 percent) stated that an "open discussion of the image and esteem of the priest today" would be "very important to me."[136] For Susan Wood, it is not surprising that there has been something of a resurgence of conservatism among newer seminarians and priests; she contends that this shift involves a "search for identity" and that "the tradition of the Church represents a rich resource to strengthen the public esteem and influence of the priesthood and to provide an identity that assures the new priest that his sacrifices are worth the effort."[137]

This resurgence is not merely a matter of newer clerics, however. As we have seen, popes and Vatican documents since the council have continued to emphasize the ways in which the ordained are superior (or called to be superior) to the nonordained, even as these popes and documents at times also emphasize a universal call to holiness. The 1994 *Directory on the Ministry of Life and Priests*, for example, announces in its first paragraph that

133. Hoge and Wenger, *Evolving Visions of the Priesthood*, 10.

134. Ibid., 31. It is worth noting that this survey took place before revelations in 2002 concerning clerical sexual abuse in Boston and subsequently around the nation.

135. Ibid., 33.

136. Ibid., 80.

137. Susan Wood, "The Search for Identity," in Hoge and Wenger, *Evolving Visions of the Priesthood*, 168.

"the entire Church participates in the priestly anointing of Christ in the Holy Spirit" but later the document refers to priests as "among the favored disciples of Jesus."[138] This *Directory* also presents guidelines for priestly dress, in order that the ordained may be distinguished from the non-ordained. The priest's

> attire, when it is not the cassock, must be different from the manner in which the laity dress, and conform to the dignity and sacredness of his ministry. The style and color should be established by the Episcopal Conference, always in agreement with the dispositions of the universal law.
>
> Because of their incoherence with the spirit of this discipline, contrary practices cannot be considered legitimate customs; and should be removed by the competent authority.
>
> Outside of entirely exceptional cases, a cleric's failure to use this proper ecclesiastical attire could manifest a weak sense of his identity as one consecrated to God.[139]

I do not wish to deny the importance of appropriate vestments for the ordained during liturgical celebrations, but I wonder if in some ways the insistence on distinctive dress at all times is symptomatic of a consumerist mode of thinking: priests and bishops must express their identity by means of what they *purchase* and wear. On the extreme end, presumably merchants would not advertise $4000 copes for bishops or $1000 copes for priests unless there was a market for these items.[140]

---

138. *Directory on the Ministry and Life of Priests* 1 and 68. In 2010, Pope Benedict XVI referred to priests as "those called to be closest to" Jesus. Pope Benedict XVI, "Proclaiming a Year for Priests on the 150th Anniversary of the 'Dies Natalis' of the Curé of Ars" (October 18, 2010), https://w2.vatican.va/content/benedict-xvi /en/letters/2009/documents/hf_ben-xvi_let_20090616_anno-sacerdotale.html.

139. *Directory on the Ministry and Life of Priests* 66. This passage has footnotes referencing statements from Pope Paul VI in the late 1960s and early 1970s and curial statements from 1976 and 1980. Church regulation of clerical dress goes back at least as far as 1215. See can. 16 of Lateran IV. Text available in Tanner, *Decrees of the Ecumenical Councils*, 1:243.

140. For an episcopal cope retailing for $3995, see "Gold Brocade Verona Cope," *Sheehan's Church Goods*, https://www.matthewfsheehan.net/gold-brocade-cope .html; for other copes retailing for $995, see "Copes Priest - Bishop," *Religious*

VI. Orders and Relationality

In an earlier chapter, I referred to the "strange configuration of sociality" of the contemporary shopping mall.[141] Lacking a firm socially embedded sense of self, shoppers are encouraged to compare themselves to ideals presented in television advertisements and displays in store windows. Rather than developing a sense of corporate identity with people around them, shoppers are encouraged to develop a *corporation* identity by displaying the newest and hippest logos on their clothing and other personal belongings. Each person undertakes this task alone, always with a competitive eye towards others. Starting with the discussion of baptism, I have argued in this book that Christian identity is public, shared, and relational. Emphasizing and reconnecting with this relational identity is one way to counteract the pull of consumerism. How does this sense of shared identity apply to the sacrament of holy orders?

We have already noted that the New Testament does not single out any believer as a "priest." Tertullian marks a distinction between ordained and non-ordained, but even so the patristic church regarded the ordained as necessarily related to a community. For example, canon 6 of the Council of Chalcedon declared that no one "who belongs to the ecclesiastical order, is to be ordained without title, unless the one ordained is specially assigned to a city or village church or to a martyr's shrine or a monastery."[142] Some 730 years later, however, Lateran Council III permitted ordinations without any requirement to be assigned to a specific community. Though many priests were in fact assigned to specific communities, in principle the relational link had been diminished.[143]

-*Apparel.com*, https://www.clergy-apparel.com/product-category/clergy-apparel/copes-priest-bishop.

141. See pp. 67–68, 76, and 83. The phrase is from James K.A. Smith, *Desiring the Kingdom: Worship, Worldview, and Cultural Formation* (Grand Rapids, MI: Baker, 2009), 96, 98.

142. Council of Chalcedon, can. 6. I am using the text in Tanner, *Decrees of the Ecumenical Councils*, 1:90. This canon builds on canon 2 of the regional council of Arles (314) and canon 15 of the Council of Nicaea (325).

143. See Lateran Council III, can. 5. Text available in Tanner, *Decrees of the Ecumenical Councils*, 1:214. For commentary on Lateran III, see Michael Mullaney, "Incardination and the Universal Dimension of the Priestly Ministry," *Periodica de re canonica* 95, no. 4 (January 2006): 567–95, esp. 569.

The history of ordination rites also indicates this diminishment. The *Apostolic Tradition*, for example, specifies that an episcopal ordination should take place on the Lord's Day in the presence of the people.[144] The ordination rites in the pontifical of 1595, however, make no reference to the presence or participation of laity.[145] Insights into ecclesiology and into the nature of sacramental worship caused a shift in the rites of ordination promulgated after Vatican II. The postconciliar rites for ordination to the diaconate, to the priesthood, and to the episcopate all state not only that the ceremonies should take place when a large number of the faithful can attend but that the setting should be arranged so that the faithful can have a "complete view" of the rite.[146] Despite these rubrics, the 2008 CARA study to which we have already referred found that 87 percent of respondents had never attended the ordination of a priest.[147] The 87 percent figure raises questions about whether ordinations are in fact scheduled to accommodate lay attendance, and also about the degree to which laity judge that participation in these rites is important. There are questions as well about how often ordinations are celebrated in the contemporary church and whether the venues for these ordinations are filled and thus unable to handle the number of laity who want to attend. More study is needed, but the numbers certainly can suggest a disconnect between laity and clergy as opposed to a strong sense of relationship.

The history of ordination rites indicates a breach of relationality in another way—but also a restoration. Paul Bradshaw observes that during the medieval period "the influence of the feudal system of the contemporary world, theological interpretations of ordination became focused on it being the conferral of specific powers on an individual and not on service to a particular ecclesial

144. See *Apostolic Tradition* 2 in Bradshaw, *Ordination Rites of the Ancient Churches of East and West*, 107.

145. See the discussion of this point in McMillan, *Episcopal Ordination and Ecclesial Consensus*, 251.

146. For episcopal ordinations, see 1968 Ordination of a Bishop 1, 9b. For ordinations to the priesthood, see 1968 Ordination of a Priest 1–2. For ordinations to the diaconate, see 1968 Ordination of a Deacon 1–2. For each rite of ordination, these directives are retained in 2012 rites of ordination. See also *Catechism of the Catholic Church* 1572.

147. CARA, *Sacraments Today*, 68.

community, and so many of the secondary accretions followed the ritual pattern of feudal appointments, the handing over of objects that symbolized the new office accompanied by impera- tive formulas expressing bestowal of the related powers, known as the *traditio instrumentorum*, a process that had begun with the minor orders and then spread to them all."[148] Indeed, the Council of Florence in its 1439 Decree for the Armenians taught that the matter of priestly ordination was the handing over of a chalice with wine and a paten with bread while the form was "Receive the power of offering sacrifice in the church for the living and the dead, in the name of the Father and of the Son and of the Holy Spirit."[149] Though Pope Pius XII was concerned about preserving "sacerdotal sanctity from the cares and pleasures of the laity,"[150] in 1947 he also revised church teaching on the matter of ordination, declaring that the "only matter" for ordination to the episcopate, the priesthood, and the diaconate was the imposition of hands. Pius also specified that "at least in the future the *traditio instru- mentorum* is not necessary for the validity of the Sacred Orders of the Diaconate, the Priesthood, and the Episcopacy."[151] The 1968 Rite of Ordination of a Priest drops reference to the reception of the power to offer sacrifice and instead, while the hands of the new priest are anointed with chrism, the bishop asks that Jesus "preserve you to sanctify the Christian people and to offer sac- rifice to God."[152] The new language situates the priest vis-à-vis "the Christian people" in a way that the former language did not.

148. Bradshaw, *Rites of Ordination*, 145–46.

149. Council of Florence, Decree for the Armenians. I am using the text in Tanner, *Decrees of the Ecumenical Councils*, 1:549.

150. Pius XII, *Sacra Virginitas* 56.

151. Pius XII, Apostolic Constitution on the Sacrament of Order (*Sacramen- tum Ordinis*, November 30, 1947) 4, http://www.papalencyclicals.net/pius12 /p12sacrao.html. By adding the phrase "at least in the future," Pius sidestepped the question about whether or how the *traditio instrumentorum* had in fact been a requirement before 1947.

152. 1968 Ordination of a Priest 24. Though this prayer is slightly expanded in the current version, the current version retains this phrasing almost exactly. See Ordination of a Priest 40 in the 2012 English pontifical.

Consumerism, however, tends to reduce people to things.[153] Especially in a church with rising ratios of parishioners to priests, this tendency can be exacerbated. As we have seen, some priests worry that they are regarded as sacramental machines or sacrament-dispensing zombies. Machines and zombies are, of course, entities without personalities. One cannot enter a vital human relationship with an entity lacking a personality. Consumer culture is also a culture of experts and spectacles. Fewer and fewer Americans, for example, can repair their cars at home; such work requires access to the cars' on-board computer diagnostic system. One must pay for the services of the expert. As we have seen, Catholic culture has long regarded the ordained as experts in the holy.[154] Hector Welgampola, whom I quoted earlier, refers to "ecclesial supermarkets" where "we now trade consumer-style payment for services."[155] In a consumer culture, these services can easily fall into the category of spectacle, as S. Anita Stauffer points out: "Much of the United States population today is highly influenced by the entertainment culture of Hollywood. One of the results is that worship is often seen not as a participatory liturgy, but as a 'program' to be observed passively—something to be watched, a time to be entertained."[156] Reinforced here is the idea that the ordained are active agents in liturgy and laity are passive spectators.[157]

Consumerism and market thinking can have an influence as well on how the ordained relate to each other. In the 2001 survey of priests, one anonymous respondent reported that "in this archdiocese the parishes really are becoming more and more owner-operated

153. See the passage from the *Program of Priestly Formation* 98; see also Pope Francis, *Amoris Laetitia* 39.

154. See the discussion in Wilson, *Clericalism*, 30.

155. Hector Welgampola, "Living Church in Asia," quoted in David Ranson, *The Contemporary Challenge of Priestly Life*, 40. See also p. 171, n. 23.

156. S. Anita Stauffer, "Contemporary Questions on Church Architecture and Culture," in *Worship and Culture in Dialogue*, ed. S. Anita Stauffer (Geneva: Lutheran World Federation, 1994), 167–81 at 173.

157. The idea that in sacramental worship clergy are active and laity are passive has roots at least as far back as Thomas Aquinas's discussion of sacramental character. See *Summa Theologiae* III, q. 63, a. 2, resp. Recall as well the impact of Nicaea's teaching on Christ's divinity and Chrysostom's lofty language about priesthood.

franchises. I don't feel there is a full-blown mission or a vision in the archdiocese. I really feel like I am operating a franchise."[158] From a different study, there is this: "Another priest said that he no longer feels that the priests in his diocese are his confreres. He said, 'We are just employees of the same company. That's the relationship I see now.'"[159] For some priests, the sexual abuse crisis worsened matters: "In the Dallas Charter, all consequences fall on priests. Nothing is in there for bishops. Diocesan priests are on their own. . . . I know of a bishop, I don't want to say who, who said to his priests, 'Our relationship is that of a CEO and an employee. If you are accused, you are on your own.'"[160]

The documents of Vatican II describe a different relationship between a diocesan bishop and the priests in his diocese. *Presbyterorum Ordinis* (the Decree on the Life and Ministry of Priests) calls on bishops to regard their priests as "brothers and friends" and *Christus Dominus* (Decree on the Pastoral Office of Bishops in the Church) directs bishops to regard priests as "sons and friends."[161] In the 1968 rites of ordination for deacons and for priests, the bishop addresses those to be ordained as "son" or "sons" in the sample homily.[162] Similarly, the sample homily in the 1968 Rite of Ordination of a Bishop advises that the new bishop should love deacons and priests as a father.[163] The 1994 *Directory* instructs bishops to have a special care for those in their first year of priesthood: "It is not superfluous to underline the fact that this year, both delicate and valuable, must favor the full growth of a rapport between the priest and his Bishop which, initiated in the seminary, ought to become a true father and son relationship."[164] One can certainly criticize those bishops who

158. Hoge and Wenger, *Evolving Visions of the Priesthood*, 34.

159. Anonymous priest quoted in Gautier, Perl, and Fichter, *Same Call, Different Men*, 102.

160. Anonymous priest quoted in ibid., 130. In light of the 2018 grand jury report on sexual abuse in Pennsylvania, some observers have renewed this critique of the Dallas Charter.

161. *Presbyterorum Ordinis* 7; *Christus Dominus* 16.

162. 1968 Ordination of a Deacon 14; see also 2012 Ordination of Deacons 227; 1968 Ordination of a Priest 14; see also 2012 Ordination of Priests 151.

163. 1968 Ordination of a Bishop 18; see also 2012 Ordination of a Bishop 39.

164. *Directory on the Ministry and Life of Priests* 82.

engaged in over-protective behavior towards priests accused of sexual abuse while one does not endorse the CEO mentality of the bishop described above. One can also raise questions about the idealized portrait of the father-son relationship as an exercise in sentimentality that stunts the maturity of priests.[165]

Perhaps *Pastores Dabo Vobis* offers a conceptual way forward by situating ministerial priesthood in a trinitarian context:

> In this way the fundamentally "relational" dimension of priestly identity can be understood. Through the priesthood which arises from the depths of the ineffable mystery of God, that is, from the love of the Father, the grace of Jesus Christ and the Holy Spirit's gift of unity, the priest sacramentally enters into communion with the bishop and with other priests in order to serve the People of God who are the Church and to draw all mankind to Christ. . . . Consequently, the nature and mission of the ministerial priesthood cannot be defined except through this multiple and rich interconnection of relationships which arise from the Blessed Trinity and are prolonged in the communion of the Church, as a sign and instrument of Christ, of communion with God and of the unity of all humanity.[166]

Later in the document, John Paul adds that "unity among the priests with the bishop and among themselves is not something added from the outside to the nature of their service, but expresses its essence inasmuch as it is the care of Christ the priest for the people gathered in the unity of the Blessed Trinity."[167] That all may be gathered in the unity of the Trinity is the heart and soul the paschal mystery that is at the root of all sacramental celebrations, including ordinations. Indeed, twice in this document John

---

165. See Wilson, *Clericalism*, 90. On the other hand, *Pastores Dabo Vobis* makes few references to the "filial" relationship a priest should have to his bishop (see 31, 41, 65) and never adverts to the obligation of a bishop to regard priests as sons. Great stress is instead placed on the priest's obligation to obey his bishop. See the discussion of this point in Leon Strieder, *The Promise of Obedience: A Ritual History* (Collegeville, MN: Liturgical Press, 2001), 116.

166. *Pastores Dabo Vobis* 2.

167. Ibid., 74. John Paul is quoting verbatim here from Proposition 34 of the synod.

Paul refers to the priest as a "man of communion,"[168] and the 1994 *Directory* holds that "the Bishop will never fail to foster communication and communion among priests."[169] This communion among priests and between priests and their bishop is not to be a matter of collective clerical navel-gazing but rather exists to promote the communion of *all* in the Trinity. The ordained are to be examples of this communion, yes, but never in a way that suggests that laity do not provide examples of communion as well. Bishops bear a primary responsibility for promoting communion in their dioceses, but far from infantilizing those over whom they have supervision (ordained or lay), this responsibility means fostering the talents and gifts of all (ordained or lay) for the good of communion.

Contexts in which communities are fragmented and communal identity is weak are contexts in which consumerism thrives, ready as it is to offer substitute methods for obtaining and securing identity in environments where the "other" is inevitably a competitor. In the case of the triune God, community is infinitely whole and communal identity infinitely strong. Ultimate reality *is* relational and so, too, should be the lives of those who minister in the name of this reality. "Relationships," says Michael Papesh, "building up the Body of Christ, are what priestly ministry is all about."[170]

VII. Conclusion

In this chapter, I have argued that consumerism presents a challenge to the understanding and practice of the sacrament of holy orders. In part, this challenge takes the shape of what John Paul II has called the hedonism of much of the contemporary world, a hedonism that works against the notions of moderation and sacrifice typically associated with the lives of the ordained. Going back to the New Testament, Christians have been warned against the siren song of "filthy lucre," and this admonition has been directed specifically to office holders in the church. Early church

---

168. *Pastores Dabo Vobis* 18, 43. The phrase appears as well in the *Directory on the Ministry and Life of Priests* 30, and in the US *Program of Priestly Formation* 76, 239.

169. *Directory on the Ministry and Life of Priests* 89.

170. Papesh, *Clerical Culture*, 98.

documents, church councils, and papal statements have repeatedly directed clerics to refrain from business dealings for personal profit, suggesting constancy in teaching but perhaps also persistent problems with the observance of these directives. In addition to episodes of profligacy in the past, recent headlines have also drawn attention to the extravagance of some in the clergy.

Yet part of what fosters present-day consumerism is the fragility of personal identity in a time when geographic, economic, and even family stability is ever harder to maintain. For more than a millennium and a half, the ordained enjoyed an elevated status in the church (and often in wider society as well), with the Catechism of Trent referring to priests and bishops as "angels" and even "gods." One can surely raise serious ecclesiological questions about such assessments, but it is just as certain that for centuries the ordained, by and large, had a clear sense of identity, reinforced by church teaching and often validated by laity. Sociological and theological changes in the twentieth century challenged and overthrew the idea of unquestioned clerical superiority, contributing to an identity crisis for the ordained at the dawn of the third millennium of the Christian era. Although priesthood can offer a guarantee of steady work in a time when many other workers must shift from job to job, the sharp decline in the number of priests—a decline associated with a crisis of identity—has given rise to a situation in which some priests worry about becoming sacrament-dispensing machines. Even with job security, there are priests who worry that running a parish (or two or three) has been reduced to running a franchise in turn run by a CEO bishop who regards priests as employees (as opposed to the tighter bond between bishops and priests envisioned in the documents of Vatican II and the 1994 *Directory on the Ministry and Life of Priests*). To the extent that priests are indeed merely sacrament-dispensing machines running parish-franchises, the consumerist tendency to reduce people to things is manifest. On an insidious level, consumerism is a challenge to human personality—to what Irenaeus referred to as the human person fully alive.[171]

171. See Irenaeus, *Against All Heresies* 4.20.7.

Is there a solution to the crisis of numbers and the crisis of identity? It would be foolish to say "no," and it would be just as foolish to claim that these problems will vanish overnight. The world is fallen but redeemed. I think part of a response is to emphasize that orders, like all sacraments, is grounded in the paschal mystery and a celebration of that mystery. That mystery is itself an expression of the mystery of the saving and communal love of the Trinity unfolding in time and space. Reflecting an ancient tradition, during the current Rite of Ordination of a Priest and speaking with reference to the eucharistic celebrations over which the priest will preside, the bishop directs the priest to "understand what you do, imitate what you celebrate, and conform your life to the mystery of the Lord's Cross."[172] These words amount to a directive to be a man of communion, a theme emphasized by John Paul and by the US bishops' *Program for Priestly Formation*. Restoring unity between God and humans is, after all, the point of the Lord's cross. At one time, being grounded in the paschal mystery meant for priests that they were the ones to offer the eucharistic sacrifice for the living and the dead. Surely, that is something that priests continue to do, but there is now a renewed sense of the priest doing so *in, with,* and *among* the Christian people. Certainly, aspects of the current crisis will abate if the numbers of ordained relative to the total number of Catholics improves. In the meantime, however, it is and will be important for all to realize anew what *Lumen Gentium* declared: "At all times and in every nation, anyone who fears God and does what is right has been acceptable to him. He has, however, willed to make women and men holy and to save them, *not as individuals without any bond between them, but rather to make them into a people* who might acknowledge him and serve him in holiness."[173]

Where consumerism divides, the saving mystery of God revealed in Christ unites.

---

172. 2012 Ordination of Priests 163. See also *Lumen Gentium* 41.
173. *Lumen Gentium* 9.

INDEX